CHRISTIAN KINSHIP

T&T Clark Enquiries in Theological Ethics

Series editors
Brian Brock
Susan F. Parsons

CHRISTIAN KINSHIP

Family-Relatedness in Christian Practice and Moral Thought

David A. Torrance

LONDON • NEW YORK • OXFORD • NEW DELHI • SYDNEY

T&T CLARK
Bloomsbury Publishing Plc
50 Bedford Square, London, WC1B 3DP, UK
1385 Broadway, New York, NY 10018, USA
29 Earlsfort Terrace, Dublin 2, Ireland

BLOOMSBURY, T&T CLARK and the T&T Clark logo are trademarks of Bloomsbury Publishing Plc

First published in Great Britain 2023
Paperback edition published 2024

Copyright © David A. Torrance, 2023

David A. Torrance has asserted his right under the Copyright, Designs and Patents Act, 1988, to be identified as Author of this work.

For legal purposes the Acknowledgements on p. ix constitute an extension of this copyright page.

Cover design: Terry Woodley

All rights reserved. No part of this publication may be reproduced or transmitted in any form or by any means, electronic or mechanical, including photocopying, recording, or any information storage or retrieval system, without prior permission in writing from the publishers.

Bloomsbury Publishing Plc does not have any control over, or responsibility for, any third-party websites referred to or in this book. All internet addresses given in this book were correct at the time of going to press. The author and publisher regret any inconvenience caused if addresses have changed or sites have ceased to exist, but can accept no responsibility for any such changes.

A catalogue record for this book is available from the British Library.

Library of Congress Cataloging-in-Publication Data

Names: Torrance, David A., author.
Title: Christian kinship : family relatedness in Christian practice and moral thought / David A. Torrance.
Description: London ; New York : T&T Clark, 2022. | Series: T&T Clark enquiries in theological ethics | Includes bibliographical references and index. | Summary: "Ideas of kinship play a significant role in structuring everyday life, and yet kinship has been neglected in Christian ethics, moral philosophy and bioethics. Attention has been paid in these disciplines to the ethics of 'family,' but with little regard to the evidence that kinship varies widely from culture-to-culture, suggesting that it is, in fact, culturally constructed."
Identifiers: LCCN 2022012246 (print) | LCCN 2022012247 (ebook) | ISBN 9780567699800 (hb) | ISBN 9780567699817 (epdf) | ISBN 9780567699831 (epub)
Subjects: LCSH: Families–Religious aspects–Christianity. | Kinship–Religious aspects–Christianity. | Linship. | Ethics. | Bioethics. | Christian ethics.
Classification: LCC BT707.7 .T67 2022 (print) | LCC BT707.7 (ebook) | DDC 248.4–dc23/eng/20220701
LC record available at https://lccn.loc.gov/2022012246
LC ebook record available at https://lccn.loc.gov/2022012247

ISBN: HB: 978-0-5676-9980-0
PB: 978-0-5676-9984-8
ePDF: 978-0-5676-9981-7
ePUB: 978-0-5676-9983-1

Typeset by Deanta Global Publishing Services, Chennai, India

To find out more about our authors and books visit www.bloomsbury.com and sign up for our newsletters.

To my beloved, Christine.

CONTENTS

Acknowledgements ix

Chapter 1
INTRODUCTION: THE NEGLECT OF KINSHIP IN THEOLOGICAL ETHICS 1
   Introduction 1
   The neglect of kinship 4
   Kinship and family in moral philosophy and bioethics: A brief overview 5
   Kinship and family in Christian theological ethics: A brief overview 10
   Kinship and family ties in John Paul II, Richard Baxter and Karl Barth 15
   Conclusion 22

Chapter 2
WHAT IS KINSHIP? 25
   Introduction 25
   American kinship 26
   A history of the study of kinship: Evolutionists, functionalists,
      structuralists and beyond 29
   Critiquing the study of kinship: Evolutionists 31
   Critiquing the study of kinship: Functionalists 33
   Critiquing the study of kinship: Structuralists 39
   Towards a definition of kinship after Schneider 44
   Conclusion 47

Chapter 3
SHEDDING BLOOD? KINSHIP AND SUBSTANCE 49
   Introduction: Substance and the folk theory of kinship 49
   Substance in Euro-American kinship 51
   Using the concept of blood in the theological ethics of kinship 57
   A genealogy of the blood tie 58
   The ugly turn in the history of the blood tie 63
   Eucharistic blood 68
   Conclusion: The disruptive blood tie 72

Chapter 4
THE CHRISTIAN HOUSEHOLD AND THE REIMAGINING OF KINSHIP — 77
Introduction — 77
Benedict in context: The household in Roman late antiquity — 78
The monastic house in *The Rule of St Benedict* — 82
Richard Baxter in context: The household in seventeenth-century England — 86
The family in Richard Baxter's *Christian Economics* — 89
A tale of two households — 94
Counter-cultural Christian households today — 100
Conclusion — 104

Chapter 5
GENDERED RELATEDNESS — 105
Introduction: Gendered relations and relative gender — 105
Christianity and gendered kinship: Augustine — 108
Christianity and gendered kinship: Karl Barth — 113
Initial theological conclusions — 122
Practising marriage, practising celibacy — 122
Conclusion — 128

Chapter 6
PERSONS IN CHRIST: KINSHIP BY BAPTISM — 131
Introduction: The anthropology of personhood and kinship — 131
Christian personhood — 133
Towards a theology of personhood for the ethics of kinship — 139
Practising baptism: Spiritual kinship — 148
Beginning and ending kinship — 151
Conclusion — 158

Chapter 7
CONCLUSION — 159
Christian kinship — 159
What about the nuclear family? — 166
The theology of kinship — 168
Final conclusions and further research — 176

Bibliography — 179
Index of Names — 192
Index of Subjects — 195
Index of Bible References — 199

ACKNOWLEDGEMENTS

This book started life as a PhD at the University of Cambridge, supervised by Michael Banner with generosity and skill. It was Michael who first taught me how the gospel is related to Christian ethics, and for that I'm deeply grateful.

The staff and students of Ridley Hall, where I was a Church of England ordinand through most of the PhD, gave me community and encouragement throughout, and the Church of England's Research Degrees Panel and Diocese of Ely provided encouragement and financial support. For further financial support, I am also grateful to Fitzwilliam College, for the Hirst-Player Studentship, and to Cambridge's Faculty of Divinity, for the Burney and Wordsworth Studentships and Steel Fund Scholarship.

Janet Soskice and Robert Song were both, in equal measure, incisive and encouraging as examiners.

I am enormously grateful to Brian Brock and Susan Parsons for receiving this book into their excellent series. It has been a pleasure to work with Sinead O'Connor at Bloomsbury and Vishnu Prasad R at Deanta.

I'm grateful to friends at the congregations of Highfield and St Denys' Churches, and the Diocese of Winchester, for affording me time away to write, and to Trinity College, Cambridge, for providing me a space to write as a visiting scholar.

Ryan Mullins, Matthew Johnson, Ip Pui Him, Matthew Lee Anderson, Jonathan Lett, Josh Hemmings, Hannah Malcolm, Luke and Jo Tarassenko, Jonathan Carter, Bobby Jamieson and Sam Carter individually provided theological friendship, in the rich research environment of Cambridge's postgraduate community. Neil Messer, Luke Tallon, Emma Wild-Wood, Gerald McKenny and Stephen Hampton each provided wise scholarly advice and encouragement.

The Society for the Study of Christian Ethics, Bob and Alice Evans's 'Religious History Conference Series', Priscilla Garcia's 'Christianity in Comparison Conference', Sotiris Mitralexis and Andrew Kaethler's 'Ontology and History Conference' and Ridley Hall's research seminar each provided early outings of ideas from this book, as well as helpful feedback and some lasting friendships. Jonathan Chaplain invited me to become a research associate at the Kirby Laing Institute for Christian ethics, affording me the chance to present as two associated conferences, and I am indebted to Jonathan for his counsel on the theology of marriage.

Christian Smith's Summer Seminar with the Notre Dame Institute for Advanced Studies gave me a new sense of how exciting interdisciplinary collaboration can be, and I am grateful to NDIAS for the financial support that made attendance possible.

I had to learn quickly about social anthropology for this project. I owe particular thanks to Joel Robbins who twice took time out of his busy schedule to talk with me. Tim Jenkins was a valued guide, as someone equally skilled as anthropologist and theologian, and through him I met others at the intersection between anthropology and theology. Patrick McKearney was my most consistent friend, guide and encourager in this exploration of his discipline. I am only a guest in social anthropology, and retain responsibility for any mistakes.

David Ford sat with me towards the end of the PhD to provide guidance on the book as a whole, and his advice was timely and helpful.

Anna Williams deserves a special mention, even though she had moved on by the time I was a PhD student. Her uncompromising focus on argumentation and deep love of historical theology, borne of a deep love of God, were an inspiration to me as an undergraduate.

Scott Thompson, Bob Eccles OP, Emlyn Williams, Sera Rumble and Tim Daulby have each, in recent years, taught me to put the ideas of this book into the context of everyday discipleship.

Sam Tranter read large parts of this as a PhD and has provided theological friendship of the highest order.

On the theme of kinship, Ariella and Martin have given us our own joyful adventure in spiritual kinship, and we are constantly schooled in the art by our son's godparents: Abi, Dan, Gina, Ben, Emma and Nick.

My brother Andrew read an early draft, giving detailed and helpful feedback. He has continually inspired me with his theological insight. Andrew, Peter and Robert have been faithful older brothers in Christ, each offering prophetic insight for my walk with Jesus.

I owe enormous debts of gratitude to Marion Foggin and Nick Smith, for always being there.

I cannot begin to offer sufficient thanks to Mum and Dad, whose love as parents pointed to the unconditional love of their Father and mine. Dad gave helpful feedback on a huge amount of this book. Mum died before I started studying theology but her influence lives on in myriad small ways in this book, as also in the lives of those she touched. She is alive with Christ.

Since then, Margaret ('Ma') has joined the family as my step-mother and, with her love and sense of fun, has been as good a proof as any that being a mother is not about biology.

Finally, my wife Christine has in countless ways enabled me to write this book and taught me about the love of God. She and John, our joy and delight, are a daily inspiration to rejoice in the Father's love.

Chapter 1

INTRODUCTION

THE NEGLECT OF KINSHIP IN THEOLOGICAL ETHICS

Introduction

Ideas of kinship play a significant role in structuring everyday life. Kinship can determine where a person lives, the company they keep, the ways they receive and spend money and the tasks that occupy them. Furthermore, kinship has greatly interested Christian thinkers, with the history of the Christian faith telling a story of profoundly critical reception of kinship norms through the centuries. This book will set out to make sense of these Christian critiques, and to discern both the logic of relatedness that Christianity might generate and the practical implications of this logic. Ultimately, the aim will be to sketch an account of how Christian faith might inform everyday practices of kinship. In offering such an account, the book will attempt to tap into the collective wisdom in the tradition, developed as successive generations of Christians through the centuries have commandeered cultural norms and refitted them for Christian use. Accordingly, the book will engage in dialogue not just with scriptural texts and great thinkers but also with social history, with particular emphasis on the theological rationale behind counter-cultural Christian practices.

When articulating a Christian account of kinship, a particular danger must be avoided: specifically, the basic assumption that kinship is a known quantity, something purely biological and therefore neither culturally contingent nor open to theological enquiry. If that assumption is wrong – and this book will argue that ideas of kinship are not a self-evident biological given – it seriously diminishes the value of ethical reflection 'downstream' on those practices informed by idioms of relatedness.

Having identified the danger of assuming that kinship is a biological given, it is necessary to state what this book is *not*. This book is not a theological broadside against the nuclear family. Rather, it is a theological engagement with what it means to be related to someone. It is certainly hoped that this might shape how the nuclear family is seen, and the book will touch on the validity of the nuclear family as an expression of Christian kinship throughout and engage with the question directly in the conclusion. However, this is not supposed to be an incursion into the culture wars, recommending that the nuclear family be protected, amended or rejected. Kinship understood rightly might be quite compatible with a range of different social structures depending on the circumstances, including the nuclear family. The question is whether ideas about kinship, in particular the idea that it is defined by reproduction (formed by blood ties or marriage), has limited the Christian moral imagination, blinding Christians to those who fall outside of the affection and obligations that go with kinship, such as the widow and orphan so commonly named in scripture.

While there have been a number of recent Christian accounts of family, some of which will be engaged later, none have delved deeply into the concept of relatedness itself. It is the contention of this book that the concept of relatedness should not be considered a given, but rather that it requires direct theological engagement in order for Christian theology to be released fully to inform those practices shaped by ideas of family.

In order to assess how the Christian faith might bear upon practices of kinship, and the underpinning ideas about relatedness, the net will be cast wide around disparate convictions that have shaped the kinship practices of Christian communities throughout history. By tracing the history of the church's engagement with kinship it is possible to observe the various pressures determining the development of Christian practice. Through engagement with the history of Christian thought and practice, these pressures will be sought out, and engaged critically, with the hope of offering a specifically Christian account of the very idea of relatedness, followed by the beginnings of an attempt to unpack this in Christian practice – again, in close dialogue with the past experience of Christians.

This book, then, will operate in dialogue with research in three different fields to engage the key question: How should Christians understand and practice kinship? First, adopting insights from social anthropology, it will be argued that kinship is culturally constructed, such that the form it takes is not a necessary entailment of human biological makeup, but that there are recurring themes in its expression cross-culturally. This will be argued in the context of a history of the social anthropology of kinship. Then, following the anthropologist Janet Carsten, the following four recurring symbols will be highlighted as important in giving meaning to kinship cross-culturally: the household, shared substance, gender and ideas of the person. This allows for a disjunctive definition of kinship: kinship is a mode of social organization that entails obligations and affections to some and not to others on the grounds of a relationship based on some mix of the following concepts: the house, gender, the person and shared substance.

Second, using social history and historical theology, the book will argue that there has been, in Christian history, recurring and significant critique of prevailing kinship norms. The development of monasticism and spiritual kinship, the introduction of wills whereby inheritance can pass out of family hands, the reshaping of marriage norms, the navigation of baptism and communion, and the endorsement of celibacy all bear witness to the uneasy relationship between Christianity and contemporary kinship norms. That said, history has also borne witness to a number of ways in which Christian convictions have been misapplied to everyday life (such as King Gunthcramn's abuse of spiritual kinship, or the popularizing of idioms of blood ties), and these will also be discussed in the following chapters. This study will not attempt to be comprehensive, and there will, of course, be sources and practices that are omitted, but it will endeavour to engage with the underlying logic of some prominent practices and arguments. It will thus serve to resource the following constructive work by introducing an ongoing discussion about the nature of Christian kinship to which this work will itself seek to contribute. Judgement about whether a practice is properly described as 'Christian' will be made on theological (rather than historical or anthropological) grounds. Nevertheless, this theological attention is merited by widely adopted and distinctively Christian kinship practices.

Third, the book will turn from the descriptive to the constructive, offering a theological account of kinship from a Christian perspective. To do so, the book will borrow resources from the social anthropology of kinship that help ethnographers structure their investigations in such a way that they avoid reading their own cultural presuppositions into the culture they seek to describe and instead can be sensitive to the internal dynamics of the culture they are studying. Similarly, it will use these same resources to guide the investigation into Christian understandings and practices of kinship, in such a way that the resulting account is preserved from alien cultural presuppositions. The key question driving this theological account is this: Is any notion of kinship theologically justifiable, and if so, what form should it take to constitute a consistent Christian vision of the world?

An anthropologist, using these tools, might write an ethnography. Nothing so specific as a '"proposed ethnography"' for Christian life can be offered by Christian ethicists, however. Any such attempt to delineate a universal, specific and radically different vision of life could not help but intrude into the finely balanced processes of everyday life as it responds to a variety of disparate real pressures. Practice is worked out in practice, not simply in the planning.

Instead, what will be offered is a toolkit for the recognition of those forms of kinship that might properly be identified as *Christian* – if, of course, there can be such a thing as Christian kinship. To put this idea of recognizing kinship another way, one ordination liturgy charges those ordained deacon to 'be faithful in prayer, expectant and watchful for signs of God's presence, as He reveals His kingdom among us'.[1] Within that vision of ministry, it is recognized that God is already at work, and His kingdom is to be sought out in order that the practitioner might participate. This toolkit might equip anyone interested in naming whether a kinship practice is a Christian practice, whether it be a Christian trying to discern God's leading, or simply a secular historian or anthropologist trying to make sense of the practices that they seek to describe.

---

1. Church of England, *Common Worship: Ordination Services* (London: Church House Publishing, 2007), available online: https://www.churchofengland.org/prayer-and-worship/worship-texts-and-resources/common-worship/ministry/common-worship-ordination-0#mm012 (accessed 21 April 2021).

So, the minister might observe and make sense of the ideas of kinship that animate and fill their own lives and those of their congregation. It will matter to the minister whether an idea is truly compatible with their Christian commitments, or whether it is an uncritically accepted cultural form. So, too, it matters to the Christian ethicist whether one of the broad range of moral problems that implicates kinship in fact arises as a result of a commitment to practices or ideas that are contradicted by even the most basic and foundational account of what forms of kinship can be said to be Christian.

The social anthropologist or historian, however, might try to make sense of the social transformations that follow widespread conversions within a society, say, or which theological ideas might promote the adoption of certain practices, such as spiritual kinship or monasticism. The social scientist might not seek to make any kind of prescriptive judgement, but the recognition of general themes in Christian kinship could certainly help them make sense as to whether the cause of a transformation is Christianity or some other factor.

What is proposed is an account of kinship that would help a minister or an ethicist working in a prescriptive key, or a social scientist working in a descriptive one, to make sense out of whether what they are presented with is, or is not, Christian. Examples will be given of such major ideas and practices – chief among them is the practice of using genetic relatedness as a prerequisite for kinship – that are incompatible with these central themes in the recognition of Christian kinship. However, the main purpose is to draw together broadly *uncontroversial* Christian ideas and practice in order to piece together a field guide for the recognition of Christian kinship at work.

Accordingly, what will be offered is a careful dismantling of some common-sense assumptions about kinship, drawn from theological investigation of the four symbols that Carsten highlights as common themes in kinship cross-culturally, and which require investigation if one is to shrug off the tight confines of one's own cultural assumptions. The result will be an account of Christian kinship that identifies the major themes that might mark out a practice or idea as Christian, and the theological logic behind them.

The neglect of kinship

In laying the groundwork for both the descriptive and constructive work described above, two tasks will help in assessing the current state of play in academic ethical reflection on issues relating to kinship. The first, to be undertaken in this chapter, is to uncover the tacit assumptions governing ethical discourse on the family. This will be undertaken through a survey of encyclopaedia entries, a select set of overviews within Christian ethics, and the investigations of major theologians. While the moral relevance of the concept of the family to a broad range of ethical issues is widely recognized, what should become apparent from this survey is that there is a serious lack of conceptual clarity on what constitutes family-relatedness. What constitutes kinship is left unstated, and instead there is a tendency for the category of 'family' to be used in such a way as to suggest that kinship is necessarily biologically determined. The second task, which will be the focus of the following chapter, will be to use field-defining research in social anthropology to expose as unwarranted the assumptions made about kinship.

The implications of this neglect are immense, as will be shown in the remainder of the book, in which it will also be argued that the history of the Christian faith bears witness to thought and practices that profoundly disrupt prevailing kinship norms. Accordingly, the beginnings of a constructive theological account of kinship will be offered, to reorient Christian ethics as it seeks to engage with the wide variety of moral issues impacted by ideas and practices of kinship.

The primary contribution of this book will be in the field of Christian theological ethics. However, the neglect of kinship is not unique to this field. As such, in addition to surveying major work on the family in Christian ethics, a brief survey will be offered of major reference works in bioethics and moral philosophy. In this way, the book will seek to expose the problems of engaging with the topic of family while neglecting to consider what precisely defines family. First, this general neglect will be exposed by an analysis of major reference works in ethics. Second, a closer study of the state of play in Christian ethics will be offered, leading to a critique of how investigations of family are approached. Finally, the book will evaluate three major thinkers in the history of theology who paid close attention to what it is that makes a family – John Paul II, Richard Baxter and Karl Barth.

By these means, neglect will be demonstrated at three levels: first, at the general disciplinary level as evidenced in encyclopaedia articles; second, at the focused sub-disciplinary level in studies on the Christian ethics of family; third, at the level of major dogmatic endeavours by leading figures in the history of theology. This is not to say that there exist no pearls of wisdom scattered throughout recent Christian theology, in biblical studies, systematic theology and Christian ethics. Rather, it is enough to say that, should a student of theology wish to sit down to study the Christian ethics of kinship, they would be led by the major relevant resources to believe that the very idea of relatedness is a natural 'given' to be accommodated, rather than a cultural norm to be theologically appraised. In other words, they would be led to believe that *there can be no ethics of kinship*. They would come to believe this, moreover, despite the vast resources available in the history of Christian thought and practice that have yet to be arranged in a systematic manner, but which suggest that the Christian faith has had and should have an impact on the understanding and practice of kinship.

This book seeks to draw attention to some of these resources, and in order to do so, it reveals the presence of a false idea – that kinship is a given – that inhibits the work of those who seek to articulate a Christian vision of kinship, and accordingly, of 'the family'.

Kinship and family in moral philosophy and bioethics: A brief overview

Turning, then, to major authoritative multi-volume encyclopaedias, there is no entry for kinship in those edited by Craig (the ten-volume *Routledge Encyclopedia of Philosophy*, recently taken over by Tim Crane), LaFollette (the nine-volume *The International Encyclopedia of Ethics*), Becker and Becker (the three-volume *Encyclopedia of Ethics*) and Reich (the five-volume *Encyclopedia of Bioethics*). They do, however, have entries relating to the concept of family. Still, even that choice of terminology reveals something of a problem, which is evident in the content of the entries.

William Ruddick, in his entry on the ethics of family in Craig's *Routledge Encyclopedia*, begins with the concept of the family, but nevertheless recognizes the challenge in engaging ethically with the category because of the 'diversity of families'. He proposes, therefore, six different conceptions – 'Metaphysical', 'Biological', 'Economic', 'Political', 'Psychological' and 'Narrative' – in order to draw on 'a plurality of approaches' which he considers may extend beyond these six. He seeks to offer a 'conceptually enriched capacity for moral reflection on family matters as they arise in context at different stages of our lives' and not a 'systematic ethics of the family'.[2]

However cautious Ruddick may look in adopting this multi-perspectival approach, his method is nevertheless determined by a basic understanding of what a family must be. For instance, Ruddick criticizes biological conceptions of the family in which gene-preserving strategies are identified as the basis for family life and instead identifies the need for 'non-biological bases' for kinship that explain these other ties, looking to economic, political, psychological and narrative conceptions. What, though, is the focus of these different angles from different disciplines? Clearly, Ruddick has an operating concept of family, because he is able to identify relevant material in each discipline, discuss their different conceptions of families and thus know what constitutes 'moral reflection on family matters'.[3] It might be a cautious and thin definition, but it is nevertheless active in the background. At best, the entry offers little to those engaging morally with 'family matters' both at the surface level, as they seek to make moral judgements about what is good to do, and at the deeper level (which resources those surface responses), as they think about why and to whom they have these obligations. At worst, the entry implies – without description or justification – the existence of a thin but nevertheless common-sense concept of family with which any reader would be familiar.

The problem with this is that any basic understanding of what constitutes a family will arise out of the cultural horizon of the reader. This means that morally pertinent questions, which will shape the final 'moral reflection on family matters', are skipped over. The necessary preparation for moral reflection is not done, because pre-existing assumptions about what supposedly 'must' constitute a family are left untouched. Ruddick's claim that the 'diversity of families, as well

---

2. William Ruddick, 'Family, Ethics and The', in *Routledge Encyclopedia of Philosophy*, ed. Edward Craig (London: Routledge, 1998), Available online: https://www.rep.routledge.com/articles/thematic/family-ethics-and-the/v-1 (accessed 15 April 2017).

3. Ibid.

as each family's complexity, may require a plurality of approaches, perhaps even greater than the six sketched here' simply leaves the question unraised: How should one understand what it means to be related?[4] Given that the very concept of relatedness is culturally contingent (which will be shown in the following chapter), this question needs to be identified as morally pertinent. As it is, it is left assumed that there is a necessary definition of family that is easily comprehensible to the one engaging in 'moral reflection on family matters', and which serves as a shared focus for different disciplinary investigations. This, however, is to skip the most basic moral question in the topic Ruddick tackles.

In order to respond to this criticism, it would be necessary for Ruddick to reflect on whether there is anything common to the various practices that he takes to concern an ethics of family. Whatever concept it is that holds the 'family matters' together would then need to be deconstructed, to see where the idea comes from, and how it might vary in describing different cultural settings. In this way, a concept that is able to describe as wide as possible an array of practices can then be used, in order that assumptions about human behaviour are not smuggled into reflection such that they determine the result. (The following chapter will identify the assumption that kinship relates necessarily to reproduction as particularly likely to generate poor description of other human possibilities.)

The best place to look in developing such a concept would be social anthropology, the subject devoted to the study of cultures, and indeed a subject which arguably originated in the study of kinship. Ruddick presents himself as consulting 'social scientists' and uses the expression 'in many cultures', but there are no social scientific studies referenced.[5] They may have shaped the entry regardless, but social science generally, and social anthropology specifically, is underrepresented in an entry that seeks to make sense of the practices and obligations associated with family.

Ruddick also writes the entry for 'Family' in the *Encyclopedia of Ethics*, edited by Becker and Becker. The bibliographies would be identical if Ekman, Ladd and Sartre were not passed over, and Archard, Parens and Plato recruited, but the content shifts to a more applied focus, attending to a range of moral questions associated with the concept of family. It pays particular attention to the problem of 'familial favoritism', summarizing the argument of the impartialists as, 'Even if kin favouritism is our biological bent, due to evolutionary genetic mechanisms, we should strive to transcend its limits in universalizing concern for all human beings. Even if blood is "thicker than water," it carries no moral weight.'[6] Neither of the objections that he describes (the 'particularist' or the 'personalist') shows any real interest in understanding how this favouritism works out in practice, or how it emerges. Rather, each engages at the level of hypothetical judgements that might

---

4. Ibid.
5. Ibid.
6. William Ruddick, 'Family', in *Encyclopedia of Ethics*, ed. Charlotte Becker and Lawrence Becker (London: Routledge, 2001), 523.

well inform moral engagement, but nevertheless are a step removed from the problems with which Ruddick and other ethicists want to engage. Given that the entry uses the concept of 'biological' relatives earlier on, without querying what this could mean, it is reasonable to suppose that the inattention to the lived reality of family emerges from a persistent underlying assumption – only occasionally questioned – that philosophers know more or less what family is and that this can, therefore, guide investigations of what family could possibly be. He avoids, on the one hand, thoroughgoing scepticism, calling into question every assumption about what constitutes family, and on the other hand, thick description, grappling with a rich description of lived reality. This means that the concept with which he operates is vulnerable to criticisms from both sides: on the one hand, the criticism that family as he imagines it does not really work like that, and on the other, the criticism that he assumes too much with his definition, ignoring moral possibilities by smuggling in assumptions about the way things have to be.

Of course, Ruddick is giving an account of the fields, and he is aware that there is something of a problem here, given his attempt in both entries to provoke dialogue with descriptive disciplines, even if social anthropology is neglected. In this way, Ruddick's entries offer a more promising picture of engagement with the question of kinship than Brighouse and Swift's entry in LaFollette's *The International Encyclopedia of Ethics*. Even though the entry calls into question whether genetic connections ought to be regarded as morally important, it does so from the perspective of justifying 'the family' and in the context of focussing on gendered relations and comparing the interests of parents, children and those of a 'third party'.[7] The focus on – to put it in anthropological terms – alliance and descent, and the casting of possible obligations to others, construes family as a mode of social organization associated with reproduction. It does so, however, without asking, first, whether kinship ought to be understood in this way, and second, whether this is, in fact, the case in practice.

Turning briefly aside from the general overviews of encyclopaedias, one finds neglect of the concept of kinship, and especially of the anthropological resources available to make sense of what it means to be related, in a recent focused treatment on the ethics of one kinship relation – that between parents and children. Brighouse and Swift write that 'The question of the nature of the interrelation between biological connectedness and social kinship (how universal? how deep?) is too big and hard for us to say more'. However, they then go on to say that 'even in a culture that puts great store by narratives involving biology, children can develop a sense of identity that will allow them to live flourishing lives without knowing much, perhaps anything, by way of specific information about their biological relations, let alone being parented by them'.[8] To put it positively, they might find

---

7. Harry Brighouse and Adam Swift, 'Family', in *The International Encyclopedia of Ethics*, ed. Hugh LaFollette (Oxford: Wiley-Blackwell, 2013), 1901.

8. Harry Brighouse and Adam Swift, *Family Values: The Ethics of Parent-Child Relationships* (Princeton: Princeton University Press, 2014), 81.

a tremendous ally in social anthropology (no anthropological text appears in the bibliography), if they wished to query the necessity of ideas of biological relatedness to the construction of the parent-child relation. To put it negatively, their later strategy of attending to the question of biological connections without due heed to social anthropology is risky, relying upon a sense of self-evidence about the nature of kinship practices that does not reckon with the cultural contingency of these beliefs. Take, for instance, the claim that 'Parenting by committee is not really *parenting*, and that remains true even if the committee is composed entirely of extended family members'.[9] This assumes a clear sense of what it means to be a parent that – if philosophical argumentation alone is used – clearly does not *have* to be universal.

Returning to encyclopaedias, consider Hilde and James Lindemann Nelson's entry on 'Family' in Reich's *Encyclopedia of Bioethics*, written principally from the perspective of family and medical care.[10] They note a general neglect of the topic of family and medicine, including the lack of an entry on family in the encyclopaedia's previous edition. The article is attentive to what 'family' might mean, and the authors offer a brief but sophisticated proposal for its definition using Wittgenstein's theory of family resemblances, which is similar to the approach to defining kinship used in the following chapter. However, it does so in a different way: one that reveals a failure to interrogate more deeply what constitutes a family. They propose that 'any social configuration that incorporates at least most of the morally significant features of, say, marital and parent-child relationships can be thought of as a family for present purposes'.[11] So, while this definition is sensitive to possibilities for variation in ideas of family, it still puts procreation at the centre without asking why this must be so. This problem is carried forward with their claim that 'none of us has chosen our blood relations', which relies upon a cultural idiom (to be explored later in this book). By assuming that kinship must be structured by procreation, they also come to make a moral assumption: this definition of kinship does not receive critical attention – to see if it is good that kinship is structured in this way – because it is assumed that it is simply necessary that kinship is that way.[12]

In each of these articles, social anthropology is notably absent as a dialogue partner, but this is not in itself the problem. Rather, the problem is that moral philosophical and bioethical issues are broadly being framed in the light of a category left undefined, so that a popular conception of family operates under the surface. In order to engage properly with the 'ought', and not merely reproduce a cultural 'is', it is necessary to gain distance from one's own cultural horizon, in order that internal cultural values might be seen as neither necessary nor necessarily good.

9. Ibid., 49.
10. Hilde Lindemann Nelson and James Lindemann Nelson, 'Family', in *Encyclopedia of Bioethics* (New York: Macmillan, 1995).
11. Ibid., 802.
12. Ibid., 804.

This study engages a selection of prominent general reviews of family, and there are moments of attention to the concept of kinship in philosophical discussions of specific ethical problems associated with kinship. For instance, attention to adoption stimulated a reference in Haslanger to the cultural constructedness of kinship, inspired by the anthropologist David Schneider.[13] However, this encouraging exception when dealing with one specific kinship practice does not overturn the general neglect of the topic in moral philosophy, especially at the thematic level in reference works. What is ultimately neglected, even in Ruddick's sophisticated philosophical critique of various ways of understanding the family, is the possibility not just that the structures of family are culturally conditioned, but that relatedness itself has no necessary form, and accordingly, that the very nature of relatedness is a moral question. It is strange, in short, that the question of whether other forms of construing relatedness are moral possibilities is so rarely asked as to be absent from major reference works in moral philosophy and bioethics.

In the next chapter, however, engagement with social anthropology – a discipline dedicated to describing social forms of practice and understanding – will reveal a long history of precisely this tendency as well, up until the 1960s. It should, then, come as no surprise that philosophers are not asking about different moral possibilities for the very concept of kinship, given social anthropologists spent a century overlooking the possibility that kinship might ever be structured by something other than procreation. There are signs of interest, especially in Ruddick, in the use of other disciplines, for securing the philosophical grasp on the slippery and complicated concept of family. This book seeks to assist in this project of handling the ethics of relatedness itself, though it will take a particular interest in theological ethics, to which this brief survey now turns.

Kinship and family in Christian theological ethics: A brief overview

Major encyclopaedias and introductions to Christian ethics do not fare much better than encyclopaedias and introductions to moral philosophy and bioethics with respect to entries on the idea of kinship, but still there are entries on family, a word liable to define a clear form and to draw attention away from what it means to be related in the first place. In Lacoste's *Encyclopedia of Christian Theology*, Lisa Sowle Cahill contributes an entry on family that is immediately attentive at least to different modes of being related: 'Knowing that family and structures of kinship take many forms across cultures, we are tempted to say that the family is only a social construction.'[14] In this way, she demonstrates a familiarity with anthropological

---

13. Sally Haslanger, *Resisting Reality: Social Construction and Social Critique* (Oxford: Oxford University Press, 2012), 176–7.

14. Lisa Sowle Cahill, 'Family', in *Encyclopedia of Christian Theology*, ed. Jean-Yves Lacoste (London: Routledge, 2005), 562.

discourse, as evidenced by the inclusion of one seminal anthropological work in the bibliography (David Schneider's *A Critique of the Study of Kinship*).[15]

Nevertheless, her attention to the anthropological literature leads her to be critical of those who consider family to be a cultural construction. She writes: 'It remains the case, however, that no known society has left human sexuality to function in a purely anarchic way, and that the multiplicity of familial structures shares one common feature: the universal existence of rules of marriage and systems of kinship.'[16] This still assumes a necessary connection between sexuality and kinship which is complex at least, and certainly not self-evident, insofar as kinship can be recognized without reference to sexual idioms. In a Christian context, the monastery would provide an obvious example, with the attribution of kinship terminology on the basis of co-residence and commitment to a shared rule (and the monastic reorganization of households ultimately testifies, it will be argued, to the recognition of one Father).

Cahill is clearly aware of the literature that proposes relatedness is not necessarily defined by procreation, and in this way, she sets herself apart from the philosophers surveyed earlier. The case for the cultural constructedness of kinship will be made in the following chapter, at which point the anthropological literature with which she disagrees will be defended. Cahill demonstrates, then, a deliberate neglect, as it were, of the ethics of kinship, because she considers relatedness to be a fact to be reckoned with, rather than a moral question to be raised. She does, however, raise the question of other modes of relatedness being made available within a 'religious conception of the family' by 'blood, marriage or adoption.'[17] While including adoption, she nevertheless seeks 'procreation and kinship as strong determinants of family ties' based on a Christian 'ethic of corporal realities.' In making sense of adoptive kinship, she elevates love, which 'prohibits us from regarding the family as a biologically grounded social mechanism for the efficient organization of reproduction, material life, and protection.'[18] She takes love, then, to ground the forms of social organization – such as adoption – that emerge from Christian commitment to hospitality. However, the call to love one's neighbour does not disrupt the basis of relatedness, which she takes to be founded on biological facts.

This is borne out in Cahill's wider work. For instance, her *Family: A Christian Social Perspective* surveys Christian ideas about family but is prefaced with the following definition: 'The family is here understood as basically an organized network of socioeconomic and reproductive interdependence and support

---

15. Her work is also well informed by historical work, and historians can also show the contingency of kinship. However, they are less equipped to do this than anthropologists, who engage in extensive comparative work for the purpose of studying, and translating for readers, a wide variety of living kinship practices.
16. Cahill, 'Family', 562.
17. Ibid.
18. Ibid., 565.

grounded in biological kinship and marriage. Kinship denotes affiliation through reproductive lines.'[19] This is not simply Cahill defining her own terminology for her own use, and using notions of family and kinship in different ways to anthropologists. She subsequently claims, 'The fact that *family* is defined primarily in terms of kinship in virtually all cultures signifies the importance of *the body* and of essential material needs in defining the family and its functions.'[20] Cahill offers no supporting evidence for this claim to universality, but particularly interesting is her use of the word 'virtually', suggesting exceptions, which is problematic in a context where universality is being used in order to defend the idea that kinship is necessarily defined by procreation.

She does, however, engage briefly with the anthropological evidence in an earlier work. In *Sex, Gender and Christian Ethics*, she considers David Schneider's reflections on the Yapese, noting that, whereas they had told Schneider 'coitus had nothing to do with the birth of children', in fact, 'Twenty years later, a colleague was given different information: coitus is necessary to conception, on the analogy of planting a seed in a garden'. Cahill grants, citing Schneider, that this shows a degree of 'variety in cultural explanations of the precise nature of male and female

---

19. Lisa Sowle Cahill, *Family: A Christian Social Perspective* (Minneapolis: Fortress Press, 2000), x–xi.

20. Ibid., xi. Halvor Moxnes makes a similar methodological move, assuming that kinship is necessarily defined by procreation. However, he also sets out to study early Christian families with recourse to households and marriage, studied on their own terms. This expansion of focus is salutary, but his methodology still assumes concepts of family connect necessarily with procreation. By assuming upfront that ideas of relatedness rely on procreation, Moxnes does not consider that early Christian practice might be shaped by other understandings of kinship, and so he cannot interpret practice in the light of possible variations in the understanding of relatedness. Moxnes's understanding of kinship is not cross-culturally applicable, and therefore hampers investigation into other cultures, as Moxnes sets out to do in studying early Christians. This critique does not serve to question every study of practice in the volume. For instance, Barclay (who adopts a slightly different methodology than Moxnes in the introduction to his chapter) describes the challenges to pre-existing concepts of kinship, and this conclusion is not strictly dependent on accurate description of those prevailing ideas of kinship. Rather, this critique serves to draw attention to the need for a work on Christian conceptions of relatedness informed by a critical account of the concept of kinship. (Cf. Halvor Moxnes, 'What is a Family? Problems in Constructing Early Christian Families', in *Constructing Early Christian Families: Family as Social Reality and Metaphor*, ed. Halvor Moxnes (London: Routledge, 1997), 14–18; John M. G. Barclay, 'The Family as the Bearer of Religion in Judaism and Early Christianity', in *Constructing Early Christian Families: Family as Social Reality and Metaphor*, ed. Halvor Moxnes (London: Routledge, 1997), 66, 72–5.). Unless otherwise stated, emphasis in quotations is in the original text

cooperation for reproduction'.²¹ However, she takes the later report as evidence of the fact that 'All societies recognize human relations built on genealogical ties, beginning with lineages of mothers and children, and including men as fathers to the extent that biological paternity is recognized'.²²

However, this is precisely what Schneider begs anthropologists not to bring to their ethnographic practice: the (false) 'Doctrine of the Genealogical Unity of Mankind, the thesis that at one level all genealogies are equal to each other, or can be treated as dealing with the same thing and so are comparable'.²³ Suffice it to say (until Schneider's own treatment of the evidence can be discussed in more detail in the following chapter), while Cahill is of course free to interpret Schneider's gathering of the evidence different, it should at least provoke pause that Cahill should use Schneider's *own* report of varying accounts of Yapese kinship in the context of proposing a completely contradictory claim about the universality of 'genealogical ties' (which Schneider argues are not universally recognized).²⁴

Don Browning is another recent theological ethicist who engages directly with David Schneider, in a posthumously published article in *Zygon* – though he does so only to present counter-evidence from the primatologist Bernard Chapais, and without engaging directly with Schneider's argument in the way that Cahill does. Cahill's and Browning's objections will both be engaged more fully in the following chapter, in the context of presenting Schneider's argument.²⁵

Cahill's moral thought with respect to the family focuses on proposing that the Christian family is a 'socially transformative family that seeks to make the Christian moral ideal of love of neighbor part of the common good' in a way that 'the nuclear family focused inward on the welfare to its own members' is not.²⁶ Cahill's work in this respect is informed and useful, and it is simply the question of kinship, or relatedness, that invites analysis.

Turning away from Cahill, another relevant encyclopaedia entry is offered by Stephen Barton in *The Oxford Companion to Christian Thought*. In the opening paragraph, Barton notes: 'Christianity inherited political ideals and patterns of social organization that accorded the patriarchal household a central role as the city-state in microcosm'.²⁷ He not only notices, then, the contingency of the forms inherited by Christianity but also goes on to explain the many ways in

---

21. Lisa Sowle Cahill, *Sex, Gender, and Christian Ethics* (Cambridge: Cambridge University Press, 1996), 102, 290n73; David M. Schneider, *A Critique of the Study of Kinship* (Ann Arbor: University of Michigan Press, 1984), 28.

22. Cahill, *Sex, Gender, and Christian Ethics*, 102.

23. Schneider, *A Critique*, 125.

24. Cahill, *Sex, Gender, and Christian Ethics*, 102.

25. Don S. Browning, 'A Natural Law Theory of Marriage', *Zygon* 46, no. 3 (1 September 2011): 752–5.

26. Cahill, *Family*, xii.

27. Stephen C. Barton, 'Family', in *The Oxford Companion to Christian Thought*, ed. Adrian Hastings et al. (Oxford: Oxford University Press, 2000), 235.

which Christian teaching inflected or critiqued what was inherited, and thus what comes to be distinctive about Christian practices of family. He surveys briefly the history of distinctively Christian thought on family and marriage, focussing on key moments, such as the emergence of monasticism.

However, he partakes in the trend found in Cahill, to assume that a 'biological family' is self-evident and that theology might go beyond it but never unsettle it. For instance, he speaks about 'monastic traditions in which the family image was carried beyond the biological family'.[28] These monastic ties are then described as taking the 'symbolism of family ties to constitute themselves as spiritual families'.[29] He makes a parallel judgement in an earlier monograph, in which he claims that, in Mark's Gospel, 'the believer's identity is defined no longer primarily in relation to his/her ties of natural kinship and household belonging . . . but in terms of ties of fictive or spiritual kinship to Jesus'.[30] Both of these share an assumption that there is a default biological kinship which might be altered, or might provide material for constructing different non-kinship ties, but might never be called into question itself. However, if supposedly biological kinship is not biological at all, but the product of Euro-American culture, then the door is opened for discerning how Christians might understand kinship in the first instance.

Barton describes clearly that the New Testament witness has profound implications for the practice of kinship, and he testifies to this in his survey of the history of the Christian faith. However, his critical orientation to the family is never allowed to penetrate properly into whether Christianity generates a distinctive understanding of what it means to be related. The question of kinship is left aside, and accordingly the encyclopaedia entry opens, 'The family and marriage have been Christian concerns from the earliest days of the church', without a definition of what this means. Barton offers an admirable survey of the history of Christian thought on the structuring of the family, and includes in this survey monasticism, suggesting an openness to the possibility that Christian theology of the family might endorse ties beyond the procreative. However, that procreative definition of family seems otherwise to be the condition for inclusion in the survey, meaning that a concept of kinship that is not investigated becomes the net that is cast around the history of Christian reflection and practice on the theme of family. In fairness, any survey is likely to be limited somewhat by the wording of the theme, and 'family' is a more recognizable word than 'kinship'. That proviso goes to all of the encyclopaedia entries assessed here. However, social anthropologists have become expert at dodging this problem, learning from myriad ethnographies of social structures in societies across the world what questions to ask in order to give a fair reflection of the subject material, as defined by its internal logic. So too, that

---

28. Ibid.

29. Ibid.

30. Stephen C. Barton, *Discipleship and Family Ties in Mark and Matthew*, Society for New Testament Studies Monograph Series 80 (Cambridge: Cambridge University Press, 1994), 123.

is the approach that this book suggests must be taken to any survey of Christian reflection on family: allow the perspective to be defined not by a normal Western use of the word but allow the internal logic of Christianity to challenge the very concept in the first place. Barton has the instinct – perhaps formed by careful analysis of discipleship in the Gospels on this very theme – to include monasticism as obviously relevant. That suggests, however, that an alternative definition of kinship might be found to structure a survey of Christian reflection on family.

Both Cahill and Barton are sensitive to the ways in which the Christian faith alters the practice of family, but each – for different reasons – does not explore how Christianity might influence the understanding of kinship itself. In so doing, their accounts are unnecessarily tied to a cultural assumption about what constitutes kinship, which is not subject to theological investigation.[31]

Kinship and family ties in John Paul II, Richard Baxter and Karl Barth

Neglect of kinship is not confined to encyclopaedias or recent monographs on the topic of family. The same sort of assumptions about what must constitute kinship find their place in the work of those engaged in large-scale treatments of Christian theological ethics. Three who stand out are Pope John Paul II, the Puritan Richard Baxter and the Swiss Reformed theologian Karl Barth.

In *Familiaris Consortio*, John Paul II writes that 'The family, which is founded and given life by love, is a community of persons: of husband and wife, of parents and children, of relatives'[32] and a little later 'Conjugal communion constitutes the foundation on which is built the broader communion of the family, of parents and

---

31. Brent Waters's treatment of the relationship between family and Christian political thought relies on similar assumptions about kinship. His mention of 'involuntary social and biological bonds imposed by the family' receives no further explanation. Even the teleological reordering of present ties – '[a]s the most basic form of human association, the family is part of a vindicated creation being drawn towards its destiny in Christ' – is not allowed to penetrate the question of kinship. Rather, the family is stated, without explanation, to be the most basic form of human association. This suggests an uncritical assumption that procreation defines kinship, also evidenced by the continual pairing of 'marriage and family'. The relationship of the family with wider political thought receives well-deserved critical theological attention in a wide-ranging survey of historical materials. However, he skips a step before asking his opening question – 'What is *the* Christian family?' – which is to raise the question as to the definition of family, and whether Christianity might offers its own answer. (Brent Waters, *The Family in Christian Social and Political Thought* (Oxford: Oxford University Press, 2007), ix–x, 1.)

32. John Paul II, *On the Family: Apostolic Exhortation Familiaris Consortio of His Holiness Pope John Paul II to the Episcopate to the Clergy and to the Faithful of the Whole Catholic Church Regarding the Role of the Christian Family in the Modern World* (Rome: Libreria Editrice Vaticana, 1981), §18.

children, of brothers and sisters with each other, of relatives and other members of the household. This communion is rooted in the natural bonds of flesh and blood.'[33] Similarly, in the *Catechism* promulgated under John Paul II: 'A man and a woman united in marriage, together with their children, form a family. . . . It should be considered the normal reference point by which the different forms of family relationship are to be evaluated.'[34] While Catholic social thought is, of course, a rich and varied tradition, it seems at these junctures to be replicating the Euro-American family (which will be described, using the work of anthropologist David Schneider, in the following chapter). In both instances, the controlling idea for the concept of kinship is the family as defined by procreation. Justification could certainly be offered for the place of marriage in forming relatedness, as will be done later in a chapter on gender, and some attention will also be paid later to possibilities of connecting conception with kinship. In neither case, however, will it be taken that this must be how kinship is construed, as though it could not be otherwise. While it might be the case for Barth and Baxter (discussed later) that they are unaware that they are making normative claims in taking kinship to be constituted in this way, the same cannot be said of John Paul II. The question remains, however, whether his preference for family constituted in this way conceals a cultural bias, given that he does not submit the concept of 'flesh and blood', for instance, to theological investigation. If so, the moral *question* of kinship is still neglected.

Richard Baxter will be discussed further in a later chapter on the household in Christian thought. At this point, it is simply his work in defining family that is relevant. In his *Christian Economics*, written in 1664–5,[35] Baxter plans the order and activities of the household in the light of Christian belief. For Baxter, Christians know from scripture to provide for their families, and from nature who counts as family.[36] For him, a family was a household composed of the governor and the governed, and, when complete, 'A father, mother, son, and servant'.[37] In this way, he focused self-consciously on the smallest of those concentric sociopolitical circles in which he was interested: 'not a tribe or stock of kindred, dwelling in many houses as the word is taken oft in scripture, but I mean a household'.[38] The theological validity of this was self-evident to Baxter: 'That families are societies of God's institution, needeth no proof.'[39] The important historical background

---

33. Ibid., §21.

34. *Catechism of the Catholic Church* (Geoffrey Chapman-Libreria Editrice Vaticana, 1994), §2202, 475–6.

35. Published in 1672–3.

36. Richard Baxter, *A Christian Directory: Or, a Sum of Practical Theology, and Cases of Conscience*, Part 2. *Christian Economics (or Family Duties)*, The Works of the Rev. Richard Baxter 4 (London: James Duncan, 1830), 69.

37. Ibid., 50.

38. Ibid.

39. Ibid., 52.

to this will be explored later, but at this point, it should be sufficient to say that Baxter does considerable work on the ordering of family-relatedness around the procreative union, without asking theologically why this must be so. There is a political philosophy in the background that draws his eyes to the ordering of wider society, and which determines his approach to the structure of the family, but Baxter gives no sense that the nature of kinship itself is in question and that the affections and obligations that attend it might emerge from more complex factors than procreative unions.

Karl Barth's neglect of kinship is particularly interesting. For Barth, any attempt to bring ethics into dialogue with 'general anthropology' – that is, accounts of human nature derived from sources other than Christian dogmatics – places the church, in its teaching, under 'an utterly alien sovereignty'.[40] If, as Barth says, 'dogmatics itself is ethics; and ethics is also dogmatics',[41] then his approach to the ethics of human ordering must be wholly determined by theological reflection on revelation, and never by observations about the natural ordering of things. Accordingly, of those surveyed, Barth is, methodologically, the most committed to caution in accepting established social norms.

Barth's thought on marriage as a separate topic will be considered later, but at this point, the key text is §54.2 ('Parents and Children'). Barth justifies special treatment of the relationship between parents and children on the basis that other relations are 'mediated' through it.[42] He is distinctly cautious, however, as to how he might define the relationship. He does this by looking at the reality that human beings are conceived and born and can, possibly, conceive as well, from the perspective of the divine command, and in this case, the fifth commandment specifically.[43] Accordingly, he dismisses as historically variable, and therefore culturally contingent, any idea of 'family' as a focus for his investigation. In so doing, he demonstrates his methodological commitment to trust entirely in revelation. He is content to speak theologically about the relationship between parents and children only because he considers it a category accepted and endorsed in scripture.[44]

Barth's focus may appear overly precise, but he justifies his caution. He is committed to avoiding the language of orders of creation, estates or mandates as found in Luther and Bonhoeffer respectively, which he deals with in §52.1 ('The Problem of Special Ethics').[45] While he commends Bonhoeffer's attempt to use the

---

40. Karl Barth, *Church Dogmatics: The Doctrine of the Word of God*, ed. G. W. Bromiley and T. F. Torrance, trans. G. T. Thompson et al., vol. I/2 (Edinburgh: T&T Clark, 1956), 782–3.

41. Ibid., 793.

42. Karl Barth, *Church Dogmatics: The Doctrine of Creation*, ed. G. W. Bromiley and T. F. Torrance, trans. A. T. Mackay et al., vol. III/4 (Edinburgh: T&T Clark, 1961), 242.

43. Ibid., 240.

44. Ibid., 241–3.

45. Ibid., 21–2.

language of 'mandates', rooted in divine commands, to avoid drawing theological conclusions from observations about the natural ordering of things, he famously finds Bonhoeffer guilty of preserving the vestiges of 'North German patriarchalism' all the same.[46] Nevertheless, their approaches are similar, with Barth describing the differentiation and relationship between childhood and parenthood as the second sphere (*Bereich*:[47] sphere, domain or area) of human fellowship after the differentiation and relationship between male and female.[48] Barth's approach is leaner, content to leave something unsaid rather than risk relying on anthropology.

It is with this in mind that Barth frames the section as an interpretation of the fifth commandment, to honour father and mother (Ex. 20.12, Deut. 5.16). Specifically, he seeks to communicate what the command means for Christians in the light of Jesus Christ, through whom he finds it to be binding to the Christian. Barth thinks the 'individual Israelite' relates to God as Father in Israel, whereas the Christian relates to God as Father in Christ. As such, Christian relationship to the fatherhood of God is not taken to be mediated by the parenthood of 'earthly parents', which defines the logic of the identity found in being members of God's chosen people.[49] As a result, further hermeneutical work is needed to make sense of the implications of the fifth commandment

---

46. Ibid., 21. Cf. Dietrich Bonhoeffer, *Ethics*, ed. C. J. Green, trans. R. Krauss, C. C. West, and D. W. Scott, Dietrich Bonhoeffer Works 6 (Minneapolis: Fortress Press, 2009), 388/392. Bonhoeffer intended something similar to Barth, however. The mandates 'depend solely on God's *one* commandment as it is revealed in Jesus Christ' in which God confronts humanity both with His love and with the reality of human guilt, and in the light of this confronts humanity with Himself and with the fellow human being. Confronted with God's love and identification with humanity in the shame of guilt, the mandates are visible as 'orders' of 'God's love for the world and for human beings that has been revealed in Jesus Christ'. (Bonhoeffer, *Ethics*, 390/394.) Furthermore, he grounds the ordering not in creation but in providence, or preservation, writing in the 1932–3 lectures, *Creation and Fall*, 'All the orders of our fallen world are God's orders of preservation on the way to Christ. They are not orders of creation but of preservation. They have no value in themselves. They are accomplished and have purpose only through Christ'. (Dietrich Bonhoeffer, *Creation and Fall: A Theological Interpretation of Genesis 1–3*, trans. J. C. Fletcher (London: SCM, 1959), 91.) Bonhoeffer himself considered the mandates an improvement on the language of the Lutheran 'order' as the latter might conjure the 'romantic conservatism that no longer has anything to do with the Christian doctrine of the four mandates'. (Bonhoeffer, *Ethics*, 389/393.) The sort of romantic conservatism Bonhoeffer had in view is evident in the Nazi slogan: 'Kinder, Küche, Kirche'. The slogan calls German women to serve the three orders of creation that might traditionally have been *their* orders: children, kitchen (or home) and church.

47. Karl Barth, *Die Kirchliche Dogmatik: Die Lehre von Der Schöpfung*, vol. III/4 (Zürich: Theologischer Verlag Zürich, 1980), 269.

48. Barth, *Church Dogmatics*, 1961, III/4, 240, 117.

49. Ibid., 248.

for Christian parental relationships. Barth warns that 'patriarchal modes of thought' in the Old Testament might have left hidden the 'spiritual nature of the command', as interpreted in Lk. 2.41-51 (a story 'not conceivable in the Old Testament'). Nevertheless, he finds the same message in the original command to Abraham in Genesis 12: 'Get thee out of thy country, and from thy kindred, and from thy father's house, unto a land that I will shew thee.'[50] Finding support in Col. 3.20 and Eph. 6.1 in which the pleasure of the Lord is connected with the rationale for honouring parents, Barth sets out to interpret the fifth commandment in light of the first, to have no other God.[51]

This provides the basis on which Barth can turn a critical eye to contemporary inflation of parental authority or responsibility. The parent is not the ultimate provider, advocate, guardian and teacher of the child, and to live properly for one's children means to 'stand before them in confidence' that it is God alone who offers these things.[52] Accordingly, any authority is only a reflection, not unlike the place of the abbot in the monastery, who takes the place of Christ for the sake of the fellow monks, but is not to view themselves as such.[53] For Barth, too, the fundamental call of the earthly parent is to witness to the one true Father.[54] This fits with the thrust of Barth's moral theology, neatly summarized nearby: 'the fulfilment of the Law which in spite of sin even sinful men are invited to accomplish through the grace of God revealed and operative in Jesus Christ, and of which they are also capable through this triumphant grace.'[55] This policy of reading ethics in the light of what John Webster characterizes as the 'ontological preponderance and inclusiveness of the history of Jesus Christ'[56] shapes the judgements Barth makes about the proper shape of human living. In this way, responsibility and gratitude to Jesus Christ are brought to determine the content of Barth's description of Christian living.[57]

Nevertheless, there is a further principle that shapes Barth's approach to parents and children. Parents are defined as those responsible for the existence of the child, in a clear allusion to generation.[58] If the interpretation of the command relied purely on the accurate observation of a supposed physical fact of parenthood, then there would indeed be little to be said, other than that

---

50. Ibid., 249.

51. Ibid., 244.

52. Ibid., 279.

53. Benedict, *The Rule of St. Benedict*, ed. Timothy Fry (Collegeville: The Liturgical Press, 1981), 2.1–40, 21–5; 64.13, 88.

54. Cf. Barth, *Church Dogmatics*, 1961, III/4, 245.

55. Ibid., 258.

56. John Webster, *Barth's Ethics of Reconciliation* (Cambridge: Cambridge University Press, 1995), 225.

57. McKenny proposes that the themes of responsibility and gratitude to Christ define Barth's ethics. Gerald McKenny, *The Analogy of Grace: Karl Barth's Moral Theology* (Oxford: Oxford University Press, 2010), 16.

58. Barth, *Church Dogmatics*, 1961, III/4, 277.

honouring parents might be consistent with the child leaving the parents. If, however, kinship is not determined physically but culturally, then there is a gap for further theological thinking about the conditions for the inception, and indeed continuity, of kinship.

Barth writes that, in interpreting the fifth commandment, 'It is not with this physical relationship as such that the command is concerned, but with a certain oversight and responsibility with regard to the children which this physical relationship implies for the parents'.[59] This claim is critical to Barth's account of the parent-child relationship. He expands his account on the basis of relatedness – the 'physical relationship' – with the observation that children stand 'immediately in a special, exclusive and lasting relationship precisely to these two persons'.[60] This may appear self-evident, and it certainly does to Barth, but what precisely generates this relationship? Is it the sharing of biogenetic substance, or responsibility attending the act of procreation, or the proximity of pregnancy (and the assumed presence of a husband), or something else altogether?

Procreative responsibility seems to stand out: 'It is to them that he owes his existence'.[61] However, while that might work for the parent to the child, further work needs to be done to substantiate the character of the relationship to bear the weight of Barth's expectations concerning the duties of the child in connection with the procreative decision of their parents. This is not to question that Christians should only seek to procreate with due concern for the children conceived. It is just that this idea cannot, in itself, sustain all that Barth wants of it, notably the building of wider kinship relationships on the basic relationship of procreator and procreated: 'We may at least remember that most men are surrounded by a greater or smaller circle of such natural relations', which are made sense of out of the 'relations between parents and children'. Why? 'These are certainly the basic forms of all the relations which arise in this connexion.'[62]

In addition to the weaker basis of responsibility in procreation, Barth offers a stronger basis for kinship: shared substance. Barth sees procreation as conferring a '*character indelebilis*', which results in the honour of sharing 'his own flesh and blood' and the obligation that attends responsibility for an event.[63] The obligation reflects that weaker basis, but the honour reflects the stronger basis: the idiom of 'flesh and blood'. The cultural contingency of the notion of the shared substance will be explored in the following two chapters, but the point here is that these

---

59. Ibid., 243.

60. Ibid., 240.

61. Ibid. While Barth adds that the 'This oversight and responsibility does not belong to the physical but, broadly speaking, to the historical order' a little later, all that he means is that it is by virtue of the fact that they are elders that they bear the responsibility – it does not serve to add any detail as to how those particular elders are parents. (Barth, *Church Dogmatics*, III/4, 243.)

62. Barth, *Church Dogmatics*, 1961, III/4, 241.

63. Ibid., 277.

ideas of shared substance do not spring directly and self-evidently from the act of procreation itself. Rather, they are more socially complex and require broader theological investigation and support than his relatively simple claim about the conferring of a *character indelebilis*.

When Barth interprets the honouring of parents as the honouring of God, drawing on Lk. 11.27-28, he allows this to trouble even 'biological fatherhood' (which would be better rendered 'vital, physical fatherhood' in order to disentangle it from recent, British-American idioms[64]). He affirms that 'physical sons' (*den physischen Söhnen*) should respect this, but that, in Proverbs and the New Testament, 'the mission of the older to the younger can seriously exist and be fulfilled' even in contexts other than 'physical parenthood' (*physische Vater- und Sohnschaft*).[65] While it is certainly not a major theme in Barth's account of the relationship between parents and children, he nevertheless does concede the possibility of kinship outside of whatever constitutes 'physical' parenthood. For instance, adoption is briefly considered, as a means by which a parental gap can be 'directly filled' for a child, as well as a small comfort for the involuntarily childless. Adoption is the exception rather than the rule and in his acceptance of it under certain circumstances, it is presented as a fictive fix in hard times rather than a deeply Christian practice, and adoption by voluntarily non-procreative couples is not considered.[66]

Barth had already clarified that the 'mission' associated with the fifth commandment can apply outside of the context of 'physical parenthood'.[67] This leads to a theological answer to the rationale for parenthood, which leads ultimately to the conclusion that 'No human father, but God alone, is properly, truly and primarily Father'. Alongside scriptural support, Barth argues that any parental duty is ultimately fulfilled by God par excellence, from being the source of the child's life to the overseer of their flourishing and salvation.[68] Barth finds, then, the theological justification which will be crucial to any account of Christianity and kinship: the siblinghood of Christians, the adoption of the Christian in Christ,[69] and the place of God alone as Father, which is itself cut loose

---

64. In the context, *Die vitale* appears to mean that the character of being physical parents provokes in the children a 'vital emotional relationship' which Barth sidelines as irrelevant to the respect due. The German there is *'eine vital emotionale Bindung'*, suggesting a vitality to the physical connection mentioned earlier with emotional ramifications, which could only be misleadingly translated in terms of 'biological fatherhood' in Barth's usage. (Barth, *Die Kirchliche Dogmatik*, III/4, 274.)

65. Barth, *Die Kirchliche Dogmatik*, 1980, III/4, 274; Barth, *Church Dogmatics*, 1961, III/4, 244.

66. Barth, *Church Dogmatics*, 1961, III/4, 268.

67. Ibid., 244.

68. Barth cites Isa. 63.15, Mt. 23.9 and Eph. 3:15. Barth, *Church Dogmatics*, III/4, 245.

69. 'But every child of man – because Jesus Christ is his Brother – is primarily and truly the child of God'. (Barth, *Church Dogmatics*, III/4, 246.)

by Jesus's exhortation to call no man father from some of the uses to which human beings put the term. Nevertheless, none of this dogmatic disruption to earthly perception of the world brings into question the basis on which earthly parents are identified.

Conclusion

The main purpose of this introduction is to show simply that the topic of kinship has been neglected in moral reflection. While the concept of family receives attention in moral philosophy, bioethics or Christian theological ethics, it generally does so without taking seriously what really constitutes the relatedness that binds families together. Different forms of neglect are evident: first, some do not question at all whether family-relatedness might be construed differently; second, some demonstrate some awareness of the variability of families but nevertheless allow an uncritical account of the family to operate under the surface; third, some take family to be straightforwardly defined by reproduction, even if they are conscious of arguments to the contrary. In each instance, the task of engaging morally with the very basis of relatedness is neglected, either deliberately or accidentally. The accounts of those for whom the neglect is deliberate – Cahill and Browning – will receive further treatment in the following chapter, in order to demonstrate that there is, in fact, a moral question to be engaged.

This introduction is not intended to be comprehensive. Rather, it serves to highlight that moral questions relating to family are widely being discussed without the question being asked whether the nature of relatedness can be taken for granted as a 'given', rather than being treated as a moral question with which to wrestle. The problem is not that social anthropology was not consulted, though anthropological evidence can alert the ethicist to the cultural contingency of relatedness, but rather that the question of what actually constitutes kinship is neglected. Accordingly, an account of family is used without sufficient recognition of the possibility of kinship being construed differently. Direct attention to the question of kinship, then, is overdue.

Within Christian theological ethical reflection – the main focus of the book – two treatments of ethical questions relating to kinship stand out as not party to this general neglect. First, while Jana Marguerite Bennett's *Water Is Thicker than Blood*, which will feature later in this study, never explicitly explores how Christianity might call into question and alter the very grounds of relatedness, she nevertheless operates with particular caution in avoiding allowing procreation to determine her use of kinship language. While there are certainly many others who are attuned to the disruptive potential of Christianity to the very idea of relatedness, Bennett is particularly consistent in this, despite never dealing head-on with the concept of relatedness itself as a topic for sustained moral theological attention. To be clear, it is no failure that Bennett does not tackle the issue head-on, as such direct engagement simply falls outside the scope of her project, but kinship is nevertheless handled well.[70] Second, Michael Banner's *The Ethics of Everyday Life* observes the 'troubling' of kinship in the New Testament, particularly in dialogue with Augustine, and attends to some of the anthropological material surveyed in the following chapter.[71] This study will attempt to complete some of the picture started there, setting out the beginnings of a Christian theological account of kinship.

When it is recognized that the ways in which family are constructed depend on a range of factors, and thus that reproduction is relativized as one factor among others, then it is possible to be alert to the different ways that family-relatedness is being construed when turning to other cultures worldwide or in history, free of the assumption that reproduction fundamentally defines kinship. Theologically, this is significant, because a range of modes of social organization that might be considered fictive – because they do not seem to call on reproduction for their meaning – can be treated as simply *kinship* (though consciously fictive kinship remains possible). There is a tradition of thought about kinship, then, that awaits consideration, either because Christian practices were not taken to challenge the very conditions for the recognition of family or because Christian practices were not taken to relate to kinship in any real way as they do not refer to reproduction.

Before exploring history for signs of distinctively Christian understandings of kinship, however, the simple question must be addressed: What is kinship?

---

70. Jana Marguerite Bennett, *Water Is Thicker than Blood: An Augustinian Theology of Marriage and Singleness* (Oxford: Oxford University Press, 2008), chap. 7.

71. Michael Banner, *The Ethics of Everyday Life: Moral Theology, Social Anthropology, and the Imagination of the Human* (Oxford: Oxford University Press, 2014), chaps. 2–3.

Chapter 2

WHAT IS KINSHIP?

Introduction

The previous chapter's brief survey of ethical investigations into the family generated a recurring complaint – namely, a question has been neglected: What constitutes family-relatedness? It is generally assumed to be too obvious to mention that reproduction explains relatedness and, if it is mentioned, insufficient philosophical or theological justification is offered for the concept of family-relatedness that is used. In other words, the question has not been asked: If families – whatever they happen to be – are tied together by kinship, what then is kinship?

Social anthropology is in a particularly good position to explain this neglect not simply because it seeks to describe cultures but also because it has a long history of precisely this neglect hampering its attempts to comprehend and communicate cultures across cultural boundaries. David Schneider's *American Kinship*, originally published in 1968 with a revised edition following in 1980, and *Critique of the Study of Kinship*, published in 1984, represent two key moments in the development of this disciplinary self-critique. *American Kinship* examines the cultural horizon that had informed American anthropology (a British equivalent was planned but never published) and presents the key move: the recognition that the ideas of kinship which anthropologists were bringing from home were themselves culturally constructed. His later *Critique* makes explicit what *American Kinship* leaves implicit: that these culturally located ideas have been superimposed on other cultures, where they do not belong.

Christian moral thought also seeks to describe a culture, as it were,[1] that has its own integrity distinct from the Christian enquirer: it seeks to describe how Christianity (which might be defined using a variety of sources) might shape

---

1. This is just an analogy. It would be more precise to say not that Christianity is a single culture, but rather that there is something that makes Christianity *Christian* that is recognizable across cultures, and which is described by the moral theologian. This quality – being the kingdom of God – need not be called a culture per se, but the Christian theologian is required to show the same caution of reading their own culture into the kingdom as the anthropologist is into the culture they study. The limitations the Christian ethicist faces

the Christian's thought and belief. Insofar as any difference is thought possible between the culture of the theologian on the one hand, and Christianity as it might consistently be lived out on the other, it is necessary for that theologian to recognize humbly their own cultural presuppositions, lest they unwittingly superimpose their own culturally contingent ideas and values on a faith that might better approach as *alien* to them. Just as the anthropologists need to be conscious of their cultural presuppositions in order to describe a culture that is not their own, theologians need to be conscious of their cultural presuppositions lest they be superimposed on the Christian life which they aspire to describe.

David Schneider's description of American kinship served to reveal some of the possible or similar cultural presuppositions of which prior and active anthropologists had not been conscious in describing kinship. Approximately the same horizon encloses the recent ethicists surveyed in the previous chapter. The same can reasonably be said about Barth and John Paul II (though it could not be said about Baxter, who instead represents a step back a little further into the history of these assumptions about what constitutes a family). Schneider took anthropologists to be asking the wrong sorts of questions about kinship in other cultures, because of their own cultural presuppositions about what kinship must be. As such, the cultural origins of those assumptions deserve some description, in order that better questions might be formed to guide the study of Christian kinship. While Schneider would conclude that kinship did not really exist – a conclusion that will be disputed for its philosophical presuppositions – his ethnographic basis will nevertheless broadly be accepted. Following this, a definition of kinship will be offered, and investigative tools borrowed from social anthropology, for the task of explicating both the historical understandings and practices of Christian kinship, and also the theological justifications that guide them, with a view ultimately to describing something of the internal logic of a distinctively Christian theology of kinship.

American kinship

American Kinship analysed American kinship as a 'cultural system',[2] exploring the symbols with which kinship is meaningful in an American context.[3] In the final chapter of the second edition he would admit to two errors: first, ignoring the

---

when describe a Christian culture of kinship are outlined in more detail in the conclusion to this book.

2. David M. Schneider, *American Kinship: A Cultural Account*, 2nd edn. (Chicago: University of Chicago Press, 1980), 1.

3. In this case, drawn from Chicago families in 1961–3 and 1965, combined with data collected from Harvard colleagues, friends, family, and a range of literature from journals to newspapers. While his main data is from Chicago, he intends to give a picture of American kinship more widely.

variation in the family form in middle- versus lower-class families, and second, ignoring the fact that ethnicity matters too, noting as examples that Greek-Americans and Japanese-Americans have been shown to have quite different cultural systems and correspondingly different ways of understanding kinship.

However, both errors cohere, rather than conflict, with the central idea that the book foregrounds: American kinship occupies its own cultural system, meaningful with reference to certain culturally specific symbols. The implication, that is spelled out more completely in his *Critique of the Study of Kinship*, is that a specifically American paradigm – of designating who is and is not a relative and what it means – is being read into other cultures with the application of a genealogical grid that is not culturally universal at all, but meaningful only with reference to the symbols that occupy the American cultural system. So, when anthropology supposedly knows what kinship really is (a mode of social organization that revolves around reproduction) and where to look for it in the non-American culture they are studying (by seeing the social ties associated with reproduction), they are in fact importing a Western idea, rather than observing how those within that culture actually understand how they organize themselves socially.

In Schneider's account of American kinship, kin are identified with reference to substance. By substance, Schneider is referring to the sharing of a blood tie, rendered more recently as 'biogenetic substance'. As the blood tie has morphed into the idea of biogenetic substance a new idea emerges: 'If science discovers new facts about biogenetic relationship, then that is what kinship is and was all along, although it may not have been known at the time.'[4] The underpinning idea is that kinship relies upon one person sharing substance with another person, the substance having been transmitted by reproduction, and this notion has shifted from blood ties to biogenetic substance.

Of course, there are kin who do not share substance, but any American child is likely to be able to distinguish uncles and aunts by blood from those related by marriage. Schneider refers to a 'code for conduct' as being the basis for kinship with those to whom one shares no blood tie.[5] In short, one *ought* to treat certain individuals – step-children, in-laws, foster children, adoptees and so on – as kin even if they are not, in American kinship, literally kin. These are kin, not according to the 'natural order of things', but according to the 'order of law'.[6]

Just as there are kin who are deemed as such by law and not by nature, there are kin who are deemed as such by nature and not by law.[7] An example of this is the genitor and genetrix ('biological parents') of a child that has been adopted by others in a closed adoption, such that the law declares that there be *no* relationship to the child, while at the same time it is meaningful for kinship language to be used.

4. Schneider, *American Kinship*, 23.
5. Ibid., 26.
6. Ibid., 26–7.
7. Ibid., 28.

The two elements of relatedness – substance and code for conduct – come together to form strong, meaningful and lasting relationships with parents, grandparents, great-grandparents, siblings, cousins and aunts or uncles by blood.

In Schneider's account of American kinship, the family is not a composite of all relatives, but rather refers to a unit composed of husband, wife and children.[8] It is not that the term 'family' could not be applied to the extended family, but these are defined differently from the nuclear family, and as such it is meaningful to say that an adult has no family (which is to say, no spouse or children) or, of an older couple, 'Their family has all grown up and is married; each has a family of his own now.'[9] This latter statement expresses an additional component of the family: living together in one place. It suggests that the child is part of one family as they grow up, and another once they move out and form their own family in a separate home.[10] The home, then, is a constituent part of the family and creates a separate realm for family to the sharply distinct realm of work.[11] Whereas work is productive and leads to a specific goal,[12] a home does not have a specific goal and is for love – which Schneider influentially renders for the American context as meaning *'enduring diffuse solidarity'*.[13] Any family that does not have these constituent parts is incomplete or broken.[14]

The family, as the site of enduring diffuse solidarity, is composed of *persons* defined in terms of their agency – their actions and their roles.[15] Persons are composites of these various roles – defined by sex, class, age, job and so on – that provide standards and guides for action. This also includes family roles – husband, wife, son, daughter – which allow for the family both to be a unit in itself and to be composed of persons, who are themselves both units and parts of a whole in the family.[16]

As kinship is based upon biogenetic substance, and biogenetic substance is transmitted by reproduction, reproduction is critical to American kinship. It is not possible to understand substance apart from reproduction if one is to make sense of the final key concept in determining who counts as a relative: distance.[17] A child is composed of substance from the father and the mother –

---

8. Ibid., 30.
9. Ibid., 33.
10. Ibid.
11. Ibid., 46.
12. While this distinction certainly does resonate today it might be troubled by the tendency to work at home so that the distinction is less sharp. Alternatively, it might well be that these cultural symbols of work and home survive and end up generating practices that retain the sharp distinction even as (or, if) working in the home becomes more common.
13. Schneider, *American Kinship*, 50.
14. Ibid.
15. Ibid., 57ff.
16. Ibid., 60.
17. Ibid., 62.

half from each.[18] This relationship of substance transmission constitutes one step of distance, with fourth-cousins, for instance, perhaps being deemed too distant really to be counted as a relative, or second-cousins beings deemed 'wakes-and-weddings relatives'[19] or something similar. It is not, however, just reproduction that is at play, and a half-sibling might be deemed to be slightly more distant than a sibling with whom one shares both parents, on the basis that the one shares more substance with the latter than the former. For American kinship, reproduction and substance are of absolutely central importance in defining who is considered natural kin, with the language of legal kinship being made meaningful by natural kinship.

Schneider does not describe all instances of American family life. Rather, he seeks to give an overview of the sort of concepts that occupy the American cultural imagination of kinship. In this way, he attempts to show how cultural ideas about reproduction and shared substance structure familiar kinship practice. This depiction of American cultural forms serves as his platform for the critique of the anthropological study of kinship, showing how ideas local to the anthropologist are read into other cultural settings in which they do not belong.

What, then, is kinship, in the cultural horizon described in *American Kinship*? For Schneider, kinship is a mode of social organization determined by the sharing of biogenetic substance, transmitted in reproduction.[20] The completeness of Schneider's description of the role of shared substance in American kinship will be discussed in a later chapter, placing it within the larger story of Euro-American connection between kinship and bodily substance. For now, this should serve to provide sufficient critical distance on what is likely a familiar way of thinking about kinship, in order to be able to detect Euro-American cultural ideas in the work of anthropologists as they seek to describe kinship outside of a Euro-American context. This, in turn, will show further why it is not appropriate to take the meaning of kinship as given, in the way that the philosophers and theologians briefly surveyed earlier have been prone to do.

A history of the study of kinship: Evolutionists, functionalists, structuralists and beyond

In his *Critique of the Study of Kinship*, Schneider examines the presuppositions operative in the anthropology of kinship, already exposed somewhat in his ethnographic description of American kinship. Schneider found anthropologists to be subscribing implicitly to the doctrine of the 'Genealogical Unity of Mankind': the idea that there is implicit in every culture a genealogical grid composed of reproductive ties (procreation and generation). Anthropologists

18. Ibid., 25.
19. Ibid., 17.
20. Ibid., 23.

might report varying practices on the precise nature in which these genealogical ties are understood and played out, but ultimately they assumed that, everywhere, 'Blood Is Thicker Than Water'.[21] Schneider takes this doctrine to underpin anthropological investigation into kinship in a sweeping survey of the history of the anthropology of kinship going back to Lewis Henry Morgan and John McLennan. While anthropologists may have recognized that a culture may have its own 'folk theory' of reproduction, he finds that even among those anthropologists most sensitive to cultural variation in theories of reproduction, they will ignore the results of the crucial question: even if the local theory affirms that a child is born of a woman, will people also affirm that this (or something else about reproduction) creates 'connectedness' between the bearer and the borne? In short, even if a culture does not believe in any implicit connection between reproduction and the making of kinship ties, anthropologists will read such a connection in anyway.[22]

Since the time of Morgan and McLennan, social anthropology has been aware of differences in the practice of kinship, with some cultures not seeming to conform, in their practice, to the supposed biological reality of kinship. What will follow is a history of the attempts to explain these differences, up to and beyond Schneider.[23] Specifically, three different kinds of theories of kinship will be outlined and rejected, with each presenting an attempt to describe kinship as universally based in some way on reproduction (either descent or alliance), but which can nevertheless accommodate cross-cultural variations. On the first, evolutionist account, kinship is a form of social organization based on the reproductive tie, with variation in kinship systems being explained by more or less advanced comprehension of this biological reality. On the second, functionalist account, kinship finds its origins in this biologically determined social reality, but the social subsequently takes on a life of its own, so that it no longer necessarily maps onto the natural. On the third, structuralist account, the universality of kinship is based on deep structures in human thought (in the case of Lévi-Strauss, reciprocity and exchange), rather than human practice, which transcend cultural boundaries, but nevertheless leave a great deal of space for variation. Each of these represents, roughly, a stage in the development of the anthropology of kinship and so, while Schneider roundly criticized all of them, it is helpful to see how theories developed in response to one another, and in response to new ethnographic evidence or puzzles like the incest taboo.

---

21. Schneider, *A Critique*, 165.
22. Ibid., 117.
23. This history owes a great deal to Sarah Franklin's history of 'conception among the anthropologists', but serves a different purpose and, accordingly, expands on or shrinks away from Franklin's history in many places. Cf. Sarah Franklin, *Embodied Progress: A Cultural Account of Assisted Conception* (London: Routledge, 1997), 17–72.

Critiquing the study of kinship: Evolutionists

The earliest of the theories of kinship named in the previous paragraph, called the evolutionists account, is found in the work of Bachofen, Maine, McLennan and Morgan. While aware of cultures in which reproduction was not given the same organizational priority in their ideas about kinship, they took this to reflect an underdeveloped understanding of nature which shaped understanding and, to some degree, practice.

Late nineteenth-century interest in other cultures of kinship was motivated by different research priorities than those that motivate most contemporary anthropologists. The principal desire was to understand the earliest origins of society. Supposedly more primitive cultures were taken as evidence of the nature of earlier stages in the development of so-called civilized societies. The hunt was on to discover whether earliest society was matriarchal or patriarchal. Despite the different investigative priorities, these figures shared an interest with modern social anthropologists in comparing living cultures of kinship. Evolutionists, with their interest in comparing what was ancient (described with help from discussions of living 'primitive' cultures) with what was more recent, set the stage for anthropologists interested in the relationship between the natural and instinctual on the one hand, and the social on the other. While this would produce attempts to describe kinship cross-culturally that, it will be argued, were flawed, it nevertheless stands as a useful starting point to make sense of later developments that might appear more convincing in the first place.

The anthropological study of kinship arguably finds its origins with Henry Maine's *Ancient Law* and Johann Bachofen's *Das Mutterrecht*, both published in 1861. These took different sides in a great contemporary debate: whether the origins of human society were patriarchal (Maine) or matriarchal (Bachofen). Reports of wildly differing cultures outside of a Euro-American cultural horizon would fuel this debate, as the supposed 'recognition' of reproduction in kinship practice became a test for how advanced a culture was.

Henry Maine sought to identify the origins of contemporary social life for the purposes of jurisprudence, using history, ancient law, and these contemporary reports of 'less advanced' civilizations from those who are more advanced.[24] He proposed that the history of kinship relationships moved 'from Status to Contract'.[25]

This was a model of progress – early in social history he found family groups with a male head, who held complete sway over the household, reflecting a natural status of power with which the father is imbued, whereas later in social history he found a move to contracts in which individuals could come to stand in contractual arrangements with one another that did not necessarily reflect this basic power dynamic. Maine was principally interested in 'Indo-European stock' and confessed that he would find it difficult to comment on whether other societies were not, in

---

24. Henry Maine, *Ancient Law* (London: J.M. Dent & Sons, 1917), 71.
25. Ibid., 101.

their earliest times, patriarchal. As such, John McLennan's scathing critique, in which he bid Maine to look beyond the Indo-European context – to Australia, for instance – seems a little unfair.[26] Moreover, McLennan shared something closely with Maine: his belief that primitive societies (his supposedly even more primitive societies in Australia) could reveal still earlier origins (which were, for McLennan, matriarchal). For both, there was a linear progression from primitive to civilized, in which other cultures served as living archaeological digs, and which could be placed along the spectrum of civility on the basis of whether or not natural kinship, determined by reproduction, was 'recognized', as it was in their own advanced societies.

Bachofen tells another story of progress, except that, in this case, it is principally sex and reproduction that brings about each new era, rather than the formation of the state, as in Maine. Though he traces the various stages carefully, with each one representing a shift from one sexual arrangement to another – from Aphroditean hetaerism[27] to Demetrian matriarchy,[28] to the Dionysian era,[29] to the Apollonian[30] – the key shift from matriarchy to patriarchy came with the 'discovery' of physical paternity.[31] Where previously the connection between mother and child was obvious, Bachofen claimed that the recognition of the role of the male in conception was brought about by a complex series of shifts in the perception of men in the context of matriarchy, and when physical paternity was culturally recognized the result was the 'father right' which could now stand against the supreme authority of the 'mother right'.[32]

These evolutionary models of linear progression provide the intellectual backdrop for Lewis Henry Morgan, who was particularly interested in systems of kinship that did not reflect the supposedly natural. Morgan was working around the same time as Maine and Bachofen, publishing his famous *Systems of Consanguinity and Affinity of the Human Family* in 1871, and building on it in his 1877 *Ancient Society*. One of his aims was to work out whether the Iroquois of North America

---

26. J. F. McLennan, *Primitive Marriage: An Inquiry Into the Origin of the Form of Capture in Marriage Ceremonies* (Edinburgh: A&C Black, 1865), 115–16. Cf. also J. H. Morgan, 'Introduction', in *Ancient Law*, ed. Henry Maine (London: J.M. Dent & Sons, 1917), xiii.

27. J. J. Bachofen, 'Mother Right: An Investigation of the Religious and Juridical Character of Matriarchy in the Ancient World', in *Myth, Religion, and Mother Right: Selected Writings of J. J. Bachofen*, trans. Ralph Manheim (Princeton: Princeton University Press, 1992), 47.

28. Ibid., 89.

29. Ibid., 100.

30. Ibid., 115.

31. This theme is developed throughout *Das Mutterrecht*, for instance, cf. Bachofen, 'Mother Right', 114.

32. Bachofen, 'Mother Right', 129.

were originally from Asia.[33] For this, whether or not kinship classifications matched a particular genealogical grid of kinship was critical. He proceeded with the kind of evolutionary model discussed earlier, taking the cultural recognition of the importance of physical paternity to be a sign of progress.[34] His research relied on the reports of other travellers – in particular, American missionaries – and Morgan's own fieldwork, involving detailed interviews with informants among the Iroquois, albeit for hours or days rather than an extended period of immersion in their culture.[35]

Morgan distinguished between the descriptive 'natural' system of kinship and the various 'classificatory' systems, with the use of kin-classifications (wife, husband, mother, father, sister, brother, etc.) in some societies coming to reflect the 'natural' and in others, rejecting descent groups, relating to great classes of people.[36] The Iroquois kin-classifications were an example of the latter, with kin-terminology used not in a 'distinct' way for other individuals who share an ancestor but rather being used more widely across tribe and nation.[37] In short, for Morgan, their kinship ceased to refer to those who were *naturally* their kin, and came to refer to those who were not.[38] Schneider puts it bluntly: 'for Morgan, the facts of blood relationship exist; it is their recognition, the discovery of their existence, that constitutes an act of human intelligence'.[39] If a culture treats as kin who are not blood kin, they have failed, for Morgan, to understand the way the world really works.

The problem, of course, is a failure to seek to understand another culture's modes of life and thought with a view to its own integrity, instead comparing ideas and practices there in a crude way with those familiar to the European or American anthropologist. Morgan predefined kinship in terms of reproduction.

Critiquing the study of kinship: Functionalists

It is with Bronisław Malinowski that one finds detailed ethnographies, paying careful attention to the other culture, informing the anthropological study of

---

33. Lewis Henry Morgan, *Systems of Consanguinity and Affinity of the Human Family*, Smithsonian Contributions to Knowledge 218 (Washington: Smithsonian Institution, 1871), 4.
34. Ibid., 470–1.
35. Ibid., viii–ix.
36. Ibid., 12.
37. Ibid., 13, 472.
38. Morgan would note some of the cultural elements informing this different strategy for naming kin, looking at communal living (Morgan, *Systems of Consanguinity and Affinity of the Human Family*, 258.) and marriage rules that separated father and son into different tribes (Morgan, *Systems of Consanguinity and Affinity of the Human Family*, 140.)
39. Schneider, *A Critique*, 168.

kinship. Malinowski, writing in the early twentieth century, was sharply critical of his evolutionist predecessors. His studies of kinship among Australian Aborigines and Trobriand Islanders were important for their distinction between natural and social facts of kinship, with the latter being treated as having its own integrity, even if Malinowski still relied upon the concept of natural kinship.

In his Australian study, Malinowski distinguished between 'physiological consanguinity' (as 'fact') and 'social consanguinity', which in European society was the recognition of this fact of physiological consanguinity.[40] He argued that, among Australian Aborigines, 'social consanguinity' in that sense did not exist between father and child because there was no knowledge of physiological paternity, and yet at the same time 'very close kinship [with the father] exists'.[41] The closeness of this relationship presented a puzzle: How could the kinship with the father be explained if there was no recognition of the blood tie he shared with the child? His conclusion would be that '*physiological* consanguinity has no direct bearing upon social facts'.[42] Instead, a range of other forces, from religious or magical belief to legal constructs, could create this social kinship.[43]

The possibility that a culture is 'ignorant' of physiological paternity would be brought to prominence in Malinowski's later work, *The Sexual Lives of Savages*, originally published in 1929. In a chapter entitled 'Ignorance of Physiological Paternity', Malinowski recounts the story of conception, in the words of an informant, Niyova, in Oburaku: 'A virgin does not conceive, because there is no way for the children to go, for that woman to conceive. When the orifice is wide open, the spirits are aware, they give the child.'[44] Malinowski, after further investigation, would elaborate: the belief seemed to be that the male made space in the female in intercourse and that space presented a place for the child to reside, inserted there by a spirit via the head of the woman. However, according to some origin traditions, there were originally only women, who came to bear children without men, but with some other form of mechanical opening – by rain, in one story.[45] In response to Malinowski's insistence of the 'truer physiological doctrine of procreation', his informants would respond with stories of women having children without intercourse, and women not having children despite intercourse.[46]

This was not merely a cultural theory but it worked itself out in behaviour – with one informant returning after over two years' absence to find a baby at home

---

40. Bronisław Malinowski, *The Family Among the Australian Aborigines: A Sociological Study*, Monographs on Sociology 2 (London: University of London Press, 1913), 177–8.
41. Ibid., 179.
42. Ibid., 182. Italics original.
43. Ibid., 182–3, 187–8, 190.
44. Bronisław Malinowski, *The Sexual Life of Savages in North-Western Melanesia*, 3rd edn., Malinowski Collected Works 6 (London: Routledge, 1932), 154.
45. Ibid., 154–5, 160.
46. Ibid., 158.

and not suspecting any adultery.⁴⁷ Additionally, the relationship with the child is established socially – hence, if the man who is biologically responsible for the existence of the child is married to the woman who bears the child he is the father, but if not he is not. As Malinowski claims, the 'husband is the father *ex officio*, but for an unmarried mother, there is 'no father to the child'. The father, then, 'is defined socially'.⁴⁸

When distinguishing between these, Malinowski did not at all wish to dispense with the study of the supposed natural facts of paternity, maternity and reproduction – he just did not want anthropologists to think that paternity requires *physiological* paternity. Malinowski still affirmed 'biological foundations' of the family, but was willing to postulate complex social arrangements for the social construction of the kinship relation, even if biology was working under the surface.⁴⁹ A functionalist, he saw the natural facts as the condition for the possibility of the social facts, and in that respect did not separate the natural and the social in the way that Schneider thought he should.⁵⁰ Malinowski's departure from Morgan and his forebears and heirs was to recognize the social definition of fatherhood, apart from the belief in physiological paternity.

In a review of functionalist accounts of kinship, particularly those of Malinowski, Spiro and Barnes (and at one point Lévi-Strauss, whom he considers to be making a functionalist claim at one point in the otherwise structuralist *Elementary Structures of Kinship*), Schneider finds that the existence of a primal natural kinship operating below the surface of cultural recognition simply has not been demonstrated. Rather, what is seen is a circular argument in which it is assumed that there is such a thing as kinship in every society: that is, a set of relationships associated with reproduction. Variation in different cultural expressions of kinship is described as having to 'adapt to' and being 'conditioned by variations in ecology, economy, demography, politics, and so on'.⁵¹

Schneider, therefore, raises the question whether the biological facts really *do* have priority over these other facts to which kinship adapts, such that it can be determined to be the base for kinship: 'What is so special about the facts of human sexual reproduction that the economy, the ecology, demography, etc., do not share? Is kinship a privileged system? Does its special privilege reside in its roots in biology or sexual reproduction? If so, just how?'⁵² In other words, kinship – defined on the basis of Euro-American cultural ideas about the social significant of reproduction – is being read into other cultures, on the basis that reproduction

---

47. Ibid., 164.
48. Ibid., 165.
49. Ibid., 172.
50. Schneider, *A Critique*, 163.
51. Melford Spiro, *Kinship and Marriage in Burma. A Cultural and Psychodynamic Analysis* (Berkeley: University of California Press, 1977), 3–4. Cited in Schneider, *A Critique*, 139.
52. Schneider, *A Critique*, 139.

is necessarily a socially significant natural fact. Kinship, defined by reproduction, is being privileged by ethnographers over other natural facts about the world, whether or not the culture being studied privileges reproduction in this way.

This argument contributes to a position taken by Schneider that this book will not ultimately affirm: that there is no such thing as kinship, after all. This will be discussed later in this chapter, but his point about privileging reproduction is important in demonstrating that kinship – whether or not one thinks it can meaningfully be said to exist – should not be taken to be inevitably defined by reproduction in the way that theologians and philosophers in the previous chapter tended to argue.

Schneider offers a useful illustration of this from his earlier research among the Yapese. In this example, one might find that *citamangen* and *fak* in Yapese culture look a great deal like 'father' and 'son', and therefore be tempted to assume that the relationship is informed by reproduction, but that would be to import an alien idea into the description of another culture:

> So far as the *citamangen-fak* relationship is concerned, then, even when coitus is recognized as a factor in conception it is not taken to 'mean' anything radically new or different; it has not changed anything. It is simply not culturally significant. And most important, it has not introduced the idea of biogenetic attributes or shared substance. That is, even with the idea that coitus plays a role in conception, the Yapese definition of the relationship between *citamangen* and *fak* remains radically different from the European cultural conception of reproduction. It is also radically different from the scientific conception of kinship which is, obviously, almost the same as the European cultural conception of kinship.[53]

The *citamangen-fak* relationship might have been immediately placed on a genealogical grid whose underlying principle is the blood tie, but with deeper probing such an action would have been entirely inappropriate to the self-understanding of the Yapese, in which there is no necessary connection between coitus and the relationship between *citamangen* and *fak*.

Christian ethicist Lisa Cahill objects to Schneider's reading of the Yapese. She claims, 'All societies recognize human relations built on genealogical ties, beginning with lineages of mothers and children, and including men as fathers to the extent that biological paternity is recognized (which it usually is, granted variety in cultural explanations of the precise nature of male and female cooperation for reproduction).'[54] After a brief, apparently appreciative nod to Malinowski's attempt at a universal basis for family in his Australian study ('the idea that family exists universally to fulfil a specific social function: the nurturance of children') she attacks David Schneider's refutation of the idea that kinship is sufficiently similar

---

53. Ibid., 73.
54. Cahill, *Sex, Gender, and Christian Ethics*, 102.

cross-culturally to be compared because of a universal basis in reproduction, with the biological always entailing 'a cultural response'.[55]

Cahill's objection is twofold: first and principally, that Schneider does not demonstrate that among the Yapese the '"blood" relationship is abolished as a factor in social organization', but rather simply 'variety, fluidity, even "strangeness" in the Yapese confluence of biological, marital, and land-based relationships', and second, in a subsidiary point made in a footnote, that Schneider's ethnographic evidence from the Yapese has in fact been disproven by later work.

With respect to the first of these, what Cahill is asking of Schneider is the proof of a negative. It is no easy thing to demonstrate that there is no trace of a blood tie in Yapese kinship, and Schneider does not seek to do so in the way Cahill requests. He simply tries to explain the culture he studies without presupposing kinship. Indeed, he offers two alternative possible descriptions of life among the Yapese: one that assumes procreation defines kinship, and another which does not. These serve to show that procreation, which is not mentioned by informants as structuring kinship like it does in American kinship, need not be taken to be tacitly making meaningful Yapese modes of thought.

So, in the deliberately flawed description, he writes:

> if the own real *citamangen* (father, mother's husband) is alive, he and only he will be referred to as *citamangen*. If he dies, he is then succeeded – perhaps by his eldest surviving *wolag* (sibling; male in this case). At that point and not before, that person will be referred to as *citamangen*.[56]

In the better description, he writes:

> The Yapese formulate the relationship between *citamangen* and *fak* in terms of authority and dependency which is either exchanged over time in certain instances, or for which a steady state of exchange is maintained. *Citamangen* provides for his *fak* when they are young and weak and without knowledge, but when the *fak* grow to near-adulthood the child returns the care and the provisions which the old person needs. A mother's husband and her child (among many others) are *citamangen* and *fak* respectively to each other. But this terminology may be reversed when the mother's husband is old, relatively helpless and dependent on his wife's son.[57]

Clearly, the two are different, and there is an obvious logic to the latter that structures the relationship between whoever is the husband of a woman and the woman's child, which relates to authority and dependency rather than relationships between bodies created by procreation. So, Schneider is able to interpret later

---

55. Ibid., 103.
56. Schneider, *A Critique*, 12.
57. Ibid., 30.

ethnographic work (which Cahill cites as undermining Schneider's earlier work) when Yapese informants say that sex is necessary to conception in the following terms: 'the view was that the man planted the seed, the woman being like the garden; the seed had to be nurtured and tended and this took place in the woman, the garden. And because the man "worked" on that garden, he had the right to the product of that garden, though that product did not belong to him; the child belonged to the mother and to her *genung*'.[58] It is still not structured by procreation. Therefore, Schneider can conclude that 'even when coitus is recognized as a factor in conception it is not taken to "mean" anything radically new or different; it has not changed anything. It is simply not culturally significant.'[59]

Schneider's *Critique* does not stand or fall on the evidence of the Yapese, though it is certainly important counter-evidence to those who take kinship universally to be ordered by reproduction. The core of the argument relies upon the ethnography, *American Kinship*, in which he describes the cultural doctrines that generate the assumptions anthropologists have taken to the field – and which this book suggests have limited the moral imaginations of ethicists. It is not possible to demonstrate beyond all doubt that a culture structures their social life in ways totally unrelated to reproduction, but it is certainly possible to argue, first, that kinship is a mode of social organization shaped by human cultural ideas which one should expect to vary from culture to culture, and second, that ethnographies of kinship in other cultures describe suspiciously Euro-American ideas at work within profoundly different cultural horizons. In that light, Schneider's explanation of Yapese social life, in which reproduction does not play the expected role, seems entirely plausible. Moreover, it seems correspondingly likely that previous anthropologists have read a cultural idea into other societies where it does not belong.

When comparing American kinship with kinship in foreign cultures, it becomes clear that different systems for organizing and understanding kinship are at work and that the strong sense of the supposed truth of biological kinship is in fact grounded in a commitment to a particular mode of social organization that exists in some places and not others. The fact that kinship is still observed in cultures in which procreation does not underpin the idea is evidence that Euro-American norms are not reducible to procreation either, as other ideas unconnected to procreation – the most obvious being the house – can be used to make kinship. Indeed, the focus on procreation has obscured not just Micronesian kinship but also Euro-American kinship, as will be argued in the following chapter, on substance. It will be argued that the Euro-American 'folk theory'[60] of kinship, which has been reproduced by anthropologists, philosophers and theologians, is

---

58. Ibid., 28.
59. Ibid., 73.
60. A term borrowed by Schneider from Scheffler and Lounsbury, but used again them, suggesting that they have relied upon Euro-American folk theories of reproduction in identifying the folk theories of reproduction supposedly operative in the cultures they study. (Schneider, chapter 10.)

precisely that: a folk theory, which certainly does not describe Yapese kinship, but also does not accurately describe Euro-American practice.

This should not be terribly surprising. Why *should* kinship be based on, say, the dissemination of genes as the sociobiologist might suggest? Human social life is incredibly complicated and affected, as Spiro pointed out, by a wide variety of other factors, as evidenced in the massive variation in forms of kinship worldwide. It might be an excellent account of very ancient origins of the human species to talk of natural selection resulting in human beings caring for those who share their genes. However, the development of societies, languages and cultures so muddies the water that it is difficult to see why so simple a system would survive.[61]

Critiquing the study of kinship: Structuralists

Schneider has certainly not been the only critic of functionalist theories of kinship. Before his critiques emerged, Edmund Leach offered a structuralist objection to Malinowski's functionalism. However, Schneider would object on different grounds to structuralist approaches to kinship. Leach decried any claim that the belief of Australian Aborigines and Trobrianders in conception without male insemination does not stem from 'innocence and ignorance' but from theology 'of the greatest subtlety'.[62]

The evidence against ignorance relies on three things: first, the fact that both Australian Aborigines and Trobriand Islanders are quite clear that copulation is key in animal reproduction;[63] second, the fact that both societies have ties with other groups whom ethnographers would not claim were biologically ignorant; third, on a reinterpretation of the ethnographic evidence inspired by a critique of a recurring error in prior anthropology. This error was to assume that religious or magical rituals that did not cause the change the participants appeared to

---

61. Geertz describes something of this complexity in delineating the role of culture in human evolution. Cf. Clifford Geertz, *The Interpretation of Cultures: Selected Essays* (New York: Basic Books, 1973), chapter 2.

62. Edmund Leach, 'Virgin Birth: The Henry Myers Lecture 1966', *Proceedings for the Royal Anthropological Institute of Great Britain and Ireland for 1966* (1966): 39. Malinowski himself would retract his theory of ignorance in the forward to the 1932 edition, because it was meant to be purely ethnography. Nevertheless, he reaffirmed its plausibility. Malinowski would use the analogy of Trobriander ignorance of Einstein's theory of relativity to defend the plausibility of the idea that they were also ignorant of a feature of 'embryology', but recommended that later anthropologists take a more parsimonious ethnographic approach, steering clear of claims of ignorance and instead populating their ethnographies with accounts of beliefs that are *present* rather than missing, and making sense of beliefs and practices in light of that information alone. Cf. Malinowski, *The Sexual Life of Savages*, xxii–xxviii.

63. Leach, 'Virgin Birth', 40.

expect (from the perspective of the outsider) was on the basis of a failed attempt to understand chains of causality in the world – that is ignorance – rather than, as Leach suggests, a way of symbolizing something.[64]

Leach's point is not that it is impossible for a practice to arise out of a failure to understand something about the world and then be sustained because of some psychological need that it satisfies. Rather, he considers it the duty of the anthropologist to try to understand the practice from within the thought-world of the culture, and to seek to determine the various purposes it serves in the culture's life and self-understanding. Indeed, the stranger the practice appears, and the more striking the supposed ignorance, the more such an approach is demanded.[65]

Having cast doubt over evolutionist accounts, or anyone for whom 'ignorance' is a satisfactory account of Trobriand belief, he turns to his own suggested method, adopted from Lévi-Strauss – 'structuralism' – which 'entails fitting the pieces together to form a pattern'. He wishes to avoid going 'the functionalist whole hog', so he does not attempt to explain all the evidence in the context of a vast theory, instead simply takes this approach to each culture in a comparative manner.[66] He takes the way in which the culture makes meaning – particularly in those instances where the outsider struggles to find meaning – and tries to find patterns in the hope of unlocking what he thinks will be an underlying order or *structure*.

For Lévi-Strauss, the premier structuralist, kinship studies should be focused not on descent (i.e. having children), but rather on alliance (i.e. marriage). Marriage, for Lévi-Strauss, arose from two key universal structures in human thought – reciprocity and exchange.[67] He focused particularly on the incest prohibition, describing it as '*the* prohibition in the most general form, the one perhaps to which all others . . . are related as particular cases'. Significantly, he adds that it is 'universal like language' and then proceeds to compare it with the development of language.[68] He would reject Malinowski's claim, also associated with Westermarck and Spiro, that incest taboos arise from the incompatibility of different biological desires, so that one cannot be both mother and wife. He argues that these roles – even within the 'biological family' – only make sense culturally, and he provides ethnographic data that suggests Malinowski's theory does not reflect the breadth of the evidence. One important piece of evidence comes from

---

64. Ibid., passim.

65. A brilliant example of a thick description of a strange practice is Geertz's classic study of Balinese cockfighting, even if Leach decried Geertz as a theologian disguised as an anthropologist. (Clifford Geertz, 'Deep Play: Notes on the Balinese Cockfight', in *The Interpretation of Cultures: Selected Essays* (New York: Basic Books, 1973), 412–54; Leach, 'Virgin Birth', 39.)

66. Leach, 'Virgin Birth', 44.

67. Janet Carsten, *After Kinship*, New Departures in Anthropology (Cambridge: Cambridge University Press, 2004), 41–2.

68. Claude Lévi-Strauss, *The Elementary Structures of Kinship*, ed. Rodney Needham, trans. J. H. Bell and J. R. von Sturmer, rev. edn. (Boston: Beacon, 1969), 493.

the Siberian Chukchee, in which a woman will be betrothed to a toddler for whom she then cares – and even nurses him alongside her own children born from relationships with temporary lovers – with the explanation being that this would, in fact, make it more likely that the toddler would look kindly on her when he grew up to become her husband.[69] He would provide supporting evidence from a number of cultures to which the respondent might respond that these are strange exceptions to the rule – but this would conflict with the universality of the claim made that certain biological desires could not be confused.[70]

The universality of the incest taboo is by no means the sole piece of evidence in what is a wide-ranging survey of a great deal of ethnographic evidence about very different kinship systems, but rather it stands as a particular ethnographic puzzle that appears to be resolved if one accepts Lévi-Strauss's suggested solution to the problem of kinship.[71] In short, that solution is this: kinship should be understood not as originating in descent, but in alliance. The implications are profound, as the idea that kinship is grounded in the relationship between parents and children, defined with reference to reproduction, is dispensed with in favour of kinship finding its meaning in reciprocity – in houses and villages, rather than in bedrooms and maternity wards. Nevertheless, Lévi-Strauss would still retain an interest in kinship as a universally explainable phenomenon – a controversial move David Schneider would reject, even if he reserved his most strident criticism for those who took reproduction to be the universal basis for kinship.

The Christian ethicist Don Browning relied on the primatologist Bernard Chapais's theory of kinship, which blends Lévi-Strauss's reflections on the universality of exogamy with an evolutionism in the tradition of Robin Fox. Browning took the work of Chapais to have demonstrated the implausibility of Schneider's thesis.[72]

Browning seeks an account of universal human nature with respect to kinship in order to offer a theory of marriage that resides on natural law. Schneider represents a threat, because he undermines the universality of kinship based on reproduction. Chapais's theories that 'humans are unique in their consolidation of biparentality and the mutual recognition of fathers and their offspring' and

---

69. Ibid., 485–7.

70. While discussions of genetic explanations for incest are relevant, and may offer some explanation for the emergence of taboos for brother-sister and parent-child incest, there are tight limits on the explanatory power of such a theory given, first, how widespread cousin-marriage is, and second, the distinction between parallel- and cross-cousins in some societies, in which parallel-cousins (children of the father's brother or the mother's sister) are likened to siblings, but children of cross-cousins (children of the father's sister or the mother's brother) are referred to as 'potential spouses'. (Lévi-Strauss, *The Elementary Structures of Kinship*, 99.)

71. Indeed, even if one were to reject the universality of the incest taboo, its commonness would still present a puzzle.

72. Browning, 'A Natural Law Theory of Marriage', 752–5.

that 'the human species is also uniquely characterized by incest avoidance and exogamous marriage'[73] are taken to support the conclusion that there is indeed such a thing as biological kinship, which is culturally universal.

Chapais summarizes his two major contributions to the debate: first, 'even when culture negates or ignores the genealogical content of a kinship bond, for example that of motherhood, it does not necessarily preclude that bond from generating preferential relationships that do map onto genealogical kinship', and second, 'the genealogical unity of humankind does exist, and much of it comes from our primate legacy'.[74]

What, then, is at stake for moral engagement with human kinship? Chapais identifies a series of propensities that may be operative in human social life, which could provoke better studies on the origins of recurring themes in human social life. This does not entail that the human conceptualities with which moral philosophers, theologians or anthropologists begin their work are necessarily semantically dependent on reproductive ties. Neither does it entail that those powerful modes of social organization described by anthropologists as kinship are, by necessity, determined by reproduction. Chapais concedes as much: 'It is true that from an anthropological viewpoint – from a strictly cross-cultural perspective – the existence of a universal set of kinship features is far from obvious. But this is because the unity is concealed beneath the extraordinary diversity of forms it has generated.'[75] In this respect, Chapais argues something similar to Lévi-Strauss, but with a biological, rather than social, basis to the concealed structure he describes. Even if the claim to universality were true, the most that could be said on this basis is that kinship has been determined to a very small degree by reproductive instincts, but has still left a very wide field on which human beings have played the game of kinship in enormously different ways, as demonstrated by cross-cultural variation recorded by social anthropologists.

As such, it can be conceded, for the sake of moving forward with the main argument, that it *could* be the case that, in the ancient origins of human social life, early human life was so much more powerfully structured by reproduction than other natural facts that – in the absence of more complex forms of social organization derived from the mediation of culturally and linguistically shaped thought – human social life everywhere was nearly identical. Perhaps this is so, but if it were indeed accurate of early human ancestors, it is no longer the case. At most one might say that there are certain ways of organizing kinship that might be more common than others. Even still, the question would remain: Why? The idea that the reality of biogenetic substance is implicitly recognized cross-culturally seems unlikely in the face of wise cross-cultural diversity, whereas the proximity of children to mothers in gestation could very easily be a natural fact with social

---

73. Ibid., 752–3.
74. Bernard Chapais, *Primeval Kinship* (Cambridge: Harvard University Press, 2008), 54–5.
75. Ibid., 56.

entailment, albeit not necessarily powerfully shaping kinship, as will be seen in the case of the Iñupiaq. To say that kinship is shaped by reproduction is in one sense obvious, though that in itself implicates a myriad of possible shaping factors (reproductive responsibility, alliance, gestational proximity alongside the explanations more likely to come from geneticists). To say that kinship is shaped by reproduction is quite a different thing to say that kinship is sufficiently explained by reproduction. That range of different factors the word 'reproduction' represents itself fits into a host of competing structuring principles – particularized by variations in cultural experience – generate varying practices that reveal a wide range of possibilities for human social structuring. This does not dispense with kinship as a meaningful concept – as will be argued later – but it does dispense with the universality of reproduction as a structuring principle.

Browning looks to Chapais in order to find 'the natural realities of human life', on the basis of which he can contribute to a natural law tradition.[76] The postulation of primal human nature lurking under a surface of cross-cultural difference could clearly serve that purpose well, and if all Browning wishes to do is advocate for a return to ancient social forms, there is not a great deal at stake – one can simply reject the idea that evolutionary origins are necessarily disclosive of good relatedness on the evidence of contradicting depictions of proper social ordering arising from scripture or the teaching of the church. (This is not to take on natural law theory, but simply Browning's particular contribution at this point.) If, however, Browning wishes to say that any alternative modes of ordering relatedness are implausible, as they cut against human nature, then there is clearly anthropological evidence of human cultures in which reproduction does not structure concepts of relatedness, and sufficient cross-cultural variability that reproduction does not have a strongly privileged role in shaping kinship practice. If Browning takes it to be necessary or inevitable that reproduction structures kinship in the way that it is taken to under a Euro-American cultural horizon, then Chapais's attention to early human ancestors does not demonstrate it, and the existence of wide cross-cultural variation makes such a proposition appear implausible.

It is not the purpose of this project to defend Schneider (and indeed there will be a point of disagreement later), so to honour the real purpose one can limit the claim to this: the possibilities for the practice of human kinship might very well be biologically restricted, but they are far more closely restricted by culture that has been shaped by a great many more accidents of history more recent than the evolution of homo sapiens, and so the moral imagination need not be very limited by biology. Practices of adoption and foster care, or celibacy and martyrdom, are entirely possible not because they have evolved in the very long term and are conducive to fitness, but because human beings are predominantly limited in their kinship practices by culture which can promote practices that can survive a very long time in that society, that run counter to the evolutionists' intuitions about the importance of disseminating genes in explaining human behaviour with regards

---

76. Browning, 'A Natural Law Theory of Marriage', 757.

to kinship. Indeed, one can take heed of Schneider's (somewhat acerbic) answer to the question, 'Why has kinship been defined in terms of the relations that arise out of the processes of human sexual reproduction?':

> It is simply that so much of what passes for science in the social sciences, including anthropology, derives directly and recognizably from the commonsense notions, the everyday premises of the culture in which and by which the scientist lives. These postulates of European culture are simply taken over and put in a form that is customary for rational scientific discourse, appropriately qualified and made slightly more explicit in places and served up as something special, sometimes in Latin. That is, the study of kinship derives directly and practically unaltered from the ethnoepistemology of European culture.[77]

In short, for the purposes of this project, the moral theologian can feel free to dispense with a great many presuppositions about what kinship must be, and instead heed a Christian theological imagination of kinship drawn from scripture and mulled over by the church. Furthermore, those who have come after Schneider even provide the tools by which it is possible for the theologian to discern as clearly as possible that which is theological versus that which comes from the theologian's own culture.

Towards a definition of kinship after Schneider

To be fully equipped by anthropology for the theological task it is necessary to identify an important criticism of Schneider. He claims that there is 'no such thing'[78] as kinship universally speaking, but rather that it is evident only in European culture (and from there exported, for instance to the United States).[79] By this, Schneider means that it is only there that one will find kinship defined in terms of reproduction and that there is no other common denominator by which kinship can be identified cross-culturally. While his critique of poor practice in anthropology is on point, it is a philosophical mistake to think the concept of kinship has no use in describing social forms in other cultures if all these cultures do not share a single common denominator.

---

77. Schneider, *A Critique*, 175. The anthropology of kinship has been so influenced by Schneider that this criticism no longer applies. Additionally, that cultural idioms are played out in scientific discourse is demonstrated in a study by Martin on how gendered ideology shapes description in reproductive biology. Cf. Emily Martin, 'The Egg and the Sperm: How Science Has Constructed a Romance Based on Stereotypical Male-Female Roles', *Signs* 16, no. 3 (1991): 485–501.
78. Schneider, *A Critique*, vii.
79. Ibid., 201.

2. What Is Kinship?

James Faubion responds to Schneider's scepticism about the usefulness of the concept of kinship in describing practices in other times and other places not by doubting Schneider's concept of *kinship* but his concept of *concept*.[80] While it might well be the case that biology is not the key factor in defining kinship in all cultures, there can still be 'family resemblances'[81] between the kinships that appear in different cultures. Not all concepts of kinship need to share the same basic feature to be understandable in a different culture. However, they must share a family resemblance. It is through the study of recurring symbols, as explored for example in Janet Carsten's work, that the cross-cultural analysis of kinship is possible. In short, while it is no mystery that concepts are not perfectly translatable from one cultural context to another, the way to bridge the divide is not to search for a universal common denominator – as blood might have been imagined to be in the case of kinship – but rather to pay heed to the variety of defining practices and symbols associated with it, that appear in different mixes in different contexts.[82]

As such, Faubion suggests that, while Schneider might have ended the 'theoretical tyranny of biologism', he notes that 'human beings very often, and very widely, treat "blood ties" as evidential criteria of what looks to be eminently translatable as "kinship", even if not the only, or always the most decisive, criteria of it. Such ties, in short, still belong to the roving interpreter's translation manual, even in the absence of a clear grammatical function or rationale.'[83] For Faubion, the lack of a 'clear grammatical function or rationale' is not a problem, but rather

---

80. James D. Faubion, 'Introduction: Toward an Anthropology of the Ethics of Kinship', in *The Ethics of Kinship: Ethnographic Inquiries*, ed. James D. Faubion (Lanham: Oxford: Rowman & Littlefield, 2001), 7.

81. Ludwig Wittgenstein, *Philosophical Investigations*, ed. G. E. M. Anscombe and Rush Rhees, trans. G. E. M. Anscombe, 2nd edn. (Oxford: Blackwell, 1958), §67, 32.

82. The focus on symbols that give meaning to relatedness is intended to resolve problems arising from false assumptions in ethics about what kinship must mean. An account will be offered of the implicit logic of Christian practices and the content of theological reflections in which they are posited as having a coherence of character and theological profundity. In this way, the account is freed to describe Christian practices that might appear to oppose 'real' kinship as simply relying on different interlocking ideas than those implicit in Euro-American practice. The account thus provides theological grounds both for thinking ethically about kinship, and indeed for faithfully interpreting historical Christian practices. With respect to interpreting reliably historical Jewish and Christian practices, Rowe and Wilhite each lay excellent anthropological groundwork for interpreting kinship in 1 Samuel and Tertullian respectively, though no equivalent exists in preparing theological ethics, beyond Banner's brief but astute treatment mentioned earlier. (Jonathan Y. Rowe, *Michal's Moral Dilemma: A Literary, Anthropological and Ethical Interpretation* (London: T&T Clark, 2011), 71–88; David E. Wilhite, *Tertullian the African: An Anthropological Reading of Tertullian's Context and Identities* (Berlin: Walter de Gruyter, 2007), 76–80.)

83. Faubion, 'Introduction', 8.

blood ties can be treated as one of the symbols that is common, but not universal, to kinship cross-culturally.[84]

How, then, does one study kinship without having this single denominator by which to identify what kinship is, how one comes to be related to others, and what affections, obligations and actions that implies? In response to the troubling of kinship by new reproductive technologies, Janet Carsten proposes a methodology for the description of kinship that involves 'traversing houses, gender, personhood, substance, idioms of kinship that are not traced to sexual procreation, and reproductive technologies'.[85] The four symbols of house, person, gender and shared bodily substance are recurring themes in ethnographies of kinship, appearing regularly in the way local informants express what it means to be related to someone, and giving it its local meaning, and therefore might reasonably be added to Faubion's proposed 'roving interpreter's translation manual'.[86] (Though it should be added that not all of these appear in every culture and their mode of 'organizing alterity'[87] that anthropologists might reasonably deem kinship.) This is not at all meant to be a flawless methodology, but it is useful for the anthropologist to focus on these idioms that are not explicitly connected to sexual procreation, drawing attention to the other modes in which cultures (including Western cultures) construct the meaning of relatedness. It should be noted, however, that this does not completely sideline procreation, but rather allows it to be studied from a different angle, not as *the* definitive foundation of kinship but as a practice that *may*, but equally *may not*, have a central symbolic and practical role in that culture's understanding of kinship.

Deconstructing kinship in this way, first, avoids reading procreation into other cultures of kinship; second, provides points of enquiry into the internal logic of the culture; and third, aids in the translation of foreign idioms to readers. Ultimately, however, the culture itself takes over, providing the ideas necessary to make sense of kinship. It would be *much* too simple, but nevertheless didactically useful, to say that one can be related in Euro-American contexts by house, by blood, by marriage and by decisions or different sorts of strong social obligations. This simply reveals the layering of ideas that structure idioms of kinship. It would be more accurate to say that the modes of thinking about relatedness rely upon these, and other, bases to be made meaningful.

For the theologian, then, this is particularly helpful, flagging up the way in which a Western paradigm is being read into scripture, while highlighting material in scripture and the history of its interpretation that is directly relevant to a Christian account of kinship. This project will return to social anthropology to make sure each symbol is properly understood as Carsten intended it, but otherwise this gives a great deal of freedom to the theologian. Noting that kinship is not beyond critique, but rather

---

84. Ibid.
85. Carsten, *After Kinship*, 185.
86. Faubion, 'Introduction', 8.
87. Ibid., 3.

is a crucial category for moral theology that should be examined, the theological material will provide the content of theological definition of the category, and not the anthropology. Whereas Barth, however cautious he is, ends up bringing his own 'folk theory' of kinship, as Schneider might call it, into his account of the relationship between parents and children, a proper understanding of the anthropology frees the theologian to engage in as purely theological a task as is possible.

Why, though, might one expect the four idioms of kinship that Carsten notes to recur as they do? Surely that would imply that there is something natural about kinship that explains such recurrence?

Carsten offers an account of the regularity of the image of the blood tie that is useful for these purposes. Commenting on blood specifically – not the biogenetic substance into which the old metaphor of the blood tie has morphed in Schneider's account – Carsten suggests that blood might provide examples of what Lévi-Strauss called things that are 'good to think'.[88] She writes:

> Blood may be particularly apt for this kind of metaphorical extension because it scores so highly in all three respects: It is visually striking, it can be seen inside and outside the body – both routinely and in exceptionally dramatic circumstances – and it can be obviously associated with life or life's cessation. The example of blood also underlines how these three different aspects are, in fact, inseparable and reinforce each other. I return to the special qualities of blood below after considering transfers of other kinds of bodily matter.[89]

It need not come as a surprise, then, that a wide variety of different ideas about blood are associated in different ways with so many practices and powerful images, least of all that it is associated with so powerful a mode of social organization as kinship. There is a series of natural facts – concerning the properties of blood – that is likely to generate certain ways of thinking and speaking about blood that in turn makes it a prime candidate for use in comprehending practices and the world.

Conclusion

Anthropologists have a great deal of experience, honed over decades of ethnographic research, of inhabiting another society, and avoiding reading their own culture into the one being studied. This experience is hugely useful to the Christian theologian. It expands the theologian's scope in discerning the Christian culture gestured towards in scripture. Carsten suggests that the roving anthropologist should ask questions about the household, gender, personhood

---

88. Claude Lévi-Strauss, *Totemism* (Harmondsworth: Penguin, 1969), 162. Cited in Janet Carsten, 'Substance and Relationality: Blood in Contexts', *Annual Review of Anthropology* 40, no. 1 (September 2011): 20.

89. Carsten, 'Substance and Relationality', 24.

and shared substance when finding out about the logic of relatedness in the culture being studied. The theologian should do this too, of scripture and the history of Christian thought and practice, to make sense of a theological account of kinship. Otherwise, when turning to theological sources, one looks only for what one expects to find and ignores what one might not expect to be relevant.

As such, the following chapters will follow this pattern. First, substance will be explored with anthropologists and historians, to trace the origins of Western notions of relatedness by substance, interrogating theologically the idea that shared substance determines relatedness. Second, two Christian visions of the house will be discussed in the light of scripture and the church's theological exploration of its faith. Third, gender will be explored, with a discussion of the role of cultural understandings of gender in the practice and theory of kinship. In the context of this theological foray into a series of vexed questions about gender, sex and marriage will be examined. Finally, the role of how a person is understood in shaping kinship will be explored, leading to engagement with relevant issues that surround the basic question: What is a person? At this juncture, in particular, how one goes about constructing an *ethics* of kinship will be explored, with an account of the place of the human being in creation and in relation to the Creator, informed by Christology.[90]

Kinship can, on this basis, be defined not only for use as an analytic term fit for clearer description of the complexities of Euro-American idioms but also for cross-cultural use: kinship is a mode of social organization (entailing obligations and affections to some and not to others) determined by perceptions of relatedness, explained with reference to some mixture of the concepts of shared substance, house, person and gender.

Using the term 'kinship' this way, these four themes will be used to guide enquiry into the history of Christian thought and practice. This is a better alternative than a history of 'family', which is, by design, inattentive to what it means to be related and to areas of life that might trouble contemporary ideas about relatedness. Instead, these four themes will be used to identify and exhibit elements in Christian traditions of kinship in such a way as to display, as it were, the internal logic of Christian kinship understood on its terms and more resistant to the imposition of foreign idioms – by the researcher and the reader – for its comprehension.

---

90. An additional anthropological category might have been spiritual kinship, which is used here to mean godparenthood, but can be used more broadly as 'kinship reckoned in relation to the divine,' (p. 3). However such a concept informs this entire work. Additionally, it is not the intention of this book to contrast the biological and spiritual. Thomas, Wellman and Malik rightly challenge the contrasting of biological vs. spiritual. The contention of this book is that reproduction has been inappropriately privileged in kinship ethics. The intention is not to privilege spiritualised forms of kinship instead. Rather, to do Christian ethics is to redescribe everything - bodily and spiritual - in the light of Christ. Cf. *New Directions in Spiritual Kinship: Sacred Ties across the Abrahamic Religions*, ed. Todne Thomas et al. (New York: Palgrave Macmillan, 2017).

Chapter 3

SHEDDING BLOOD?

KINSHIP AND SUBSTANCE

Introduction: Substance and the folk theory of kinship

The idea of shared substance is, for David Schneider, of defining importance for the folk theories of American kinship. He argues that the blood tie of old has become shared biogenetic substance today. This folk theory, that shared substance determines kinship, has skewed the anthropological picture of other cultures. However, it will also be claimed that this folk theory of kinship does not fit Euro-American *practice* either, even if the notion of transmitted bodily substance grounding kinship operates as a powerful popular *theory* of how kinship is practised.

For Schneider, in American kinship, and subsequently in the anthropological imagination (which has been extended here to have influenced the moral imaginations of philosophers and theologians), 'kinship is defined as biogenetic. This definition says that kinship is whatever the biogenetic relationship is. If science discovers new facts about biogenetic relationships, then that is what kinship is and was all along, although it may not have been known at the time.'[1] The basis of this disruptive role of scientific discovery is that 'A relative is a person who is related by blood or marriage. Relatives by blood are linked by *material* substance; husband and wife are linked by *law*.'[2] As introduced briefly earlier, there are some people who ought to be treated as kin, according to the 'order of law', and there are others who are in fact kin, according to the 'natural order of things', in which the transmission of bodily substance through reproduction creates a relationship between two bodies that requires social recognition.[3]

This broad-brush picture of American kinship theory will, in this chapter, form the basis for a more detailed investigation of the place of substance in Euro-American kinship thought and practice. This investigation will look beyond Schneider, to the anthropology of assisted reproductive technologies (ARTs)

---

1. Schneider, *American Kinship*, 23.
2. Ibid., 37.
3. Ibid., 26–7.

and Marilyn Strathern's discussion of how theories of knowledge inform the comprehension and practice of relatedness. Subsequently, the cultural contingency of this use of substance will be discussed, in order to show that there is nothing necessary or inevitable about its use in defining kinship. This, in turn, raises the question as to whether there is a Christian heritage to the place of substance in the folk theory of kinship. Accordingly, the anthropology of substance will be looked to for the questions necessary to investigate the place of substance in the history of Christian kinship.

This investigation into the relationship between kinship and ideas of substance will set the stage for a discussion of whether or not relatedness by substance has a legitimate place within a Christian moral imagination. This will involve two moments – one descriptive, and the other constructive – with a theological prescription for Christian ethics of kinship emerging from reflection on the history of the relationship between shared substance and kinship in Christianity. In this way, it will follow Michael Banner in investigating whether the blood tie has a place in a Christian imagination of social life, given the seeming conflict with the sacraments of baptism and the Eucharist, with the former 'displac[ing] kin by blood' and the latter 'mak[ing] us kin to Christ, and thus to one another, by sharing in his blood'.[4]

Whether shared substance should be recognized as, in any way, constitutive of kinship has direct bearing on polarizing moral debates. Indicative of the power of concepts of shared substance in constructing kinship is the phenomenon of 'chasing the blood tie', to borrow a phrase from Helena Ragoné used to describe surrogacy.[5] Michael Banner points to two related ideas that power the chasing of the blood tie with ARTs: 'first, that of 'the desperation of childlessness'', and second, 'that that desperation can be best addressed by obtaining "a child of one's own"'.[6] Accordingly, to follow Janet Carsten's suggestion that ethnographers of kinship examine substance leads the theological ethicist into familiar territory, even if only to examine the cultural ideas that construct the experience of those using ARTs.

A clear example of 'chasing the blood tie' is found in mitochondrial donation, which is conducted in the UK through the use of one of the two different technologies approved by the House of Lords on the 24th of February, 2015. Frederick Curzon, then Parliamentary Under-Secretary for the Department of Health, introduced the bill thus: 'My Lords, the purpose of the regulations is to enable women to have their own genetic children, free of terrible disease caused by disorders in their mitochondrial DNA. The regulations do so by allowing healthy mitochondria from a donor to replace the unhealthy mitochondria in a woman's egg or embryo.'[7]

4. Banner, *The Ethics of Everyday Life*, 59.
5. Helena Ragoné, 'Chasing the Blood Tie: Surrogate Mothers, Adoptive Mothers and Fathers', *American Ethnologist* 23, no. 2 (May 1996): 352–65.
6. Banner, *The Ethics of Everyday Life*, 37.
7. 759 Parl. Deb., H. L. (2014–15) 1569.

Curzon's summary highlights the fact that is particularly pertinent to this study: the technologies would enable women (mitochondrial disorders are transmitted via the egg) to have 'their own genetic children'. This chapter will not be concerned with the morality of technologies legalized in this bill, even if resources will be introduced in the course of this chapter that might reasonably be used as part of a case against the necessity of mitochondrial donation. Rather, it stands as the perfect example of the significance of shared bodily substance for some cultural ideas of kinship. After all, the sole advantage mitochondrial donation confers over, for example, egg donation (a technology posing many, but not all, of the problems posed by mitochondrial donation) is shared genetic material between mother and child.

The idea of the significance of shared substance was – implicitly or explicitly – defended at great cost. The bill was controversial, not just because of questions over the status of the embryo but also because of the medical risks (which were deemed, in the end, proportionate to the benefits), the financial cost of the procedure to the NHS and the emotional cost to those receiving the treatment, which is well described in the context of IVF at least, as evident in the comment of a woman after a failed round of fertility treatment: 'After acknowledging that it was the worst experience of my life, I decided to do it again.'[8]

Most interesting is the media reception of mitochondrial donation, with the idea of 'three-parent' babies catching the public imagination. This phrase was used as a criticism of the practice, but tacitly endorses the grounds on which the debate was premised: that genetics makes kinship. To borrow a point from Michael Banner, mitochondrial donation does not represent a great, technological *troubling* of the norms of kinship as might be imagined, but, in fact, it *re-inscribes* those kinship norms. Writing on ARTs more generally, Banner comments: 'ARTs for all their supposed subversive potential, are in fact chiefly put to the service of the very notions of kinship, which, on the epochal view, they are set to undermine.'[9]

Substance in Euro-American kinship

Schneider's picture of the place of substance in Euro-American kinship will be accepted as presenting a good picture of how Americans and Western Europeans *think* they think about kinship, which is what skews the anthropological picture of other cultures. However, the experience of Americans and Western Europeans using ARTs demonstrates that there is more complexity in the use of notions of substance when it comes to informing actual practice.

---

8. Gay Becker, *The Elusive Embryo: How Women and Men Approach New Reproductive Technologies* (Berkeley: University of California Press, 2000), 132; Banner, *The Ethics of Everyday Life*, 50.
9. Banner, *The Ethics of Everyday Life*, 50.

The problem Carsten finds with Schneider's use of the idea of shared substance is that he slips too freely between very different concepts – blood, biogenetic substance, heredity – without explanation. For instance: 'Two blood relatives are "related" by the fact that they share in some degree the stuff of a particular heredity. Each has a portion of the natural, genetic substance.'[10] She sets this alongside a contemporary example (admittedly from northwest England rather than Chicago, where Schneider collected data, but it illustrates the point), from Jeanette Edwards, in which a woman theorizes about the effects of an artificial womb in laboratory conditions on the baby:

> Somebody somewhere must be creating this artificial womb. A baby reacts to what you're feeling – if your heartbeat is faster then the baby's heartbeat is faster. It could be fed on just vegetables – how would it react then, through the placenta – not what you fancy like crisps, or salad, or chewitts [sic] on the bus, like cravings at different times – vegetables, sweets, alcohol whatever it takes to make a baby. It will have no feelings because no feelings are going through it.[11]

What this reveals is something more complicated than simply the transmission of substance. Either blood or some other imagined fluid is implied in the woman's comment, flowing through the baby and shaping it in the process. It is not kinship that is at stake in this example, but rather the feelings of the baby – the informant does not say that the baby would not be related to the mother if it does not have this shaping flow of what the mother eats going through the baby. What it hints at, however, is the possibility that there is more going on tacitly, nuancing and expanding the meaning of the blood tie in ways different to that of shared substance.

Given that Schneider is clear that he is speaking about cultures, and about the symbols that compose the cultural imagination,[12] this might produce quite a significant critique. That is, he had not considered the fact that symbols like blood are not interchangeable with anything, let alone biogenetic substance, because they are profoundly 'overdetermined', to borrow a term from Sarah Franklin.[13] Nevertheless, such a problem always exists in the deployment of language – clearly 'blood' is associated in instances of kinship with biogenetic substance, and the fact that it is not an exact synonym does not in itself undermine Schneider's account, provided he uses the terms correctly. It does, however, reveal a deeper problem

---

10. Schneider, *American Kinship*, 24; Carsten, *After Kinship*, 112.

11. Jeanette Edwards, 'Explicit Connections: Ethnographic Enquiry in North-West England', in *Technologies of Procreation: Kinship in the Age of Assisted Conception*, ed. Jeanette Edwards et al. (Manchester: Manchester University Press, 1993), 59; Carsten, *After Kinship*, 113.

12. Schneider, *American Kinship*, 1.

13. Sarah Franklin, 'From Blood to Genes? Rethinking Consanguinity in the Context of Geneticization', in *Blood and Kinship: Matter for Metaphor from Ancient Rome to the Present*, ed. Christopher H. Johnson et al. (New York: Berghahn Books, 2013), 292.

of understanding which applies as much to blood as to genes – are these merely substances, or do they – additionally or alternatively – convey information?

This can be understood using Edwards's example: what the mother eats shapes the baby's feelings, transmitting something that is form, rather than substance, from mother to child, by the substance of blood. This gives a sense of the metaphorical richness of the idea of blood. Genes are an even more obvious example, given their information-transmitting quality. The anthropologist Carles Salazar borrows a phrase from Lee Silver, a molecular biologist who specializes in social, political and ethical implications of advances in his field, saying that to share genes means – for the molecular biologist – sharing 'intangible, non-material information'.[14] Salazar points out that this is simply quite different from the idea of sharing 'natural substance'.[15] Salazar is quoting a specialist who habitually uses the word 'gene' in a way that is informed by greater awareness of a hinterland of meaning (informed by scientific reading) that is nevertheless accessible to be drawn upon and to shape the understanding of the layperson, and which – importantly – is a different hinterland of meaning than that behind the concept 'blood'.

For Carsten, Schneider was, by shifting between blood and biogenetic substance, taking himself to be shifting between 'the symbol and what is allegedly symbolized', but was doing so without examining the depth of meaning attached to blood and biogenetic substance.[16] Schneider neglects the different uses of blood, biogenetic substance and heredity.

The trouble is that the idea of substance suggests a gold standard for kinship, something fixed and unchangeable. Marilyn Strathern discerned, in American, UK and Australian contexts, a more flexible language of kinship, which allows room for people to make decisions about to whom they are related. The language of blood, genes and heredity can express the gold standard of substance-based kinship, but it can also be used in describing kinship relations that are determined by choice, as will be seen later. What this language retains in common with ideas of shared substance is that they describe a fact about a person, on the basis of which one can 'know' that they are kin. David Schneider, reflecting on his career, confided that he had not noticed, when writing his major works on kinship, 'how much the Euro-American notion of knowledge depended on the proposition that knowledge is *discovered*, not invented, and that knowledge comes when the "facts" of nature, which are hidden from us mostly, are finally revealed'.[17]

14. Lee M. Silver, 'Confused Meanings of Life, Genes and Parents', *Studies in History and Philosophy of Science Part C: Studies in History and Philosophy of Biological and Biomedical Sciences* 32, no. 4 (December 2001): 652.

15. Carles Salazar, 'Are Genes Good to Think With?', in *European Kinship In The Age Of Biotechnology*, ed. Jeanette Edwards and Carles Salazar (New York: Berghahn, 2008), 181.

16. Carsten, *After Kinship*, 112.

17. David M. Schneider, 'Afterword', in *Schneider on Schneider: The Conversion of the Jews and Other Anthropological Stories*, ed. Richard Handler (Durham: Duke University Press, 1995), 222.

Accordingly, Euro-American theories of knowledge have implications for how kinship is construed, especially as it pertains to concepts associated with shared substance. How does one 'know' that a person is kin? Schneider's reflection on a Euro-American theory of knowledge – loosely defined – suggests that for someone to know something there must be objective grounds that are there regardless of what one chooses to believe, and which must be revealed. Kinship can be thought of in those terms – there are kinship criteria that can be met, and if they are met, then the person is kin, and if not, they are not kin.

This, of course, suggests a very fixed definition of the role of substance in kinship: a person is known to be kin because there is a natural fact about them that makes them so. However, Euro-American theory of knowledge is not so simple in practice. Judgements about whether the criteria for kinship are met are not straightforward. They are informed by the kinds of relationships that the agents want, while at the same time operating under strict criteria that limit choice, especially once a judgement has been made. Joan Bestard describes the position of Marilyn Strathern on this well, that 'kinship knowledge is a form of constitutive rule: 'once known [it] cannot be laid aside'"[18] – but its initiation as well as how it is understood in complex situations has an element of choice about it.

Joan Bestard provides an example of this in the story of Esperança, a woman using egg donation, who is therefore faced with the prospect of a child who shares the 'genetic endowment of another woman', combined with that of her husband. She comments on the fact that the child will not have certain family features, but weighs that up against the fact that the child will also not 'inherit certain things I don't like at all of my family'. She worries that the child will be her husband's – 'his, not mine'.[19] The husband commented that his family was thrilled – because, as a Latin American of Spanish descent now living in Spain, he would re-establish the connection with Spain, after a gap of three generations. An added degree of continuity was celebrated on one side of the family, while Esperança struggled to find the means by which she could claim the child as 'mine'. After the birth, a sense of continuity was assisted by those friends who did not know about the egg donation and spoke of her likeness to the child. Esperança would conclude that *pregnancy* was crucial: 'She had been pregnant, given birth and fed her child. Across these very biological and cultural actions she has passed on substances of her body and has identified herself with the child. Therefore the child resembles her and she thinks in terms of continuity.'[20] This confirmed an earlier prediction, as she had worried about the nature of her relationship with the child:

18. Joan Bestard, 'Knowing and Relating: Kinship, Assisted Reproductive Technologies and the New Genetics', in *European Kinship in the Age of Biotechnology*, ed. Jeanette Edwards and Carles Salazar (New York: Berghahn, 2008), 22. Citing Marilyn Strathern, *Property, Substance and Effect* (London: Athlone Press, 1999), 79.

19. Bestard, 'Knowing and Relating', 25.

20. Ibid.

I'll carry the child nine months in my womb, how could he/she not be mine? You have carried it inside you, you have nourished it, fed it . . . you have passed your feelings, thoughts, emotions on to him/her during these nine months, you will give birth to him/her, . . . well, I do not know whose this child can be if it is not mine. I know, the genetic endowment . . . in the end it's relativised, isn't it?[21]

Genes in this example were not ignored, but were wrestled with because of their apparent relevance to kinship. In the end, they are played down in favour of other factors, and other means of sharing substance and shaping the child. Seeing shared substance as *part of* the picture fits neatly with Strathern's notion of 'cutting and splicing' in kinship, and she borrows and refits a notion from Sarah Franklin, of the 'recombinant' relation. The idea of the 'recombinant' family allows access to the connections that persons make (and which are the object of study for social anthropology) as well as the disconnections they make at the same time.[22] The way in which this happens, and the resources upon which these social agents draw, when faced with the need for recombination, reveal something about the notion of kinship at work. In order to reveal this dynamic, Strathern puts a humbler phenomenon – divorce – alongside biotechnology, to show the ways in which connections and disconnections are managed.

For divorce, she borrows an example in which paternal grandparents sue the mother for greater access to their children after the parents divorced and the father subsequently passed away. The usual boundaries of kinship were transgressed and the courts used ideas of 'parental determination' and 'nuclear family' (which contained a new husband, a child from that union, three from another earlier marriage of hers and two from his, meaning eight children from four unions) to resolve the case.[23] In more regular cases of divorce, similar recombination is necessary, as the old order passes and decisions need to be made about how one distinguishes full-siblings, half-siblings, step-siblings and those one does and does not live with. 'Recombination', for Strathern, describes what happens when the relationship between marriage and filiation is complexified by divorce, or filiation and conception by ARTs.[24] Members of 'recombinant families'[25] become skilled at something kinship demands: 'managing two kinds of relations at once, not just connections but disconnections as well'.[26]

So, returning to Esperança, she intended a connection and drew on the components that would provide kinship, whereas the donor – one presumes – did not intend a connection, and so ignored the usual social implications of sharing

---

21. Ibid., 26.
22. Marilyn Strathern, *Kinship, Law and the Unexpected: Relatives Are Always a Surprise* (Cambridge: Cambridge University Press, 2005), 25.
23. Ibid., 15–16, 22.
24. Ibid., 24.
25. Ibid., 22.
26. Ibid., 32.

DNA. Schneider is basically right in saying, of the Euro-American context, that 'kinship was thought to be the social recognition of the actual facts of biological relatedness, give or take a few errors'[27] but those last six words should be replaced with the caveat: facts of biological relatedness are socially recognized in kinship, but there is a degree of interpretative freedom given to the person, though not the freedom to invent entirely. Needless to say, in what has been said the subject of discussion has been the majority position that determines the rules of the use of kinship language, which suggests that adoptive, foster or spiritual kin are fictive kin, rather than *real* kin, and that childlessness is a tragedy.

Contrary to the expectation that ARTs provide solace to those suffering 'desperate' childlessness, research by Sarah Franklin suggests that ARTs, in fact, intensify the desire for children and with it 'peace of mind' made ever more elusive by increasing avenues of marginal hope.[28] Franklin cites comments from women going through fertility treatments. One woman said, 'I don't want to get to menopause and feel I haven't tried everything.' Another: 'To know we've done everything [helps] to come to terms with [infertility].' In short, there is a theme of those who 'wanted to dispel any doubt by knowing that at least they'd "given it a shot"'.[29]

These interpretative 'fixes' of those involved in ARTs, however, are still reliant upon something like a blood tie, even as it finds new ways to affirm and seek it. In short, ARTs are put to the service of a long-standing, slow-to-adapt way of negotiating social life. Even adoption can do this – Elaine Tyler May records the practice of adoption agencies in the United States after the Second World War, in their attempt to create 'pseudo-biological relationships': 'The idea was to construct an entirely new family – not an overtly adoptive family, but a fictive genetic family in which everyone "matched" as closely as possible.'[30]

Strathern's diagnosis concerning Euro-American kinship norms, then, is particularly insightful: '*Kinship*, though, is where Westerners think about connections between bodies themselves.'[31] This is enabled in the West, argues Strathern, by the overlap between the notions of *conceptual relationship* on the one hand and *social relationship* on the other.[32]

There are, at times, junctures in which connections and disconnections can be recognized by choice. However, these choices are bounded by the rules for use of the meaning-making symbols that resource and inform this process. Indeed

---

27. Schneider, 'Afterword', 222.

28. Sarah Franklin, 'Making Miracles: Scientific Progress and the Facts of Life', in *Reproducing Reproduction: Kinship, Power, and Technological Innovation*, ed. Sarah Franklin and Helena Ragoné (Philadelphia: University of Pennsylvania Press, 1998), 112–13.

29. Ibid., 112.

30. Elaine Tyler May, *Barren in the Promised Land: Childless Americans and the Pursuit of Happiness* (Cambridge, MA: Harvard University Press, 1995), 142–3.

31. Strathern, *Kinship, Law and the Unexpected*, 26.

32. Ibid., 64–7.

it is the coherence of these symbols and their rules that show kinship to be a meaningful analytic term. Those symbols develop uniquely in each culture, in different forms and different arrangements, but Carsten has shown that there are nevertheless themes that recur across cultures.

Where does this leave shared bodily substance as a category for making sense of relatedness? There are a number of ways in which bodies can be conceptually 'related' – they might share a particular substantial 'stuff', they might share a likeness (transmitted by genes, or shaped by behaviour of those around the child *in utero*), or two bodies might relate to one another in the sense that they both, for nine months, shared a physical space. Each of these represents a distinct basis for proposing relatedness between bodies themselves, and each of these deals in unchosen factors (unchosen substance, likeness or past proximity). Accordingly, if people are thought to be constituted in large part by their bodies, then these factors have the appearance of offering an almost scientific basis for kinship. However, the variety of options, and the opportunity to choose which unchosen factors matter, provide the culturally agreed-upon notes by which a person can improvise. Thus, kin-making can become a process of discovery about entities in the order of nature, but a process that is nevertheless informed by the order of law.

Using the concept of blood in the theological ethics of kinship

What does this mean for moral investigation into the place of substance with respect to kinship? It reveals a huge degree of complexity in the working out of the Euro-American folk theory that 'kinship is defined as biogenetic. . . . If science discovers new facts about biogenetic relationship, then that is what kinship is and was all along, although it may not have been known at the time'.[33] Accordingly, even in Euro-American cultures of kinship, biogenetic substance does not straightforwardly determine who is related to whom. Ideas of relatedness are determined not only by a range of notions other than shared biogenetic substance but also by a complex interplay between objective description and subjective desire.

This should not surprise anyone who ascribes any influence over practice to the mediation of human thought, which is itself socially supported and structured by culture. After all, it is not simply instincts that determine whom one treats as deserving the affections and obligations of kinship, but a series of socially supported decisions about how the world should be ordered.

Carsten finds blood to be a useful category for capturing these variances in the concept of substance. In her descriptions of Malay ideas about blood, she elides the concept of substance with that of blood, which carries with it possibilities of 'mutability, transferability, vitality, essence, content'.[34] Her admission of the ad hoc

---

33. Schneider, *American Kinship*, 23.
34. Carsten, *After Kinship*, 131.

way in which she thus deploys substance as a category is disarming, but need not be altogether embarrassing. Pairing the analytical concept of substance with the rich symbol of blood aids in tracking how different concepts of substance are used. There are a variety of different but similar concepts of substance to look out for in turning to Christianity. The flexibility of the language of blood – which in one place grants substance, in another forms the child, and in another feeds them – and its capacity for deployment in a range of metaphors makes it an excellent focal point in studying substance in Christian kinship.

Accordingly, a genealogy of the concept of the blood tie will be offered, both to explore the origins of the ideas of biogenetic relatedness that have tacitly informed theological reflection and to explore whether and how Christianity might connect kinship with ideas of substance. The recognition, as mentioned, of the diversity of notions of substance within Euro-American kinship practice (remaining more or less silent on kinship cross-culturally) makes clearer the radical contingency of the idea that shared biogenetic substance makes kinship. This contingency is also visible historically. This next section will explore its roots in the symbol of blood to reveal its association with Christian thoughts and practices through the centuries.

A genealogy of the blood tie

There are two main aims to offering a genealogy of the blood tie. First, it will provide further evidence of the cultural contingency of ideas of substance-relatedness. Second, it will identify the place of the Eucharist in popularizing the idea of the blood tie, which in turn has promoted the concept of relatedness by biogenetic substance. This will then set the stage for the subsequent recovery in the final section of the social implications of the Eucharist for kinship.

Shared substance, though culturally vital for establishing 'real' kinship, has a flexible meaning. The idea of shared substance can create a demand for ARTs, but precisely what it means to share substance can also adapt when the normal way of making kin is disrupted. The notion of 'blood' reflects the origins of Euro-American idioms of substance and kinship and also conveys this flexibility. As Sarah Franklin comments: 'This "loose" quality of the blood tie is what enables its continual negotiation, or social "adjustment" – indeed this is what might be imagined to facilitate the use of blood to "make and unmake kin" because, like a bicycle, the blood idiom is ready to hand, and can be made to go 'off road' quite easily.'[35]

Some history is required to plumb the depths of the meaning of the blood tie, and discover the reason for its hold on Euro-American kinship and its connection with the Christian faith. The historians David Sabean and Simon Teuscher criticize anthropologists on this front: 'today's anthropological studies of Western constructs such as "blood", "substance", and "relatedness" display the same ahistorical point

35. Franklin, 'From Blood to Genes?', 295.

of view'.[36] They propose that anthropologists could better understand their own terms if they heeded history. What history serves to offer this project, though, is more than just the sharpening of anthropological tools that Sabean and Teuscher aim for but also an account of the relationship between the Christian faith and notions of the blood tie, as the symbol of blood, and its connotations and uses, is followed through the centuries.

What follows, then, is the background to the ugly turn in the history of the concept of the blood tie. A picture will emerge of blood as an uncommon term for the description of kinship, until shifts in the practice of the Eucharist – formalized at the Fourth Lateran Council in 1215 – prompted the enormous growth in the use of blood as a symbol for kinship. The following detailed survey of where blood *was* used for describing kinship serves to demonstrate the rarity of this usage in the West until – ironically – changes in the practice of the Eucharist created the conditions in which blood became a major kinship symbol.

Early uses of blood in the Latin-speaking world can be found in Republican Rome.[37] The term *consanguinei* was attached to property, so that according to the 'Twelve Tables, Rome's earliest law code, dating from the 450s BCE' sons and daughters of the fathers who had died intestate both their independence and equal claim to property, and were called *consanguinei*.[38] Coming from *sanguis*, the etymology of it at least expresses a relationship of blood. However, it was a rare term, being reserved for this extremely specific situation, in the second and third centuries *after Christ*, carrying on the tradition of the Twelve Tables.[39] The small group of *consanguinei* would become more important in the second century BC, when the inheritance rights of female *proximi agnati* (closest agnates, which is to say, those descending from the *paterfamilias*) were revoked, with the exception of these *consanguinei* who survived an intestate father. Cognates would later be given rights to inherit, at the end of the Republic, but only after a series of other claims had been met.[40] The priorities evident in the system, and which defined the legal use of the term *consanguinei*, were the 'transmission of family property, name, and cult within the kinship group'.[41] There was a suitably large class into which the elite could marry, and so while financial interests did not generate household

---

36. David Warren Sabean and Simon Teuscher, 'Introduction', in *Blood and Kinship: Matter for Metaphor from Ancient Rome to the Present*, ed. Christopher H. Johnson et al. (New York: Berghahn Books, 2013), 2.

37. Covering approximately the first five centuries before Christ.

38. Ann-Cathrin Harders, 'Agnatio, Cognatio, Consanguinitas: Kinship and Blood in Ancient Rome', in *Blood and Kinship: Matter for Metaphor from Ancient Rome to the Present*, ed. Christopher H. Johnson et al. (New York: Berghahn Books, 2013), 22.

39. Philippe Moreau, 'The Bilineal Transmission of Blood in Ancient Rome', in *Blood and Kinship: Matter for Metaphor from Ancient Rome to the Present*, ed. Christopher H. Johnson et al. (New York: Berghahn Books, 2013), 44.

40. Harders, 'Agnatio, Cognatio, Consanguinitas', 22–3.

41. Ibid., 23.

endogamy, it did generate 'social endogamy', in which marrying kin to retain claims to property was not required, but marrying those within one's class was.[42] Why, then, was this all linked to *sanguis*, to blood?

The agnatic, rather than cognatic, nature of the relationship of *consanguinei* might be tied to perceptions of the relationship between semen and blood. Aristotle describes semen as the 'foam of blood' and the seventh-century Isidore of Seville expands on this with a definition of *consanguinei* as 'those of one blood, i.e. those who are of one father's semen. For the semen of man is the foam of blood'.[43] However, these emerge out of wide-ranging debates in ancient medicine, which Harder warns are unlikely to elucidate the connection between *sanguis* and *consanguinei*.[44]

Instead, she follows the deployment of the latter word via Cicero, who uses it in one instance to distinguish what might be termed 'relations' compared to *parentes* (parents), *liberi* (children), *coniuges* (spouses) and *supplices* (supplicants).[45] In another instance, within the same work, he divides *cognatio* into *consanguinei* and *maiores*, with the former being horizontal cognates and the latter vertical cognates.[46] Livy, writing after Cicero's death, records different deployments of the term, in some instances in political arguments that concern ties between nations, in others blood (*sanguis*) is used to describe descent, looking at Hannibal and Perseus and their descendants, and in still others, *sanguis* is used to describe the corrupting power of plebeian blood over patrician blood in marriage.[47]

The noticeable difference between Livy and other sources like Cicero is that the former is describing history and broad groups of people, whereas Cicero and legal sources are more focused and careful in their language, concerning themselves with legal issues in which *cognatio* and *agnatio* were more useful. *Consanguinitas* in the sense found in Livy had little value, Harders concludes, in a legal context. Blood was used by Cicero in order to make sense of Roman social ordering as he imagined the relation of reproduction to wider society in *De officiis* 1.53-55, writing in political philosophy, but it does not in itself have a determining role in shaping the legislation of kinship, in which it is treated 'not as a given natural fact, but as a social process'.[48] For instance, *consanguinitas* was used in a legal context to describe the socio-legally important practice of adoption, and *manus* marriage, stretching its use beyond the use of *sanguis* in Livy and in Cicero's political philosophy. The transmission of blood from the father, then, is not drawn upon to ground the ordering of kinship practices in a legal context, which suggests the weakness of this idea about blood in determining social practice, even if it makes

---

42. Ibid., 25.
43. Ibid., 26. Citing Isidor of Seville, *Etymologies*, 623, 9.6.4.
44. Harders, 'Agnatio, Cognatio, Consanguinitas', 26–7.
45. Ibid., 28. Citing Cicero, *De Inventione*, n.d., 1.103.
46. Harders, 'Agnatio, Cognatio, Consanguinitas', 28–9. Cf. Cicero, *De Inventione*, 1.35.
47. Harders, 'Agnatio, Cognatio, Consanguinitas', 29–30.
48. Ibid., 34.

a cameo appearance in explaining the importance of reproduction for Cicero's vision of society.

Moreau nevertheless finds evidence of blood's binding quality. Ulpian, who lived across the turn of the second to third century, refers to the 'affection for blood' when advising judges presiding over matters of provision not just up the patrilineal line but also the matrilineal. The legal question is not the issue – what matters is that it reveals a concern for the possibility that the 'affection for blood' might entail obligations.[49] This is a small piece of evidence on the basis of which one might claim that kinship affections were associated with the notion of blood, but which is, in Moreau's judgement, a far cry from later medieval preoccupation with *consanguinitas* in structuring kinship. Roman family law is strongly informed by factors other than blood, and uses *consanguinitas* in a narrow range of cases. Blood, *sanguis*, appears when describing 'globally cognatic system and implies transmitted identity and compulsory identity, but which was never used, in common conceptions, as the basis for a corporate group or for an abstract category of kinship'.[50] An example – not from Moreau's research – might be Augustine's use of the term (in late antiquity) to guarantee Christ's descent from David 'according to the flesh [*carnem*]' (Rom. 1.3), by arguing that Mary indeed shared *consanguinitatem* 'with the line of David'. The idea of *consanguinitas*, then, was at least familiar to Augustine (and it is unsurprising that a mainly legal term would be familiar to Augustine given the nature of his academic work in Milan). Interestingly, though, Augustine uses the expression precisely while stating the irrelevance of procreation to the kinship of Mary to David, just as in the kinship between Joseph and Jesus.[51]

The main takeaway from this section of the genealogy, however, is to demonstrate that blood *did not yet* have the symbolic power that it later had. Moreau suggests this symbolic power might be Germanic on the one hand and Christian on the other, but it was only later historical developments that allowed blood to become a powerful symbol structuring kinship practices.[52]

The near-absence of blood from the Roman imagination of kinship is striking, not just in comparison with the later medieval preoccupation with blood, but also given the roughly contemporary presence of blood in Greek kinship language. Caroline Johnson Hodge finds several examples in Greek: in 4 Macc. 13.20 ('these brothers remained an equal time [in their mother's womb] and were formed ... for the same period and increased by the same blood [αἵματος]...'[53]), in the Iliad 6.211

---

49. Moreau, 'The Bilineal Transmission of Blood in Ancient Rome', 50.
50. Ibid., 52.
51. Augustine, 'Agreement among the Evangelists', in *New Testament I and II*, trans. Kim Paffenroth, The Works of Saint Augustine: A Translation for the 21st Century, I/15 and I/16 (Hyde Park: New City Press, 2014), 2.2.4, 170.
52. Moreau, 'The Bilineal Transmission of Blood in Ancient Rome', 52.
53. Caroline Johnson Hodge, *If Sons, Then Heirs: A Study of Kinship and Ethnicity in the Letters of Paul* (Oxford University Press, 2007), 24. Her own translation, amending Brenton.

(Glaukos describes the 'lineage (γενεῆς) and the blood (αἵματος) from which he is born'[54]), in the Nicomachean Ethics viii.12.3 ('Brothers love each other as being from the same source . . . which is why we speak of "being of the same blood" or "of the same stock" (ταὐτὸν αἷμα καὶ ῥίζαν)'[55]), in Philo's *On the Virtues* 195 ('In the court where truth presides, kinship . . . is not measured only by blood [αἵματι], but by similarity of conduct and pursuit of the same objects'[56]), in Philo's *Embassy to Gaius* 54 ('all my kinsmen by blood (οἱ ἀφ᾽ αἵματος'[57]), and in Herodotus' *Histories*, 8.144.2 ('The Greek people . . . are of the same blood (ὅμαιμον) and the same tongue'[58]). This language of blood must have provided the backdrop against which some of Paul's writings on kinship in Christ would make sense, as blood is omitted in favour of flesh and bone in Hebrew Bible kinship language.

That is not to say that this Greek tradition did not *in any way* inform later speech. Anita Guerreau-Jalabert has described the process by which *consanguinitas* in Medieval Latin became, for the Carolingians, a less-common 'equivalent of *cognatio*', denoting a *group* rather than a *tie*.[59] The main way of speaking about kinship was in terms of flesh, *caro*, while *sanguis*, borrowed from the classical period, would become a variant with little independent meaning in the High Middle Ages, both in Latin and in Old French.[60]

It was only around the fifteenth century that blood would start to loom large in kinship language, appearing particularly in the context of talking about bloodlines, on the one hand, and royal blood, on the other.[61] Still, though, it retained a slimmer range of meaning than the more dominant language of flesh. While 'blood relatives' was, according to Bettina Bildhauer, an expression used in Medieval Latin and contemporary accounts of conception, the connotations of blood to kinship were not as commonly drawn upon during the period than those of violence and sacrifice, and the notion of noble blood would take some time to develop.[62] The use of blood as a symbol was infrequent, and generally connected with violence.[63]

---

54. Ibid. Her own translation, amending Lattimore.
55. Ibid., 25. Her own translation, amending Rackham.
56. Ibid., 39. Translation from Colson, cf. Philo, *Works*, trans. F. H. Colson (Cambridge, MA: Harvard University Press, 1962).
57. Hodge, *If Sons, Then Heirs*, 95. Translation from Colson.
58. Ibid., 50. Her own translation, heavily amended from Godley.
59. Anita Guerreau-Jalabert, 'Flesh and Blood in Medieval Language about Kinship', in *Blood and Kinship: Matter for Metaphor from Ancient Rome to the Present*, ed. Christopher H. Johnson et al. (New York: Berghahn Books, 2013), 63–4.
60. Ibid., 64–9.
61. Ibid., 69.
62. Bettina Bildhauer, 'Medieval European Conceptions of Blood: Truth and Human Integrity', *Journal of the Royal Anthropological Institute* 19 (1 May 2013): 572.
63. Bettina Bildhauer, 'We Have Never Been Unbloody', *Syndicate Theology* (blog), available online: https://syndicate.network/symposia/theology/blood/ (accessed 26 July 2019).

The ugly turn in the history of the blood tie

Blood would become a powerful and popular metaphor for kinship in Western Europe, but so far this genealogy has not yet encountered the origins of this shift. Blood was not unheard of as a symbol for kinship in the West, but neither was it common. The spark for the dramatic rise in blood as a symbol for kinship in the West would find its origins, ironically enough, in the practice of the Eucharist.

Guerreau-Jalabert looks to the connection of three concepts in order to explain the evolution of blood as a symbol for kinship: *anima* (spirit), *caro* (flesh) and *sanguis* (blood). When contrasted with spirit, then flesh and blood were tied together. However, on their own, flesh and blood were different, because they had different connotations: the Old Testament associated spirit (this time *anima*) with blood (Gen. 9.4-6; Lev. 17.11 and 14 – in the Vulgate what the NRSV renders 'life' is rendered *anima*, spirit), and in the Eucharist the bread was taken to feed the flesh, and the wine the *anima*.

Take, for instance, Aquinas, who writes: 'the flesh of Christ under the form of bread is offered for the well-being of the body, the blood under the form of wine for the well-being of the soul.' He then ties up the two issues by closing with the words: 'As we read in Leviticus, the animal's soul is in the blood.'[64]

This logic would be applied to the church as imagined as the body. The priests, *in persona Christi*, were placed at the head of the body, receiving both wine and bread, and the layperson received only the bread.[65] This conceptual connection between Christ's blood in the church is made even more plausible by the declaration by the Council of Vienne in 1311-12, that the Bride of Christ, which is to say the church, springs from the side of Christ (alluding both to the creation of Eve and

---

64. Thomas Aquinas, *Summa Theologiæ*, trans. William Barden, vol. 58 (London: Blackfriars, 1965), 3a. 74, 1 ad 3. A similar logic is applied in a discussion of consanguinity in the *Supplementum*. Responding to the objection that blood was sourced in food, implying greater kindred with food than with those from whom one was born, he points to 'likeness', which 'depends more on form whereby a thing is actually, than on matter whereby a thing is potentially'. Food, he argues, merely impacts the accidents, rather than the substance, of the person. He looks to Aristotle's account of the relationship between semen and blood to argue that blood transmits form, meaning it is more precise to speak of a relationship by blood than by flesh. Accordingly, Aquinas took blood to transmit the essence. (Thomas Aquinas, *Summa Theologiæ*, trans. Fathers of the English Dominican Province, vol. 5 (Allen: Christian Classics, 1948), Suppl. 54, 1. ad. 3-4. For a brief discussion, see Simon Teuscher, 'Flesh and Blood in the Treatises on the Arbor Consanguinitas (Thirteenth to Sixteenth Centuries)', in *Blood and Kinship: Matter for Metaphor from Ancient Rome to the Present*, ed. Christopher H. Johnson et al. (New York: Berghahn Books, 2013), 86.)

65. Guerreau-Jalabert, 'Flesh and Blood in Medieval Language about Kinship', 73.

the piercing of Christ's side on the cross) so that the church is one body, stemming from Christ's blood.[66]

Bildhauer picks out the Fourth Lateran Council in 1215 as a key juncture in the shift that Guerreau-Jalabert also describes, in which not only the church's identity as a group of communicants sharing in Christ's blood was clarified but also its hierarchical structure was reinforced, leading to the exclusion of the laity from sharing in the blood at communion.[67]

There lies the problematic turn in the genealogy of the blood tie. It was through the development of these spiritual associations that blood became closely associated with the kinship of flesh, according to Guerreau-Jalabert. The introduction of blood as a higher principle reserved for the social elite explains the burgeoning use of blood to describe *royal* kinship. From there, it trickled down the social chain, not least under the influence of the priesthood of all believers in the time of the Reformation, and the collapsing of spiritual hierarchies. The spiritualizing of social relationships was already prominent, as spiritual, or baptismal, kinship had gone mainstream, and so the conditions were ripe for the more spiritual blood to become prominent in discussions of royal kinship. While Guerreau-Jalabert admits that her case 'still remains to be settled',[68] Teuscher calls it 'most convincing', and it chimes with Ruiz's proposal discussed later, as well as Bynum's description of the rising symbolic significance of Christ's blood in worship.[69]

What is so interesting about the picture, though, is the deep irony. Blood had become the stuff of ties under the influence of Eucharistic theology, and with it came social exclusions and barriers. These exclusions and barriers, however, *contradicted* the relativization of pre-existing kinship that the Eucharist demands as it proclaims membership of Christ's body. This irony will be discussed theologically later, but for now there is more of the story to be told in order to understand how the popularization of blood as a symbol would come to shape twenty-first-century kinship practice.

---

66. Bettina Bildhauer, *Medieval Blood*, Religion and Culture in the Middle Ages (Cardiff: University of Wales Press, 2006), 137. This language is also found in Augustine: 'A wife is made from the side of the sleeping man; the Church is made for the dying Christ from the sacrament of the blood that flowed from his side when he was dead.' (Augustine, *Answer to Faustus, a Manichean*, ed. Boniface Ramsey, trans. Roland Teske, The Works of Saint Augustine: A Translation for the 21st Century, I/20 (Hyde Park: New City Press, 2007), 12.8, 130.)

67. Bildhauer, *Medieval Blood*, 154–6.

68. Guerreau-Jalabert, 'Flesh and Blood in Medieval Language about Kinship', 73–4.

69. Teuscher, 'Flesh and Blood in the Treatises on the Arbor Consanguinitas (Thirteenth to Sixteenth Centuries)', 98. Cf. Caroline Walker Bynum, *Wonderful Blood: Theology and Practice in Late Medieval Northern Germany and Beyond* (Philadelphia: University of Pennsylvania Press, 2007), 1–9.

After the adoption by nobility of blood to describe kinship groups, urban elites followed suit, as Ruiz finds is the case in Castile from the late twelfth century.[70] This was married with fraught relationships between dominant Christians and their Jewish and Muslim neighbours, with the power of the latter waning considerably in that period. The language of tainted blood followed, as descent from the Visigoths combined with the pride of military victory and boasting in their faith, and was vaunted over Jews and Muslims who had rejected the Christian faith, were weak in battle and were cursed as a race, parsed in terms of tainted blood. Under persecution, many Jews converted, with one effect being the opening of privileges to those of Jewish descent. There followed a renewed focus on race, rather than religious affiliation. New 'cleanliness-of-blood statutes' came into force in 1449, which were controversial but still popularized the idea of tainted blood.[71] Having shifted from minority metaphor to organizing principle among the nobility, blood went mainstream, not just joining groups but also marking social status as well as *essence* and *identity*, and new potential for both inclusion and exclusion on the basis of blood.

Gérard Delille argues much the same, but on different terms. It was piety concerning the shed blood of Christ that led to the infusing of blood with the idea that it bore identity. In the fifteenth century, Franciscans and Dominicans debated furiously whether the blood of Christ ought to be adored. The former argued that *cruor* ('shed' blood) was 'severed from the Divinity, from the Word', in a way that *sanguis* ('internal blood') was not, on the grounds that *sanguis* was the bearer of life – the *anima* – only when united with the body. The latter argued that *because* blood, *sanguis*, was the bearer of life it could not be separated from the divine breath or life, meaning that, in the case of Christ's blood, there was no distinction between *cruor* and *sanguis*.[72] Somewhat confusingly, it was the *Franciscans*, rather than the Dominicans, who looked more favourably on the devotion of blood relics (though Bynum remarks that Dominicans would also often honour those in their possession, rather inconsistently), because the blood could then reveal a *real* sacrifice, in which Christ's blood was *really* shed. A sign of sacrifice was worthy of devotion. For the Dominicans, however, the blood could not be separated from God, because otherwise it would not be able to pay so great a price as was owed by humanity, and as such if there were a 'miraculous transformation' of spots on the bread then it was simply some sort of corruption, because the saving blood was 'in

---

70. Teofilo R. Ruiz, 'Discourses of Blood and Kinship in Late Medieval and Early Modern Castile', in *Blood and Kinship: Matter for Metaphor from Ancient Rome to the Present*, ed. Christopher H. Johnson et al. (New York: Berghahn Books, 2013), 112.

71. Ibid., 114–15.

72. Gérard Delille, 'The Shed Blood of Christ: From Blood as Metaphor to Blood as Bearer of Identity', in *Blood and Kinship: Matter for Metaphor from Ancient Rome to the Present*, ed. Christopher H. Johnson et al. (New York: Berghahn Books, 2013), 126.

glory', whereas for the Franciscans it was an occasion for devotion, revealing the saving – and *shed* – blood of Christ.[73]

With this Dominican denial of the distinction between *cruor* and *sanguis* of Christ came the association not just of life but of particular sorts of 'qualities' in the transmission of blood.[74] In fifteenth-century France a new 'naturalist theory' of blood justified the notion of noble blood, so that it could be claimed to be a 'substance capable of transmitting' in the way that semen and milk were already taken to be, and which was easily justified with recourse to Aristotelian thought.[75] This transition was opposed by the church, with its affirmation of the 'unity of the human species', and by the state, with its idea of *political* nobility, but it nevertheless remained popular.[76]

It is a curious puzzle that agnatic kinship and patrilineal inheritance grew in popularity between 1400 and 1700, strengthening thin lines of descent, even though ancient science of conception, popular in the seventeenth century, proposed that women produced the blood, and the Bible proposed that husband and wife were one flesh anyway.[77] Bossuet, the great seventeenth-century French preacher, very much assumed that blood came from the mother when he argues that God forms Mary's blood into Christ, giving Him the same substance as God shaped as though in the divine 'womb' but from Mary's blood (while Mary receives the pure blood that Christ needed to receive from Christ Himself).[78] Nevertheless, the blood kinship language promoted by the theory of mother-to-child transmission of blood to express kinship ties was borrowed. When combined with increasingly patrilineal transmission of property, blood was then used to describe ties between fathers and sons, or even fathers and sons-in-law, as well as alliances between houses and other kinship or political groups.[79]

Among French colonists of North America, the transmission of blood was important. This can be seen in eighteenth-century Louisiana, with fears about mixing 'French blood' with that of local 'Indians' leading to a ban on missionaries blessing such marriages. This incurred the wrath of a visiting clergyman from Quebec – where eighty years before there had been unsuccessful attempts to promote marriage between French men and local women, in order to support the growth of the colony[80] – who argued that French blood was

---

73. Bynum, *Wonderful Blood*, 128–9.
74. Delille, 'The Shed Blood of Christ', 126.
75. Ibid., 129–30.
76. Ibid., 132.
77. David Warren Sabean, 'Descent and Alliance: Cultural Meanings of Blood in the Baroque', in *Blood and Kinship: Matter for Metaphor from Ancient Rome to the Present*, ed. Christopher H. Johnson et al. (New York: Berghahn Books, 2013), 145–6.
78. Ibid., 146–52.
79. Ibid., 153–6.
80. Guillaume Aubert, 'Kinship, Blood, and the Emergence of the Racial Nation in the French Atlantic World, 1600–1789', in *Blood and Kinship: Matter for Metaphor from Ancient Rome to the Present*, ed. Christopher H. Johnson et al. (New York: Berghahn Books, 2013), 177.

not harmed in the mixing. The argument for intermarriage from the need to increase the population failed to convince those concerned about the damage done to the purity of blood.[81] Similar policies discriminating against whites who married those of African descent were imposed in Saint Domingue and Martinique.[82] There were efforts by the *Société des Amis des Noirs*, and attempts at emancipation at the end of the eighteenth century, to curb the racist use of blood. Whether or not successful, this dark side of the history elevated further the use of blood to mark out social groups, identity and boundaries, including kinship and race.[83]

In France, blood as an expression of kinship was undergoing a 'demotion' compared to the more popular term *famille*, not just with the anti-aristocratic backlash in the 1789 Revolution, but shortly before.[84] The importance of distinguishing between relatives by blood and by marriage ebbed. This followed the recognition of younger or female heirs and a decrease in the power of the father and the importance of the father's bloodline.[85] In the early nineteenth century, on the back of transitions of power in the Revolution away from the aristocracy and the church, only two families were upheld: the private and the public, with the state being described in familiar terms. Blood shifted from kinship to a 'racialized nation'.[86] Evidence for this is found in the late-eighteenth-century historical search for the origins for this French nation/race, which was 'given "scientific" validity by biology'.[87]

Similar trends emerged in twentieth-century Germany. The 'bureaucratic arithmetic of blood' pushed the 'quarter-Jew' to marry 'a full-blooded Aryan' to dilute Jewish blood and eradicate it from the German race. '[H]alf-Jews' were to marry one another, so as not to pollute Aryan blood.[88] When the murder of 'full-Jews' was at its peak, the question of 'half-Jews' remained active, with Himmler suspecting that Jewish blood might be, as it were, 'dominant', corrupting German

---

81. Ibid., 182–3.
82. Ibid., 184–5.
83. Ibid., 189–91.
84. Christopher H. Johnson, 'Class Dimensions of Blood, Kinship, and Race in Brittany, 1780–1880', in *Blood and Kinship: Matter for Metaphor from Ancient Rome to the Present*, ed. Christopher H. Johnson et al. (New York: Berghahn Books, 2013), 198–9.
85. Ibid., 200–1.
86. Ibid., 202.
87. Ibid., 216. For a fascinating reading of a late-nineteenth-century American Christian challenge to those concerned about tainted blood in adopted orphans, see Amy Laura Hall, *Conceiving Parenthood: American Protestantism and the Spirit of Reproduction* (Grand Rapids: Eerdmans, 2007), 395–9.
88. Cornelia Essner, 'Nazi Anti-Semitism and the Question of 'Jewish Blood'', in *Blood and Kinship: Matter for Metaphor from Ancient Rome to the Present*, ed. Christopher H. Johnson et al. (New York: Berghahn Books, 2013), 236.

blood for more generations than his 'racial experts' suggested. This led to the decision to sterilize 'half-Jews'.[89]

Discussing the blood tie alongside racism is not designed to critique the former by association. Rather, it is a necessary part of the story in which blood would come to be associated with both social belonging and scientific ideas of biogenetic substance. The genealogy as a whole shows the historical contingency of the idea of the blood tie, complementing prior arguments from social anthropology for its cultural contingency. The genealogy also disclosed how practices of the Eucharist would play a vital role in securing blood as a powerful symbol of social belonging and exclusion.[90]

It should come as no surprise, as will be argued next, that the Eucharist should be associated with social belonging, though it is ironic that it would contribute to the forms of social organization implied by the modern language of blood ties. In the next section, the social logic of the Eucharist will be teased out, as properly ordering social life in quite a different way than occurred through the historical accidents recorded in the aforementioned genealogy.

Eucharistic blood

Kinship thinking is complex, with notions of relatedness being constructed from a series of meaning-making symbols, and the symbol of blood does not capture everything that can be said in relation to ideas of how procreation might be interpreted as creating a connection. Other connections will be discussed in a later chapter on the relationship between personhood and kinship. At this point, it is sufficient to say that this genealogy of the blood tie suggests that the way in which the concept of shared substance is used in Euro-American kinship is neither necessary, nor inevitable, nor – it will now be argued – good.

This genealogy reveals a Christian theological objection to social organization based on shared substance, transmitted down lines of descent. Specifically, the Eucharist has been written into Euro-American kinship norms, drawing out and strengthening notions of ties by blood. Blood is a thing which is 'good to think',[91] and it should come as no surprise that it is found in Greek kinship language. However, it was rare in Latin kinship language, only to receive its exalted status under the influence of the binding power of the Eucharistic blood.

The contribution the Eucharist made in the history of Euro-American kinship is, however, curious. The Eucharist might have served to strengthen ideas of the

---

89. Ibid., 241.

90. Blood symbolism is discussed extensively by the anthropologist Anidjar, who remarks on the Christian roots of anthropological assumptions, describing Morgan as basing his 'science of kinship' on a 'Eucharistic "community of blood"' (Gil Anidjar, *Blood: A Critique of Christianity* (New York: Columbia University Press, 2014), 43.)

91. Carsten, 'Substance and Relationality', 19.

blood tie, but it originally served an opposing function: to open access to a set-apart community whose membership was determined principally in terms of descent. In the early church, the Eucharist was at the centre of a debate about how the 'new covenant in my blood' (Lk. 22.20) related to the covenant with Israel, and the corresponding separation of Jew and Gentile.

Caroline Johnson Hodge argues persuasively that, in the writings of Paul, 'lineage, paternity, and peoplehood are the salient categories for describing one's status before the God of Israel'.[92] She details extensively the place of patrilineal descent in the cultural context, but it should come as no surprise that Paul was working with such categories, given the reference in Gal. 3.29 to those who belong to Christ being 'Abraham's offspring [σπέρμα: seed], heirs according to the promise'. In the background, here, is God's covenant with Abraham and his seed (cf. Gen. 17.9).[93]

The nature of God's covenant relationship with Abraham and the kinship practices of God's partner in this covenant constitute too large a topic for discussion here. However, it should be sufficient to note that while some membership of God's covenant with Abraham was made available to his offspring, recorded in genealogies determined by some notion of descent, membership of the new covenant is taken to be organized in a different way, mediated by Jesus Christ. One feature of this new covenant membership is being grafted into the lineage of Jesus. This is certainly not to say that this exhausts the benefits of the new covenant, made available to both Jew and Gentile, but – referring to the 'grafting' in of the gentile olive shoot in Romans 11 – Hodge explains: 'The adoption of the gentiles incorporates a new people into an already existing kin group'.[94] Hence, those who belong to Christ become Abraham's offspring, siblings in Christ, who are welcomed to the same table, to share in the blood of the new covenant that binds them.[95]

The new covenant in Jesus' blood, remembered in the Eucharist, drew together Jew and Gentile into a descent line, but it did so through adoption in Jesus Christ.[96] It is profoundly ironic, then, that the Eucharist, which signifies the opening of

92. Hodge, *If Sons, Then Heirs*, 4.
93. In Gal. 3.29, Paul's use of seed refers back to his Christocentric re-reading of the seed of Abraham in v. 16, the basis of which is brought to light in Richard B. Hays, *Echoes of Scripture in the Letters of Paul* (New Haven: Yale University Press, 1989), 85.
94. Hodge, *If Sons, Then Heirs*, 77.
95. For further work on the connection between blood and kinship, see Hodge's work on the significance of ritual blood (sacrifice or circumcision) in marking relatedness with the father in both Jewish and Greek symbolic worlds in the first century. (Hodge, *If Sons, Then Heirs*, 27–8.) Hodge sees this ritualized kinning as serving as the background for Paul's connection between baptism and adoption by the Spirit. (Hodge, *If Sons, Then Heirs*, 76.)
96. 'Gentiles are made descendants of Abraham not through physical acts of procreation but through kinship with Christ'. (Hodge, *If Sons, Then Heirs*, 63–4.)

the descent line of Abraham, should come to serve the purpose of emphasizing exclusive membership of kinship construed in terms of descent.

As church practice and doctrine developed, the Eucharist would continue to have this significance, uniting in Christ, and cutting across pre-existing kinship ties. Augustine serves as a valuable guide to precisely this theology of the Eucharist, being one of the principal architects of later Christian theology of the sacrament.[97]

Augustine, when speaking about the Eucharist, strongly emphasizes the binding quality of Christ's body and blood. Just as baptism has 'the same value as being buried with Christ' then so too the Eucharist has value beyond 'fill[ing] the belly' – 'it nourishes the spirit'. It is 'the sacrament of unity'.[98] He reiterates this, labouring the point, describing individual participants as grains and grapes, merged in the process of making bread and wine into one.[99] In a sermon preached at Hippo Regius his claim that in the sacrament 'one thing is seen, another is to be understood' is fulfilled by the participant submitting to the body of Christ in their joining, alongside their fellow participants.[100]

Augustine used the Eucharist against the Donatists, pointing out that at its institution Jesus did not single out his betrayer for exclusion, but gave to all.[101] Any split would display pride, whereas the giving of Christ's body and blood taught humility.[102] With rich rhetoric, Augustine describes the sharing of Christ's body and blood as the realization now of the future community that will be experienced by the faithful.[103]

---

97. Augustine's influence hardly needs to be established, but is evidenced by Aquinas' repeated use of Augustine in his own statement on transubstantiation. (Aquinas, *Summa Theologiæ*, 1948, 5:3a. 75.)

98. Augustine, *Sermons (184-229Z)*, ed. John E. Rotelle, trans. Edmund Hill, The Works of Saint Augustine: A Translation for the 21st Century, III/6 (New Rochelle: New City Press, 1993), 229A.1, 269-70. A similar parallel between the reality of burial at baptism and the reality of the body and blood of Christ is found in Letter 98. Cf. Augustine, *Letters 1-99*, ed. John E. Rotelle, trans. Roland J. Teske, The Works of Saint Augustine: A Translation for the 21st Century, II/1 (Hyde Park: New City Press, 2001), 98.10, 431-2.

99. Augustine, *Sermons (184-229Z)*, 229A.2, 270. Cf. also Augustine, *Homilies on the Gospel of John 1-40*, ed. Allan Fitzgerald, trans. Edmund Hill, The Works of Saint Augustine: A Translation for the 21st Century, I/12 (Hyde Park: New City Press, 2009), 26.17, 463-4.

100. Augustine, *Sermons (230-272B)*, trans. Edmund Hill, the Works of Saint Augustine: A Translation for the 21st Century, III/7 (New Rochelle: New City Press, 1993), 272, 300. Preached on Pentecost or Easter between the years 405 and 411.

101. Augustine, *Letters 1-99*, 44.5.10, 178.

102. Augustine, *Expositions of the Psalms 33-50*, ed. John E. Rotelle, trans. Maria Boulding, The Works of Saint Augustine: A Translation for the 21st Century, III/16 (New York: New City Press, 2000), 33.2.7, 29.

103. Augustine, *Homilies on the Gospel of John 1-40*, 26.15, 463.

Sharing in this unity is a serious affair with responsibilities – those who share in the body of a prostitute do not share in the body of Christ.[104] Augustine draws on the words of Jn 6.56, 'Those who eat my flesh and drink my blood abide in me, and I in them,' to warn that for those who do not abide in Christ in day-to-day life, the sacrament is one of condemnation, not sanctifying union.[105]

However, even as Augustine raises the stakes of participation in the Eucharist, he identifies its nature as communicating forgiveness, with his striking statement on Christ's executioners: 'Their hands were impious and stained with Christ's blood, but he whose blood they had spilt washed them. These people, who had looked upon his mortal body and hounded him, were now joined to his body, the Church. They spilt their own ransom so that they might drink their own ransom, for many of them were afterward converted.'[106]

For Augustine, then, the Eucharist offers, among other things, unity in forgiveness by Jesus, and obligation to those who receive. The costliness of the communion that the Eucharist invites the participant into is immediately obvious, and was not lost on Augustine. Augustine observed this horror, remarking upon Jesus' words, 'Those who eat my flesh and drink my blood have eternal life, and I will raise them up on the last day; for my flesh is true food and my blood is true drink,' that 'The disciples who were following him were appalled.'[107] In this respect, Judaism 'clearly parted company' with Christianity, notes David Biale on the history of the use of blood-language: 'whereas Judaism retained the biblical horror at the consumption of blood, Christianity ultimately made the "eating" of its founder and the "drinking" of his blood a central sacrament.'[108] The Eucharist points to a sacrifice received, not performed, by the communicant, as Jesus serves both as High Priest and as offering.[109]

The response? Augustine bids Christians to recognize that they are the passive party, remembering a sacrifice they did not offer and receiving the effects they did not bring about.[110] Augustine bids his congregation at Easter in a special way to 'make constant reflection' on Christ's sacrifice, and especially without neglecting

---

104. Augustine, *City of God*, trans. Henry Bettenson (Harmondsworth: Penguin Books, 1984), 21.25, 1010.

105. Augustine, *Homilies on the Gospel of John 1–40*, 26.18–19, 464. Cf. also 1 Cor. 11: 27, 29.

106. Augustine, *Expositions of the Psalms 73–98*, ed. John E. Rotelle, trans. Maria Boulding, The Works of Saint Augustine: A Translation for the 21st Century, III/18 (New York: New City Press, 2002), 93.8, 24.

107. Augustine, *Expositions of the Psalms 33–50*, 33.1.8, 19. Cf. Jn 6.60.

108. David Biale, *Blood and Belief: The Circulation of a Symbol Between Jews and Christians* (Berkeley: University of California Press, 2007), 44.

109. Augustine, *Sermons (184–229Z)*, 228B.2, 261.

110. Augustine, *Sermons (94A–147A)*, ed. John E. Rotelle, trans. Edmund Hill, The Works of Saint Augustine: A Translation for the 21st Century, III/4 (Brooklyn: New City Press, 1992), 136C.2, 368. Cf. also Augustine, *City of God*, 17.20, 756.

the remembrance of Christ whenever they share in 'his body and blood as our daily banquet' in any other time of the year.[111]

Augustine's theology is rich with the language of blood. The blood of Christ unifies, joining Christians in partaking of the Eucharist, just as they are joined as sinners in need of His sacrificial offering, or debtors for whom Christ's blood is payment. Blood appears in the language of violence, whether it flows through the veins of the forgiven sinner even as it stains their hands in the murder of Christ, or whether it spills from the side of Christ's body, the church, synecdochically in the martyr as they lay down their life.[112] Blood flows through that body – Christ's blood, which unites all who receive from Him in one body.

Conclusion: The disruptive blood tie

Neither Paul's account of the new covenant in Christ's blood nor Augustine's rich imagery of blood in the Eucharist lend themselves to the conceptuality of exclusion. Writing about the obligations that the Eucharist implies for those who partake, William Cavanaugh draws on 1 Cor. 11.27-29 to write, 'Those of us who partake in the eucharist while ignoring the hungry may be eating and drinking our own damnation.'[113] This is because in the Eucharist 'we become one with others and share their fate'.[114] Similarly, Cavanaugh draws on Mt. 25.31-46 – particularly the words 'For *I* was hungry and you gave me food' – to identify the pain of those excluded from care (in this case, the hungry) with the pain of Christ. As such, any temptation 'to spiritualize all this talk of union, to make our connection to the hungry a mystical act of imaginative sympathy' is firmly rejected. The Eucharist has social consequences because it changes the identity of those who receive. Cavanaugh uses Augustine's aphorism to summarize the logic of the change the Eucharist brings about: 'God is the food that consumes us.'[115]

With blood imagery, Augustine offers expositions of the core practices of the Christian faith – baptism and the Eucharist – as well as the central event of the Christian faith, Christ's death on the cross. In neither event are existing kinship ties elevated. Rather, baptism and the Eucharist disrupt contemporary kinship norms, reflecting the chief identity that the Christian has, as one redeemed by the

---

111. Augustine, *Sermons (184-229Z)*, 229D.2, 278–9. In a similar vein, see also Augustine, *Answer to Faustus, a Manichean*, 20.18, 278.

112. Augustine, *Expositions of the Psalms 73–98*, 85.1, 221; 93.8, 384; Augustine, *Homilies on the Gospel of John 1–40*, 7.6, 149; Augustine, *Expositions of the Psalms 33–50*, 40.1, 225.

113. William T. Cavanaugh, *Being Consumed: Economics and Christian Desire* (Grand Rapids: Eerdmans, 2008), 98.

114. Cavanaugh, 95. See 1 Cor. 10.16-17.

115. Augustine, *Confessions*, Oxford World's Classics (Oxford: Oxford University Press, 2008), 7.16, 124. Cited in Cavanaugh, *Being Consumed: Economics and Christian Desire*, 95.

blood of Christ and brought to share in Christ's Sonship with the Father through adoption.

Strangely, kinship ties have been elevated, through accidents of history, through metaphorical accretions to the meaning of blood in connection with kinship that contradict those Augustine attaches to blood when describing the Eucharist. The unifying Christian imagery of blood which runs through one body was appropriated to describe social bodies of exclusion: the elite of the church, then royalty and the aristocracy, then down through the social hierarchy to urban elites, then to describe kinship, which in turn came to define Christian 'races' against inferior 'races' – first the Muslim and the Jew, and then the Native American or the slave of African descent.

Blood came to be a key personal identifier, telling the person who they were, and connecting them with their kin. In that context, the inability to have children biologically becomes a tragedy to be alleviated by the creation of a blood tie. This blood tie was biologized as biogenetic substance – under race science as much as genetics – but with the flexibility that allows the seeker to 'discover' a solution to their kinship needs. Blood could transmit likeness by flowing through the child *in utero*, or it could transmit substance, depending on whether you were egg donor or recipient, and whether you want there to be a connection. It motivates the proliferation of ARTs, guiding the public imagination to support attempts to alleviate the condition of those unable to have children biologically – even those for whom another option delays the closure of knowing they have tried everything.

It is an ironic narrative. The Eucharist has promoted an ideology that gave birth to the practices of godparenthood and which unites Christians of all ethnicities, genders and households into one body. However, in the development of the concept of the blood tie it would also beget practices that deny the existence of real kinship without the sharing of something associated with the processes of conception, perhaps substance, form or the proximity of pregnancy.

What are the alternatives to this ideology of blood? One might turn, in radical form, to St Basil, who makes it clear that, in the monastery, companions (*familiares*), blood relatives (*consanguinei*), relatives in the flesh (*carnalibus propinquis*) and neighbours (*proximi*) were no longer kin in any special sense.[116] Or one could look at the kinship from the font of spiritual kinship, in which non-kin were selected as baptismal parents, with responsibilities, in the time of Caesarius of Arles, for teaching their charge the Creed and Lord's Prayer,[117] and in the last century, in a Greek Orthodox village, responsibility for naming and anointing of the child at baptism, with the parents themselves being absent, waiting for children to run

---

116. Basil of Caesarea, *The Rule of St. Basil in Latin and English: A Revised Critical Edition*, trans. Anna Silvas (Collegeville: Liturgical Press, 2013), 33.1–2, 136–7.

117. Caesarius of Arles, *Sermons, Volume 1 (1–80)*, trans. Mary Magdeleine Mueller, Fathers of the Church 31 (Washington: Catholic University of America Press, 2010), 13.2, 75.

from the church to tell them the name.[118] Suffice it to say that Christians certainly *should* believe in blood ties, but the blood in question is Christ's blood, and it flows through all members of His body.

Does this rejection of biological blood (or, to use the more biological-sounding metaphor, 'biogenetic substance') 'disparage the truth of our animality, our biological connection and regard for specificity and recognition' as Susannah Cornwall has warned against (while offering wise counsel not to allow it 'to become ultimate').[119] There is no need to dispute the animality of humans. However, a multi-generational project in the anthropology of kinship suggests that human biology is not very restrictive at all of human social relationships, as evidenced by the vast diversity of kinship practices across cultures, recorded by social anthropologists. Does this mean that this book engages in the 'over-relativization of biological relationship' that Cornwall warns against? Quite simply, this is not over-relativization but a measured and appropriate relativization which gladly concedes that human biology may well restrict human kinship practice in some ways. However, the evidence suggests that even if there is such a restriction, it is minimal, because human biology has permitted a vast array of understandings and practices of kinship cross-culturally. Accordingly, Cornwall is also quite correct in her further warning that over-relativization of biology should not be used to portray women 'who strongly desire the experiences of pregnancy and birthing as irrational' or of men who feel the same. Such a portrayal should indeed be rejected: that desire is not irrational, it is *cultural*.[120]

Culture is immensely powerful in shaping human desires. A British person could no more wake up tomorrow and shake off an inculturated desire for the kinship their culture describes as biological than they could wake up tomorrow and think in all the ways that a Trobriand person thinks. The power of the feeling, even when experienced physically, does not prove the biological origins of that drive. Rather, the anthropological evidence suggests that human biology allows a wide diversity of practices, ideas and desires. When Michael Banner, whose seminal theological work on kinship Cornwall is criticizing, interacts with the cultural ideas underpinning ARTs and the cultural ideas underpinning spiritual kinship, he never claims that those using ARTs need to just stop wanting to be pregnant and instead acquire a god-child. He is simply claiming that there is a friction between a Euro-American culture of kinship that generates the need for morally complex and difficult practices, on the one hand, with cultural practices of kinship that are clearly traceable to Christianity, such as godparenthood, on the other.

---

118. Juliet du Boulay, *Cosmos, Life, and Liturgy in a Greek Orthodox Village*, The Romiosyni Series 18 (Limni: Denise Harvey, 2009), 210–11.

119. Susannah Cornwall, *Un/Familiar Theology: Reconceiving Sex, Reproduction and Generativity*, Rethinking Theologies (London: Bloomsbury, 2017), 115.

120. Ibid., 116.

The freedom facing all who want Christian social logic to critique and alter their own outlook on relationships is to allow Christian ideas and practices to have full sway in their own lives and decisions. So, the socially disruptive influence of the Eucharist is captured in William Cavanaugh's description of its celebration in Chile under Pinochet: 'To participate in the eucharist is to live inside God's imagination. It is to be caught up into what is really real, the body of Christ.'[121] The reason the Eucharist is disruptive is because, in sharing in the body of Christ (as opposed to a sociologically described 'body' of persons), the church 'receive[s] itself as a gift of God who is Other in the Eucharist.'[122] If practice is defined by a sense of identity that is bestowed by God in Jesus Christ, then the state is strictly limited in its capacity to define and control with torture.[123]

Similarly, the social imagination provoked by the practice of the Eucharist also disrupts cultural ideas and practices altogether less brutal than those used under Pinochet. When the self-understanding and practice of Christians come to be determined by membership of the body of the living Christ, then this can displace the rationales for those social structures that might compete. In this instance, concepts of descent – whatever form they take – are vulnerable to a competing social logic, in which the obligations and affections of kinship might be organized in a number of ways, but are grounded in membership of Jesus' body. Needless to say, the social implications of participation in the Eucharist are not straightforward, and do not set out a clear alternative mode of kinship practice. Nevertheless, the Eucharist has provoked the development of Christian kinship practices such as monasticism or spiritual kinship.

This chapter has asked a series of questions. First, what does substance mean, and how does it connect with kinship, in the contemporary West? Second, to what extent is this meaning and connection with kinship culturally contingent? Third, how has substance come to connect with kinship in this way? Fourth, has Christianity played a part in this story? Finally, fifth, does this historical role reflect the true social logic of the Christian faith, and if not, how should Christians relate substance with kinship, if at all? Ultimately, these all feed into a straightforward main question: Is the sharing of bodily substance a theologically justifiable basis for determining kinship? It appears that, while concepts of shared substance have been important for Christians over centuries for defining kinship, there is nothing necessary, inevitable or theologically justifiable about it. Conversely, the

---

121. William T. Cavanaugh, *Torture and the Eucharist: Theology, Politics and the Body of Christ*, Challenges in Contemporary Theology (Oxford: Blackwell, 1998), 279.

122. Ibid., 271.

123. Ibid., 279. Rogers, in a short article that anticipates a forthcoming book on blood in Christianity, argues that this is original to the Last Supper, with Jesus 'subverting a structure of violent oppression (crucifixion) to make it a repeated feast (communion)', with blood becoming a symbol of this costly subversion. (Eugene F. Rogers, 'The Genre of this Book', *Syndicate Theology* (blog), available online: https://syndicate.network/symposia/theology/blood/ (accessed 26 July 2019).)

practice of the Eucharist suggests a competing justification for social organization: membership of Christ's body orients participants in love to all – Jew or Gentile – to whom the body is made available.

It has been contended that the idea of substance-relatedness familiar in Euro-American kinship, and visible in the rationale for the use of ARTs, is neither necessary, nor inevitable, nor good. The idea that kinship is determined by shared biogenetic substance is not culturally universal, and in the Euro-American case has been supported by the misapplication of the binding power of the Eucharist. That being said, this argument does not pretend to be sufficient to persuade those seeking to use ARTs not to do so, not least because there are likely to be other factors for the seeking of ARTs than the belief in the kinship-making properties of genes. The place of the *proximity* of pregnancy, for instance, in forming a social tie will be explored later in the chapter on personhood. At this juncture, the aim is simply to bracket out the factor of shared substance in determining kinship as neither necessary nor inevitable nor good.

Should we be related by bodily substance? Yes, but it is by Christ's body, not our own bodies. There are a number of ways in which this relatedness might manifest itself, and many of these may look like familiar Western family forms, under the influence of factors other than conceptualities of shared substance – proximity in pregnancy, duties attached to reproduction, sharing of houses – which are still to be discussed. Nevertheless, the shedding of the blood tie opens a wide margin for other forms of kinship that more directly take their rationale from the social theologies of baptism and the Eucharist. If theological ethicists look beyond the very tightly defined ideas about substance-based kinship used in public discourse today, they might see the emergence of monasticism or of spiritual kinship as examples of how kinship informed by baptism or the Eucharist might provoke new practices. Alternatively, and more recently, one might look to Chilean Christians under Pinochet, as described by William Cavanaugh. The potential for new social forms to arise out of the combination of situational demands and properly free theological imagination is visible in such cases. Conversely, the argument of this chapter might offer a word of freedom to those labouring under the cultural prescription to organize affections and obligations around arbitrary factors such as the sharing of biogenetic substance. Should the Christian theology affirm the existence of the blood tie? Certainly, but it is Christ's blood that binds.

The idea of sharing in the body of the living Christ will be revisited in a later chapter on kinship and personhood. In the next chapter, on kinship and the house, some of the implications of this new social logic of the Eucharist will be explored, showing where an abstract idea that is nevertheless intuitively graspable has shaped thick practices of living together. There, the practical outworking in history of competing visions of social organization in the light of the Christian faith will be described and the theological rationale that has begun to be opened here will be teased out.

Chapter 4

THE CHRISTIAN HOUSEHOLD AND THE REIMAGINING OF KINSHIP

Introduction

This chapter will be chiefly descriptive, serving to highlight within the history of Christian thought and practice the connection between kinship and house. Nevertheless, it will be argued that the same disruptive logic described in the previous chapter is evident in the practice of monasticism as prescribed in St Benedict's *Rule*, with origins traced back to the New Testament. An alternative history will be offered for the vision of the house offered by Richard Baxter – briefly mentioned in the introduction – which taps into a tradition determinative of the house pictured in *American Kinship*. The disciplinary counterpart in this chapter, then, will chiefly be history, rather than social anthropology, both because the analytic concepts are simpler and because the alternative ways of living and thinking are easier to imagine than theologically altered concepts of substance, gender or personhood.

Nevertheless, this chapter will address normative questions as well, chief among them: To what extent should a Christian ordering of the house impact ideas and practices of relatedness? The previous chapter asked how Christians have thought and should think about being related by shared bodily substance, and this chapter will ask how Christians have thought and should think about being related by co-residence.

This chapter will not, in serving its descriptive function, offer a genealogy of the sort offered when investigating the blood tie. Rather two key texts – Benedict's *Rule* and Baxter's *Christian Economics* – will be set in their respective social and intellectual historical contexts and examined. Each text has within it both a prescriptive and descriptive element, taking contemporary practices (for Benedict, the monastery, and for Baxter, a seventeenth-century household), which they modify in the light of theological critique and prescribe to their readers (for Benedict, in the form of a monastic rule, and for Baxter, advice for the faithful).

The life and structure of the household were high on the theological agenda in the early church. As such, it provides a rare insight into a topic – kinship – that is frequently beneath the surface but rarely noticed, not least in the family values rhetoric associated with the Puritans who colonized the New World. How

Benedict reimagined the sixth-century home and Baxter the seventeenth-century home provides an opportunity to uncover two theologies of kinship and two answers to the question, 'Who are my mother and my brothers?'[1]

Benedict in context: The household in Roman late antiquity

St Benedict composed his *Rule* at the monastery in Monte Cassino in the first half of the sixth century.[2] This was an era of transition: Rome had been sacked a century before and things were changing – under a religious revolution instigated by Constantine and under the centralization of power to an imperial bureaucracy extended under Justinian.[3] The household forms of the fourth century were, nevertheless, relatively intact come the sixth century. In addition to this sociopolitical background, behind Benedict stood Basil and Cassian – to whom he refers directly – and the theological giant Augustine.[4]

The traditional Roman family of the later Roman Empire was a vital economic institution, composed of those who owned property (the *paterfamilias*), those who owned *no* property (his wife, children, bonded labourers and boarders) and those who *were* property (his slaves). The household was the organizing unit of society and was itself tightly organized under the *paterfamilias*.[5]

Both Roman law and Cicero's political theory recognized procreative relationships as the foundation on which the state was built: procreation led to children, which led to households, which led to the state.[6] Women could be *manus* wives under the authority of their husband, *sine manu* wives under the authority

---

1. Mk 3.33.

2. Marilyn Dunn, 'Asceticism and Monasticism, II: Western', in *Constantine to c. 600*, ed. Augustine Casiday and Frederick W. Norris, The Cambridge History of Christianity, vol. 2 (Cambridge: Cambridge University Press, 2007), 681.

3. Kate Cooper, *The Fall of the Roman Household* (Cambridge: Cambridge University Press, 2007), 23–4; Geoffrey Nathan, *The Family in Late Antiquity: The Rise of Christianity and the Endurance of Tradition* (London: Routledge, 2000), 5–6.

4. Benedict, *The Rule of St. Benedict*, 73.5, 95.

5. Brent D. Shaw, 'The Family in Late Antiquity: The Experience of Augustine', *Past & Present* 115 (May 1987): 11, 14; Augustine, *Expositions of the Psalms 51–72*, ed. John E. Rotelle, trans. Maria Boulding, The Works of Saint Augustine: A Translation for the 21st Century, III/17 (New York: New City Press, 2001), 60.6, 197.

6. Shaw, 'The Family in Late Antiquity', 11n16; Cicero, *On Obligations* (Oxford: Oxford University Press, 2000), 1.54, 20. Marriage and procreation were also strongly encouraged under marriage laws in place since Augustus Caesar. (Susan Treggiari, 'Marriage and Family in Roman Society', in *Marriage and Family in the Biblical World*, ed. Ken M. Campbell (Downers Grove: InterVarsity Press, 2003), 150.)

of their father, or they could be concubines, slave or free.⁷ Single women could even be the *paterfamilias*, but in a restricted legal sense that meant simply that they owned property that constituted a *domus*, but which did not give them *potestas* over children.⁸ They would be *paterfamilias* in what was clearly seen as a legal fiction, but not *materfamilias*, which denoted an honourable woman who was married to a *paterfamilias*.⁹

The *paterfamilias*, legally, had total control, though whether they *really* could do all that the law allowed them is an important question into which contemporary sermons and letters allow insight. In any case, they owned everything in the house, including their children, whose marriages they could arrange, and their slaves, to whose bodies they had unhindered access.¹⁰ A child could be emancipated or escape by joining the army. Until that point, the *paterfamilias* had full use of corporal punishment and could command loyalty with the promise of inheritance. Inheritance, then, was key to the nexus of power between *paterfamilias* and heir, guaranteeing the outgoing *paterfamilias* care in old age and honour after his death.¹¹ The core of the Roman household, defined by procreation, was small,¹² and the extended family did not have a hugely important role, except when it came to bragging about illustrious ancestors or asking uncles to step in as guardians.¹³

That was the fourth century, but by the time of Benedict, this form of the family would have undergone extensive ecclesial critique, as well as being affected by economic change. Kate Cooper offers a narrative in which there are two formative influences changing the Roman household: first, the 'religious revolution' instigated by Constantine (306–37) and, second, the changes brought about by Diocletian

---

7. Richard P. Saller, *Patriarchy, Property and Death in the Roman Family* (Cambridge: Cambridge University Press, 1997), 76.

8. Richard P. Saller, 'Pater Familias, Mater Familias, and the Gendered Semantics of the Roman Household', *Classical Philology* 94, no. 2 (April 1999): 188.

9. The exception to this is Ulpian who would sometimes use not only this definition but also *materfamilias* to denote a female *paterfamilias* (Saller, 'Pater Familias, Mater Familias, and the Gendered Semantics of the Roman Household', 193–4.) This legal fiction could also apply to prepubescent boys who similarly could not be *pater* and therefore could not hold *potestas*. (Richard P. Saller, 'Symbols of Gender and Status in the Roman Household', in *Women and Slaves in Greco-Roman Culture: Differential Equations*, ed. Sandra R. Joshel and Sheila Murnaghan (New York: Routledge, 2005), 86; Saller, 'Pater Familias, Mater Familias, and the Gendered Semantics of the Roman Household', 184.

10. Shaw, 'The Family in Late Antiquity', 12.

11. Ibid., 23.

12. Richard P. Saller, 'Roman Kinship: Structure and Sentiment', in *The Roman Family in Italy: Status, Sentiment, Space*, ed. Beryl Rawson and Paul Weaver (Oxford: Clarendon, 1997), 31. Its size was partly determined by the fact that most Roman men lost their fathers by the age of twenty-five, and the remainder were mostly emancipated by then. (Cooper, *The Fall of the Roman Household*, 110–11.)

13. Nathan, *The Family in Late Antiquity*, 167–8.

(284–305), who brought in co-emperors leading to greater communication with the provinces and thus the centralization of power in Rome.[14] The collapse of middle classes, decline of imperial power and impoverishment of Rome made the carefully structured Roman household vulnerable, setting the scene for Christian critique.

St Ambrose was a critic of exaggerated kinship loyalty, speaking approvingly to a girl that had gone forward for consecrated virginity against the wishes of her family: 'Conquer family-loyalty first, my girl: if you overcome the household, you overcome the world.'[15] Augustine nuanced the position, endorsing marriage as a good,[16] but still endorsing consecrated virginity as a choice for women – a rare opportunity for a woman to defy her *paterfamilias*, and apparently a popular option among the rich.[17]

Augustine addressed inheritance and property explicitly by castigating those who cited the social requirement to build a large inheritance for the children in order to 'justify their stinginess' to the poor.[18] While very much in favour of the *paterfamilias* disciplining his children, he reframed the relationship of inheritance to discipline, forbidding using it as a tool for control but instead calling it a grave responsibility for which children needed to be prepared.[19] Augustine also addressed the problems of inheritance and property implicitly, through his support for monasticism. The monasteries of Augustine in the West and Basil in the East were not, as might be expected, principally designed for the management

---

14. Cooper, *The Fall of the Roman Household*, 23–4.

15. Ambrose, *De Virginibus*, I.ii.65–6 and I.ii.63. Cited in Peter Brown, *The Body and Society: Men, Women, and Sexual Renunciation in Early Christianity* (Chichester: Columbia University Press, 2008), 344.

16. Augustine, 'Continence', in *Marriage and Virginity*, ed. John E. Rotelle and David G. Hunter, trans. Ray Kearney, The Works of Saint Augustine: A Translation for the 21st Century, I/9 (Brooklyn: New City Press, 1999), 9.3, 207; Augustine, 'The Excellence of Marriage', in *Marriage and Virginity*, ed. John E. Rotelle and David G. Hunter, trans. Ray Kearney, The Works of Saint Augustine: A Translation for the 21st Century, I/9 (Brooklyn: New City Press, 1999), 3.3, 34.

17. Dunn, 'Asceticism and Monasticism, II: Western', 670.

18. Augustine, *Expositions of the Psalms 121–150*, ed. Boniface Ramsey, trans. Maria Boulding, The Works of Saint Augustine: A Translation for the 21st Century, III/20 (New York: New City Press, 2004), 131.19, 168.

19. Augustine, 'Tractates on the First Epistle of John', in *Tractates on the Gospel of John 112–24; Tractates on the First Epistle of John*, trans. J. W. Rettig, Fathers of the Church 92 (Washington: Catholic University of America Press, 1995), 7.8, 223; Shaw, 'The Family in Late Antiquity', 22; Augustine, *Sermons (1–19)*, ed. John E. Rotelle, trans. Edmund Hill, The Works of Saint Augustine: A Translation for the 21st Century, III/1 (Brooklyn: New City Press, 1990), 13.9, 313.

of sex but for the management of property.[20] Augustine's *Praeceptum* – a sort of proto-Rule – opens thus: 'The chief motivation for your sharing life together is to live harmoniously in the house and to have one heart and one soul seeking God.'[21] Inspired by the church in the book of Acts, he prescribed that all be held in common and inheritances be renounced, not just to divide property equitably but because he saw it as the best context for Godly community to flourish.[22] Augustine would still adapt to pastoral need, not only calling back Laetus who had left the monastery after his father's death but also insisting he see his old family provided for.[23]

From the year 434, legislation was enacted to allow monasteries to act as entities in themselves, independent from their members, like little corporations.[24] Monasteries were shocking, reminiscent of 'slave barracks' to Roman eyes, and St Cassian approvingly compared monastic obedience to a slave under a 'harsh and powerful master'.[25] Benedict's *Rule* would temper this, offering a sensitive and highly structured attempt to deal with everyday problems in the monastery. By the sixth century, suspicion of monasticism had waned, and the power of the church

---

20. Brown, *The Body and Society*, 303; Augustine, *Expositions of the Psalms 73–98*, 93.17, 394.) Willemien Otten contrasts Augustine with Cassian, finding Cassian to be focused on personal perfection and Augustine on 'the community's love and concord'. (Willemien Otten, 'Augustine on Marriage, Monasticism, and the Community of the Church', *Theological Studies* 59 (1998): 403.) This is backed up by Marilyn Dunn, who contrasts Augustine's *Rule* with an Origenist theology of self-transformation through renunciation. (Dunn, 'Asceticism and Monasticism, II: Western', 672.)

21. Augustine, 'Praeceptum', in *Augustine of Hippo and His Monastic Rule*, ed. George Lawless (Oxford: Oxford University Press, 1990), 1.2, 81.

22. Augustine, 'The Works of Monks', in *Treatises on Various Subjects*, ed. Roy Joseph Deferrari, The Fathers of the Church 16 (New York: Fathers of the Church, 1952), 1.2. Cited in Bennett, *Water Is Thicker Than Blood*, 110. Cf. also Augustine, 'Praeceptum', 1.3–5, 80.

23. Augustine, *Letters 211–270, 1*–29* (Epistulae)*, The Works of Saint Augustine: A Translation for the 21st Century, II/4 (Hyde Park: New City Press, 2005), 243.6–9, 167–8.

24. Kate Cooper, 'Approaching the Holy Household', *Journal of Early Christian Studies* 15, no. 2 (Summer 2007): 140–1. Indeed, the issue has not been straightforwardly resolved as to whether the monastic property was *owned* by the bishop/abbot. Kate Cooper, 'Poverty, Obligation, and Inheritance: Roman Heiresses and the Varieties of Senatorial Christianity in Fifth-Century Rome', in *Religion, Dynasty, and Patronage in Early Christian Rome, 300–900*, ed. Kate Cooper and Julia Hillner (Cambridge: Cambridge University Press, 2007), 174.

25. John Cassian, *The Institutes*, trans. Boniface Ramsey, Ancient Christian Writers (Mahwah: Newman Press, 1997), 19.1, 87. Cf. Peter Brown, *Through the Eye of the Needle: Wealth, the Fall of Rome, and the Making of Christianity in the West, 250–550 AD* (Princeton: Princeton University Press, 2012), 416.

increased as bishops collected to themselves soft power that counterbalanced the hard power of the *paterfamilias*.[26]

The imperial bureaucracy grew, as taxes on the curial middle classes increased, incentivizing *curia* to seek tax-exempt senatorial status by becoming civil servants. This led to the collapse of the 'honeycomb of carefully graded social statuses'[27] leading to a 'brutal binary model'[28] of rich and poor. It also decreased the power of the *paterfamilias* who stayed back to manage the estates while sending their sons to the major cities.[29] Landowners under financial pressure would sell out to richer neighbours and would avoid slave and tenant labour in favour of wage labour, which incurred no obligations out of season.[30]

Even as poverty increased, the meaning of 'giving to the poor' shifted to upholding justice, as bishops exploited the rhetoric while petitioning rulers on behalf of the clergy.[31] Nevertheless, people remained captivated by the possibility that beggars were the anonymous Christ, and it is *this* that underpins Benedict's call to 'relieve the lot of the poor, clothe the naked, visit the sick . . . and bury the dead'.[32]

The monastic house in The Rule of St Benedict

Around 496, Benedict of Nursia left Rome, where he had been studying, and retreated to a cave in Subiaco.[33] Gregory the Great, basing his account on the testimony of some of Benedict's disciples, recounts Benedict being asked by the monks of the local abbey to be their superior. He reluctantly gives in, but things turn sour. After trouble in Subiaco, he moves to Monte Cassino and founds a monastery there based on his *Rule*.[34] This *Rule*, first, is a theologically informed recommendation for how life might be lived; second, is practically informed, having been drawn from experience in Monte Cassino; third, it provides evidence of early enquiry into the nature of kinship in the light of Christian theology. Indeed, it points back to still older sources.

There are five key features of the organization of the monastery in the *Rule* that establish its significance as a form of counter-kinship: first, the use of kinship

---

26. Brown, *Through the Eye of the Needle*, 505.
27. Ibid., 508.
28. Ibid.
29. Cooper, *The Fall of the Roman Household*, 27.
30. Ibid., 103–5.
31. Brown, *Through the Eye of the Needle*, 509.
32. Benedict, *The Rule of St. Benedict*, 4.14–18, 27. Cf. Mt. 25.36.
33. Jacques Fontaine, 'Education and Learning', in *The New Cambridge Medieval History, Vol. 1, c.500–c.700*, ed. Paul Fouracre (Cambridge: Cambridge University Press, 2005), 743.
34. Gregory the Great, 'Dialogue Two', in *Dialogues*, trans. Odo Zimmerman, Fathers of the Church 39 (Washington: Catholic University of America Press, 1959), 8, 74.

language within the monastery; second, the cutting of prior kinship ties; third, the commitment to a shared social life, instead of separation in an eremitic life; fourth, the careful and thorough attention to the everyday needs of the monks; fifth, children were raised in the monastery.

With respect to the first and second of these features, members of the monastery in Benedict's *Rule* adopted the language of kinship. Monks would submit to the abbot as father, to practice submission to their true Father, God. Using 'brother' for one another was not a fiction, because they were co-adoptees of God,[35] and they cut all prior ties, including inheritance[36] and exclusive loyalties between birth kin in the same monastery.[37] Here, Benedict follows Basil's instructions for monks (collected by Rufinus, hence the Latin): companions (*familiares*), blood relatives (*consanguinei*), relatives in the flesh (*carnalibus propinquis*) and neighbours (*proximi*) were no longer kin in any special sense. Why? Because Jesus's response to the request, 'Master, first let me go and bid farewell to those at home' was 'No one who puts his hand to the plough and looks back is fit for the kingdom of heaven'.[38]

Basil's continued work with his brother, Gregory, who in turn wrote a hagiography of their sister, Macrina, could be read as inconsistent.[39] Rebecca Krawiec has explored the problem, and writes that 'despite the "default" mode of renunciation of biological kinship, we still find "profamilial" calls for family loyalty'.[40] She claims, 'Even in the case of a typical "hate your family" argument like Augustine's to Laetus, the biological family was not wrong but limited.'[41] Basil's suggestion that relatives are to be left behind except in the case of pious upbuilding

---

35. Benedict, *The Rule of St. Benedict*, Prologue.5, 15.

36. Ibid., 33.1-8, 56; 59.1-7, 81. In practice, as early as the 370s and 380s property was managed in such a way as to ensure that it remained in the family and that ascetics took no property with them (to be donated to the monastery) when they left the family (Brown, *Through the Eye of the Needle*, 295.). However, the monastery, with its counter-logic of kinship, was used by others to reinforce prevailing kinship norms, in the form of enforced renunciation for competitors for the family inheritance. Indeed, in 458, Emperor Majorian stepped in to make it illegal to force a young girl to become a nun. (Brown, *Through the Eye of the Needle*, 439.)

37. Benedict, *The Rule of St. Benedict*, 66.6-7, 91; 67.6, 92; 69.1-4, 92-3.

38. Lk. 9.61-2, Basil of Caesarea, *The Rule of St. Basil in Latin and English*, 33.1-3, 138-9. As a telling sign of this new life, seniority was determined not by age but by year of entry (with the exception of the abbot, who was the most senior, and was appointed). (Benedict, *The Rule of St. Benedict*, 63.5-6, 85.)

39. Gregory of Nyssa, 'The Life of Macrina', in *Ascetical Works*, trans. Virginia Woods Callahan, Fathers of the Church, a New Translation 58 (Washington: Catholic University of America Press, 1967), 161-91.

40. Rebecca Krawiec, '"From the Womb of the Church": Monastic Families', *Journal of Early Christian Studies* 11, no. 3 (Fall 2003): 286.

41. Ibid., 305.

(which might happily cover Basil's own relationship with Gregory) leaves open the possibility that relationships are maintained, but with the point being underlined – by his objection to 'human satisfaction' – that there is something problematic about normal kin loyalties.[42]

Third, Benedict was committed to the principle of living together. While he does not criticize hermits directly, nowhere in his *Rule* does he recommend graduation from his 'school for the Lord's service'.[43] He extols the virtues of 'cenobites', in contrast to 'sarabaites' and 'gyrovagues' who did not submit to a rule of household but are accountable to no one, and also the 'anchorites or hermits', who 'have built up their strength and go from the battle line in the ranks of their brothers to the single combat of the desert'.[44] What is striking is the ambiguity with which these two groups – one admirable and the other unacceptable – are distinguished. A plausible interpretation is that Benedict – himself a hermit for a few years between monasteries – quietly opposed monastic life outside of community, but was unwilling to criticize so many heroes of the faith, whether out of intellectual humility or to avoid an unnecessarily controversial position. Regardless, he uses the distinction between the groups as a vehicle to promote the ideal of living out the monastic life in community. This life, for Benedict, was the ideal means by which the service of the Lord can be instilled, and part of this service is hospitality to the stranger, in whom Christ is welcomed.[45]

Fourth, the careful attention to the everyday needs of the monks supports the plausibility of the monastery as an alternative to the household. This can be seen in small remarks from Benedict – to avoid overindulgence not just because of greed but to avoid indigestion, and to sleep clothed and belted, ready for the day, but not with their knives lest they cut themselves in the night.[46] Monks were to sleep in the one place,[47] cook for one another,[48] eat together,[49] share their belongings and own nothing themselves,[50] care for one another when sick,[51] work together,[52] receive

---

42. Basil of Caesarea, *The Rule of St. Basil in Latin and English*, 33.2, 139.
43. Benedict, *The Rule of St. Benedict*, Prologue.45, 18.
44. Ibid., 1.3–5, 20. These distinctions can be traced to Jerome and Cassian. For a historical overview of the likely forms of early monasticism, cf. Samuel Rubenson, 'Asceticism and Monasticism, I: Eastern', in *Constantine to c. 600*, ed. Augustine Casiday and Frederick W. Norris, The Cambridge History of Christianity, vol. 2 (Cambridge: Cambridge University Press, 2007), 644–7.
45. Benedict, *The Rule of St. Benedict*, 53.1–2, 73.
46. Ibid., 39.7–9, 62; 22.5, 49.
47. Ibid., 22.3, 49.
48. Ibid., 35.1, 57.
49. Ibid., 43.15, 66.
50. Ibid., 33.1–7, 56.
51. Ibid., 36.1–10, 59.
52. Ibid., 48.1, 69.

guests together,[53] raise children who had been brought to the monastery and care for the elderly,[54] and of course pray together.[55]

Fifth, the monastic household was not simply a place of adults, that admitted those raised in other households. Celibacy did not prevent monks rearing children, but the children were welcomed as sisters or brothers, rather than daughters or sons. Children were treated more or less the same as adults, though Benedict made allowances for more food to be given to children and at an earlier time, 'Since their lack of strength must always be taken into account'.[56] A ninth-century commentary on the *Rule* also allowed for more sleep, and an hour of play in a meadow either once a week or once a month.[57] Children would be offered at a young age by their parents, and this would entail the cutting of inheritance ties (and, indeed, limiting the number of heirs was often the motive for this practice of 'oblation').[58] In time it would only be oblates (children committed to the monastery as members) who would be cared for in the monasteries. Two centuries after the composition of the *Rule*, Charlemagne decreed that the only children who could reside in monasteries were oblates, in order to prevent them being used as nurseries.[59]

Oblation was permanent. There was some opposition at the highest level to the forcible oblation of children, with Pope Nicholas I arguing that monastic life must be voluntary. He requested that oblates be given the opportunity of leaving the monastery at a certain age, should they wish. However, the Council of Worms rejected this in 868, the year after his death, reaffirming the fourth council of Toledo, and allowing for the use of force in retaining oblates or any who had made monastic vows, should it be deemed necessary.[60]

Boswell compares the life of an oblate to that of a student at a strict religious boarding school of the time, but with the addition of extensive liturgical duties.[61] It was a childhood of hard work, but there would at least be guaranteed food. However, the guarantee of food and the protection of the patrimony were certainly not the only motives for oblation.[62] The religious life was considered to be a

---

53. Ibid., 53.1–3, 73.

54. Ibid., 37.2–3, 60.

55. Ibid., 43.1–3, 65. Common prayer is mentioned throughout the *Rule*.

56. Ibid., 37.2, 60.

57. Colin Heywood, *A History of Childhood: Children and Childhood in the West from Medieval to Modern Times* (Cambridge: Polity, 2001), 14.

58. John Boswell, *The Kindness of Strangers: The Abandonment of Children in Western Europe from Late Antiquity to the Renaissance* (Chicago: University of Chicago Press, 1988), 240.

59. Ibid., 243–4.

60. Mayke De Jong, *In Samuel's Image: Child Oblation in the Early Medieval West* (Leiden: Brill, 1996), 96–7.

61. Boswell, *The Kindness of Strangers*, 249.

62. Ibid., 239. Cf. Benedict, *The Rule of St. Benedict*, 59.3–8, 81.

good life for a child.[63] Oblation was, Boswell argues, 'the most humane form of abandonment', not just replacing exposure but also arising, at least in part, from the belief that the monastic life was a *good* life:

> Both the ideal of nonbiological, fostering love and the possibility of success despite humble beginnings were built into oblation and virtually never left to chance, as they were in the case of other forms of abandonment. The very idea of monasticism entailed the creation of a voluntary family, the application of familial affections and relationships by and to persons whose responsibility for each other was voluntarily assumed rather than inherited. . . . Oblates were *alumni* in a family in which *all* the children were adopted: ecclesiastical legislation even referred to them as the church's *alumni*.[64]

Though harsh, even the oblation of children displays the logic of Christian kinship at work: first, real kinship could be had in the monastery; second, the monastery represented a viable and honourable alternative to the ordinary household; third, human persons were not disposable but were created for a purpose – to be children of God and to worship Him – and the exposure of children represented a problem for which oblation represented an answer.

Benedict confronts the Fall with a theologically conceived life lived in the light of Christ: 'In his goodness, he has already counted us as his sons, and therefore we should never grieve him by our evil actions.'[65] Framed in this way, monks were now in a household dedicated to a heavenly *paterfamilias*, underpinned by a rejection of contemporary presumptions about who was and was not kin.

Richard Baxter in context: The household in seventeenth-century England

Richard Baxter's *Christian Economics*, written in 1664–5[66] as part of Baxter's grand *Christian Directory*, is a different take on a similar project: ordering the household in the light of Christian belief. It stands as one of the most important and detailed works in the Puritan theology of the family, which informed Puritanism in the Old and New Worlds, which in turn shaped modern American kinship.

It may seem strange, though, to skip over a millennium of cultural change when switching from Benedict to Baxter. However, both presented particularly relevant work, and both mark moments of intellectual confluence fed by more original thinkers whose ideas they brought together and distributed widely. Benedict was fed by Cassian, Augustine, Basil and others, and shaped profoundly the monasticism that followed. Baxter was part of an English Puritan tradition fed

---

63. Boswell, *The Kindness of Strangers*, 266.
64. Ibid., 239.
65. Benedict, *The Rule of St. Benedict*, Prologue.5, 15.
66. Published in 1672–3.

by both Reformed and humanist ideas, which reshaped their own country, helping to form the culture of the New World – particularly that of its political elite. Baxter distinguished himself within this tradition partly because he paid such detailed attention to questions of domestic life, and partly because he stood in an awkward position between conformity and non-conformity, bringing a critical voice to public discourse while being, at various times, sufficiently acceptable to command wide readership with less trouble than his more radical counterparts.

Baxter was a complex figure, fighting for Parliament in the Civil War and seeing Cromwell as his ticket to a Holy Commonwealth, but opposing the execution of the king and refusing to swear an oath to Cromwell.[67] His definition of kinship would remain the same, though, whether it be in the *Holy Commonwealth* that would be burned after the Interregnum, or *Christian Economics* written later. In the *Holy Commonwealth*, Baxter describes the natural emergence of kinship from procreation: 'Nature immediately makes an inequality in our procreation and birth, and subjecteth children to their Parents as their undoubtedly rightful Governours.' When it came to the obedience of wives and servants he cites both 'Law of Nature and Scripture', displaying his belief that what he is saying is so obviously natural that it required little scriptural basis, though he still wished to affirm that what he was saying was consistent with scripture.[68] This was one half of what Lamont calls the 'schizophrenic Baxter' that followed 1660. There was the private Baxter who urged the use of *Holy Commonwealth* and that, in letters, suggested Grotius, Bilson and Barclay be read as a counter to the *overreliance* on scripture of his interlocutors. Then there was the public figure of the *Christian Directory* who is politically more cautious, making sure his advice to families was on a defensibly scriptural footing (which will be explored later), while discouraging 'clergymen from meddling in things they don't understand'.[69]

Baxter saw the family as the key to the proper ordering of society, writing in *The Reformed Pastor*, 'The life of religion, and the welfare and glory of Church and State, dependeth much on family Government: and duty.'[70] He was writing after the 1640s and 1650s when it was popular to critique the contemporary family. There was Milton favouring freer divorce;[71] antinomian Ranters arguing

---

67. William Lamont, 'Introduction', in *A Holy Commonwealth*, ed. Richard Baxter, Cambridge Texts in the History of Political Thought (Cambridge: Cambridge University Press, 1994), x–xi.

68. Richard Baxter, *A Holy Commonwealth*, ed. William Lamont, Cambridge Texts in the History of Political Thought (Cambridge: Cambridge University Press, 1994), 64–6.

69. Lamont, 'Introduction', xix–xx.

70. Richard Baxter, *Gildas Salvianus; The First Part: I.e. The Reformed Pastor. Shewing the Nature of the Pastoral Work; Especially in Private Instruction and Catechizing)* (London: Printed by Robert White, for Nevil Simmons, 1656), 83. Cf. Christopher Durston, *The Family in the English Revolution* (Oxford: Basil Blackwell, 1989), 166–7.

71. Durston, *The Family in the English Revolution*, 10.

against family duty;[72] Quaker endorsement of women's equality; and proponents of polygamy, incest and casual sex.[73] In response to these, Jeremy Taylor, also writing in the 1640s and 1650s, offered arguments similar to Baxter in defence of marriage.[74] He claimed, for instance, that 'Marriage is a school and exercise of virtue; and though marriage hath cares, yet the single life hath desires, which are more troublesome and more dangerous, and often end in sin . . . if single life hath more privacy of devotion, yet marriage hath more necessities and more variety of it, and is an exercise of more graces'.[75] Meanwhile, radical, but ultimately failed, experiments were going on among Puritans on the famous Plymouth plantation in the American colonies, in which property was shared and ranks removed. Clearly, however, patriarchal attitudes remained: 'And for mens wives to be commanded to doe servise for other men, as dressing their meate, washing their cloaths, etc., they deemd it a kind of slaverie.'[76]

Ideological ferment aside, the form of the family remained stable, and legal reforms in the 1650s sought to strengthen and protect the family.[77] Brought about by Puritans, these reforms were intended to protect the family against various kinds of disorder, from conduct in alehouses, through sexual immorality, to blasphemy, with each being described as in some way an assault not just on God but on the *family* – in the case of blasphemy it was the example that the parents set for children, endangering their salvation, that made this an urgent legal matter.[78] It reached its pinnacle in the Act of 1650, imposing the death penalty for female adulterers and their male lovers, and prison for premarital sex, though this rarely enforced.[79]

What norm did the law seek to promote? In upper-class families, it referred to a group of parents, children, servants and, ideally, three generations of the extended family. Families were self-sufficient, except in education. Rank within the family was determined on the basis of sex, age and birth order, with the father and master

---

72. Ibid., 10–13.
73. Ibid., 14–20.
74. Ibid., 24.
75. Jeremy Taylor, 'The Marriage Ring; or the Mysteriousness and Duties of Marriage', in *Sermons*, ed. Charles Page Eden, The Whole Works of the Right Rev. Jeremy Taylor, D.D., vol. 4 (London: Longman, Brown, Green, and Longmans, 1861), 211.
76. This is shortly followed by a claim of total defeat: 'Let none objecte this is men's corruption, and nothing to the course it selfe. I answer, seemingly all men have this corruption in them, God in his wisdome saw another course fiter for them.' (William Bradford, *Bradford's History of the Plymouth Plantation 1606-1646*, ed. W. T. Davis, Original Narratives of Early American History (New York: Scribner, 1908), 146-7.)
77. Bernard Capp, 'Republican Reformation: Family, Community and the State in Interregnum Middlesex, 1649–60', in *The Family in Early Modern England*, ed. Helen Berry and Elizabeth Foyster (Cambridge: Cambridge University Press, 2007), 41.
78. Ibid.
79. Ibid., 49, 55.

at the core.[80] Wet-nurses and nannies were common,[81] as was sending children to other houses to be raised.[82]

Baxter would alienate these upper classes by criticizing their wealth.[83] However, Alexandra Walsham has argued, compellingly, that unpopularity was key to the Puritan identity, and indeed a sign that one was doing things right, so if not a victory in itself it may not have been such a loss to be mocked.[84] Nevertheless, Baxter would enjoy support for two of his works – *Catechizing of Families* and *Poor Man's Family Book* – and thus he bridged the gap to mainline Anglicans, and could appeal to wide audiences.[85]

The family in Richard Baxter's Christian Economics

Baxter never had children, but still spoke from experience as the head of a household with a wife and servants,[86] supplementing his experience in parish ministry in Kidderminster.[87] Much like Benedict, he pays close attention to the

---

80. Patricia Crawford, *Blood, Bodies and Families in Early Modern England* (Harlow: Pearson, 2004), 217.

81. Miriam Slater, *Family Life in the Seventeenth Century: The Verneys of Claydon House* (London: Routledge & Kegan Paul, 1984), 29. Lancy affirms this shift, though he focuses more on lower classes and child labour than the control of children in the upper classes. He also records the tipping of this scale from 'gerontocracy' to 'neontocracy', with the child becoming both a more burdensome and a 'must-have' item. (David F. Lancy, *The Anthropology of Childhood: Cherubs, Chattel, Changelings*, 2nd edn. (Cambridge: Cambridge University Press, 2015), 26–74.)

82. Slater, *Family Life*, 108–9.

83. J. T. Cliffe, *The Puritan Gentry: The Great Puritan Families of Early Stuart England* (London: Routledge & Kegan Paul, 1984), 9.

84. Alexandra Walsham, 'The Godly and Popular Culture', in *The Cambridge Companion to Puritanism*, ed. John Coffey and Paul C. H. Lim (Cambridge: Cambridge University Press, 2008), 290.

85. Alexandra Walsham, 'Holy Families: The Spiritualization of the Early Modern Household Revisited', in *Religion and the Household: Papers Read at the 2012 Summer Meeting and the 2013 Winter Meeting of the Ecclesiastical History Society*, ed. John Doran, Charlotte Methuen, and Alexandra Walsham (Suffolk: Boydell, 2014), 143.

86. Baxter was married in 1662 at the age of forty-seven to the twenty-seven-year-old Margaret Charlton. They had no children and so in that sense, in Baxter's own estimation, were not a complete household, but *A Christian Directory*, which was written mostly in 1664–5 (but published in 1672–73), could still have been informed by his relationship with his wife and servants. (J. M. Lloyd Thomas, *The Autobiography of Richard Baxter, Abridged by J.M. Lloyd Thomas*, ed. N. H. Keeble (London: Dent, 1974), 173–4, 262–77.)

87. John Spurr, 'Richard Baxter', in *Puritans and Puritanism in Europe and America: A Comprehensive Encyclopedia*, ed. Francis J. Bremer and Tom Webster, vol. 1 (Santa Barbara: ABC-CLIO, 2006), 19–20.

daily rhythm of life, defining the right amount of sleep,[88] limiting dressing time[89] and suggesting a servant or child read scripture to the master when eating or dressing, all with the aim of maximizing time for prayer and for work. Work was to be done conscientiously with breaks being devoted to conversations on spiritual matters with colleagues.[90] Sin was to be confessed immediately,[91] and temptation could be avoided with a variety of (not quite serious) Godly 'life-hacks' such as writing on the walls of the dining room:

> BEHOLD THIS WAS THE INIQUITY OF SODOM; PRIDE, FULNESS OF BREAD, AND ABUNDANCE OF IDLENESS WAS IN HER, neither did she strengthen the hand of the poor and needy.[92]

Daily rest was limited to necessity, and included the task of 'look[ing] to the special duties of your several relations'.[93] While work may have been dedicated to the poor, it was duties within the household that were enshrined in the daily pattern of life of the household. When addressing the rich, he offers ten directions on the avoidance of the temptations of wealth, followed by a single direction on its distribution, in the form of employing more servants to allow them more time for prayer.[94] While he offers a slightly nebulous instruction to serve one's neighbours, he is quick to clarify: 'your care must be in a special manner for your children and families'.[95] In another work, *Christian Politics*, he forbids readers from 'maintain[ing] and provid[ing] for others as your own'. Why? Because 'the common good' and 'God's command' required that 'the expressive part' be ordered thus.[96]

Underlying this is an important *truth* – affections need to be divided, being held especially for kin, and this is no different from the affections Benedict expects within the monastery. But how does one determine who one's kin are?

Baxter's short answer is that the Christian knows from *Scripture* to provide for their families, and from nature who counts as family.[97] For Baxter, a family was a household composed of governor and governed, and, when complete, 'A

---

88. Six hours if healthy, seven if not and eight for the elderly and infirm. (Baxter, *Christian Economics*, 230.)
89. Baxter, *Christian Economics*, 230–1, 238.
90. Ibid., 235.
91. Ibid., 237.
92. Ezek. 16.49. Baxter, *Christian Economics*, 236–7.
93. Baxter, *Christian Economics*, 237.
94. Ibid., 394.
95. Ibid., 395.
96. Richard Baxter, *A Christian Directory: Or, a Sum of Practical Theology, and Cases of Conscience, Part 4. Christian Politics, (or Duties to Our Rulers and Neighbours*, The Works of the Rev. Richard Baxter 4 (London: James Duncan, 1830), 430.
97. Baxter, *Christian Economics*, 69.

father, mother, son, and servant'.⁹⁸ This was self-evident to Baxter: 'That families are societies of God's institution, needeth no proof.'⁹⁹

His mode of operation is reminiscent of his earlier avowed dependence on the political philosophy of Grotius, Bilson and Barclay. Baxter offers a clear definition of the term 'family' with which he will operate: 'not a tribe or stock of kindred, dwelling in many houses as the word is taken oft in scripture, but I mean a household'.¹⁰⁰ Working systematically, the starting point he takes in offering his definition is the identification of the two necessary conditions: a head of the family (male or female) and one governed (servant or child). A complete family, though, he would expect to include at least is 'A father, mother, son, and servant'.¹⁰¹ There is, to put it simply, a secular logic here, in which he works with a variety of concentric sociopolitical circles – tribe, stock, household – followed by a careful analysis of this smallest circle to identify its necessary parts. He does all this with the assumption that the family he was looking at *was* Christian and that the households he knew were divine institutions for which no greater proof was needed. Baxter would defend this definition with scripture, but before turning to that it is worth pausing to ask why Baxter went to so much trouble, and what it was about his context that stimulated so great an interest in the household.

Baxter was partly interested in societies on the basis of a Reformation argument that God's covenant was with a group – the church – of which a household was a small but complete part.¹⁰² This did not just entail family worship but the formation

---

98. Ibid., 50.
99. Ibid., 52.
100. Ibid., 50.
101. Ibid.
102. The theological background can be found in Calvin for Baxter's attempt to prove 'That Christian families are sanctified to God', by writing, 'We find in Scripture not only single persons, but the societies of such sanctified to God'. (Baxter, *Christian Economics*, 58.) In an essay on Calvin and the church, Walker writes: 'Calvin asserts that God deals, not so much with isolated individuals, as with people in community. Natural groupings, by families and nations, are embraced in His design.' (G. S. M. Walker, 'Calvin and the Church', in *Readings in Calvin's Theology*, ed. Donald K. McKim (Eugene: Wipf and Stock, 1998), 220.) This is based on Calvin's comment on Paul's greeting of Aquila and Prisca 'with the church that is in their household' (1 Cor.16.19): 'What a wonderful thing to be put on record! – that the name "*Church*" is applied to a single family; and yet it is fitting that all the families of believers should be organized in such a way as to be so many little churches.' Calvin proposed, against Erasmus, that this meant *Church* and not *congregation*, so that a Christian household bears the hallmarks of the body of Christ. (John Calvin, *The First Epistle of Paul the Apostle to the Corinthians*, ed. David W. Torrance and Thomas F. Torrance, trans. John W. Fraser, Calvin's Commentaries (Grand Rapids: Eerdmans, 1996), 356.) This connects with Calvin's famous 'third use of the law' for Christians, in a connection that J. T. Johnson has argued was especially important for Puritan ethics. (James Turner Johnson, 'Marriage As Covenant in Early Protestant Thought', in *Covenant Marriage in Comparative*

of all through catechesis and discipline.¹⁰³ Alongside the Reformation, Christian humanism sits in the background, as Baxter contributed to a tradition of 'domestic advice' books revived by Richard Whitford's in 1530, continued with Perkins's *Christian oeconomie* in 1609, Gouge's *Of domesticall duties* in 1622 and Griffith's *Bethel* in 1633, from origins with Aristotle and Xenophon.¹⁰⁴ Baxter joined with humanist Catholics in their emphasis on the importance of the household as church, as part of a simultaneously Calvinist Reformed but also Erasmian Catholic humanist critique of church institutions.¹⁰⁵ Graeco-Roman ideas, of the family as the building block of society, were Christianized with the family becoming the 'seminary of the church and commonwealth'.¹⁰⁶

The placement of husband and wife at the centre, defining the household, was standard fare, though the Puritans would arguably elevate the role of the woman by placing responsibility for their holiness with them rather than with their husbands.¹⁰⁷ However, even in this they were part of a tradition shared among contemporary Catholics and drawn not from the Reformation but from Christian humanists.¹⁰⁸ Baxter, for his part, would defend his wife's more public work, pointing out that it was for church and charity, and indeed would later lightly criticize his wife for not talking about religion enough around others.¹⁰⁹ This is set

---

Perspective, ed. John Witte Jr. and Eliza Ellison (Grand Rapids: Eerdmans, 2005), 131.) The third use of the law reveals what it means to stand in covenant relationship with God, and what is expected as the recipient of this grace. Whereas the first use of the law condemns the Christian, acting 'like a mirror', and the second use, as civil law, restrains those who will not restrain themselves, the third use offers knowledge of the divine will for humanity. Here Calvin is speaking of the law as given to Israel through Moses. (John Calvin, *Institutes of the Christian Religion*, ed. John T. McNeill, trans. Ford Lewis Battles (Louisville: Westminster John Knox Press, 1960), I.ii.7.6–13, 354–61.) Returning to Baxter's reception of Calvin, he, too, turns to the covenant community of Israel (quoting Deut. 7.6): 'Thou are an holy people unto the Lord thy God, he hath chosen thee to be a special people to himself above all people that are upon the face of the earth'. Israel 'did all jointly enter into covenant with God, and God to them'. The point here is that Calvin's third use of the law, which describes the appropriate response to membership of the new covenant, is interpreted in the light of the old covenant, where God takes all of Israel collectively as His covenant partner, issuing the law to all collectively.

103. Baxter, *Christian Economics*, 105.
104. Walsham, 'Holy Families', 128–9.
105. Margo Todd, *Christian Humanism and the Puritan Social Order* (Cambridge: Cambridge University Press, 1987), 115–17.
106. Ibid., 101–2.
107. Ibid., 113.
108. Ibid., 116.
109. Ann Hughes, 'Puritanism and Gender', in *The Cambridge Companion to Puritanism*, ed. John Coffey and Paul C. H. Lim (Cambridge: Cambridge University Press, 2008), 298. Cites Richard Baxter, *A Breviate of the Life of Margaret, the Daughter of Francis Charlton*

against the background of women being generally confined to the house as their realm, but at the time that was not a closed-off realm, particularly if one were wealthy, in which case one's house would be an important institution locally as a site of influence and economic power, as well as providing a place of work. Puritan women specifically were likely to have within their sphere of influence their own children, household servants and neighbours while being encouraged to honour the duty they had to their own sanctification in penitential prayer and the reading of scripture.[110]

In defining the family, Baxter cites not only nature but also scripture's commentary on family relationships in the household codes, focussing particularly on Eph. 5.21–6.9.[111] However, the Ephesians code only acted as supporting evidence, helping him clarify what these relationships should look like. While Baxter is happy to reform the practices within the household, the basic organization of contemporary households is reflected in his reading of scripture. Having a clear idea of what a family was, he did not bring other relevant parts of scripture to bear upon the issue.[112] By pre-judging what a family must be, based

---

of Apply in Shropshire, Esq. and Wife of Richard Baxter (London: Printed for B. Simmons, 1681), 20, 64, 66, 79, 85.

110. Hughes, 'Puritanism and Gender', 299.

111. Baxter, *Christian Economics*, 61.

112. This relates to the selection of the Ephesians household code, rather than its content, but the latter demands some attention, even with limited space. Eph. 5.23 reads: 'For the husband is the head of the wife just as Christ is the head of the church, the body of which he is the Saviour.' What does this parallel between husband and wife on the one hand, and Christ and the church on the other, imply? While vv. 22 to 24 address wives, the passage seems to say as much to husbands. The wife is not pointed to the church as though its stellar obedience is a fitting example, but rather is pointed to Christ, who exercises his headship of the church by dying for it. The implication for the wife is that they ought to be as the church is – the recipient of sacrifice. This implies the response of v. 24: 'Just as the church is subject to Christ, so also wives ought to be, in everything, to their husbands.' This verse is sandwiched between two reminders of what Christ has done – 'the body of which is the Saviour' in v. 23, and 'Husbands, love your wives, just as Christ loved the church and gave himself up to her' in v. 25. Husbands are taught to love their wives (as sharing their flesh) with this entailing that they give themselves for their wives, while wives are told to be subject to and to respect their husbands. These are the ways in which Paul applies his opening statement in v. 21: 'Be subject to one another out of reverence for Christ'. Mutual submission reveres Christ, because it reflects Christ's self-emptying, as described richly in Philippians 2. Ephesians 5 permits the husband to live out their culturally expected headship *only insofar as* it reflects Christ's headship, in a similar way when Paul instructs slaves to obey earthly masters 'as you obey Christ' (Eph. 6.5). This same logic can be applied to very different social structures, as indeed it is applied within the school of the Lord's service that is the Benedictine monastery. Nevertheless, Paul's advocacy of submission relates here only to the normal Christian household in first-century Ephesus or Colossae.

on nature, he unintentionally cherry-picks scripture for support of this definition, ignoring the passages that *Benedict* considered critical. This results in a surface-level critique that, by piling on duties within the household, massively strengthens the household whose foundations Benedict, inspired by scripture, digs up and redesigns.

Baxter affirms, 'your own house is your castle; your family is your charge.'[113] Why not instead challenge this, saying, with Jesus, 'Here are my mother and my brothers. For whoever does the will of my Father in heaven is my brother and sister and mother' (Mt. 12.49-50)? Might not the words, 'Whoever comes to me and does not hate father and mother, wife and children, brothers and sisters, yes, and even life itself, cannot be my disciple' (Lk. 14.26), inspire a vision in which traditional family obligations are challenged and re-described? It is especially surprising because Baxter was so keen to affirm that a person's children were primarily 'children of God',[114] which seems much more consistent with Benedict's approach to household social structures.

A tale of two households

For both Benedict and Baxter, their vision of the household determines the practice of kinship they prescribe. On the one hand, Baxter conforms the shape of the household to a certain political ordering, though he clearly also takes the nature of the family to be both self-evident and theologically justifiable.[115] It is, at bare minimum, composed of the governor and the governed, and, when complete, 'A father, mother, son, and servant'.[116] Baxter retains a view of kinship beyond the household (and so distinguishes a family from 'a tribe or stock of kindred'[117]) but offers a vision of the household in which servants join the special affections, obligations and structures of accountability within a 'family'. The household is certainly not the only kinship-forging force in Baxter's vision of the family, with reproduction clearly being assumed to play a determinative role. However, Baxter's

---

Instead of being read as endorsing similar household structures (contemporary to Paul, Baxter or the present day), it should be read as critiquing what could make these structures oppressive, while at the same time not casting aside the entire structure, to be replaced, among his readers, with something as vulnerable to the sort of oppression he tackles. For a discussion of household codes in 1 Timothy and Titus, focused less on gender and more on the relationship between trends of social critique and social entrenchment in the early Church, and its ambiguous legacy in relation to these trends, see Barclay, 'The Family as the Bearer of Religion in Judaism and Early Christianity', 77–8.

113. Baxter, *Christian Economics*, 103.
114. Ibid., 112.
115. Cf. Ibid., 52.
116. Ibid., 50.
117. Ibid.

desire for clear political ordering solidifies the place of shared living as kinship-making.

On the other hand, Benedict conforms kinship within the monastery to the social logic described in the previous chapter, reorganizing kinship in the light of membership of the body of Christ. While Benedict was contributing to an established monastic tradition, he is nevertheless clearly purposeful and self-conscious in offering an alternative way of life to that practised by his wider social context.

Nevertheless, he still – like Baxter – thinks the house bestows special affections, obligations and structures of accountability. This is because the properly ordered Christian life must, for Benedict, involve submission to a rule and to those in authority, as evident in his denunciation of the sarabaites and gyrovagues. The abbot is to 'hold the place of Christ in the monastery',[118] so that monks might practice obedience 'as promptly as if the command came from God himself'.[119] Accordingly, he cites, for his theological justification of social organization under an abbot, both Rom. 8.15, in which the adoption of Christians as children of God is described, and Luke 10, in which Christ sends out the apostles to declare the kingdom, with the words – as quoted by Benedict – 'Whoever listens to you, listens to me' (Lk. 10.16).[120] Benedict sees organization within a smaller community as necessary if Christians are to submit to Christ and enjoy kinship in Christ, as they should. Benedict takes the absorption of the logic of adoption in Christ to require not just a relativization or even renunciation of existing ties, but also the establishment of new ties, organized on a different basis, but nevertheless limited in their scope, according to the requirements of submission to authority and the enjoyment of social life.

For both Baxter and Benedict, relatedness is – as it were – bestowed by the house. Baxter implicitly upholds reproduction as limiting relatedness, and Benedict explicitly upholds kinship in Christ as expanding relatedness, but, in both cases, they prescribe a form of relatedness determined by the requirements of shared living and submission to authority within a house. However, Benedict's justification is explicitly theological, citing the universalization of siblinghood in Christ and the need to obey Christ now in obeying fellow Christians, and in this way tapping into a rich vein of social critique in the theology of late antiquity, with origins in the New Testament. Baxter's justification for the organization of the household reveals the hallmarks of a humanist political philosophy which looked for its terms of reference to pre-Christian political philosophy.

This is not to criticize such political philosophy. Clearly, Baxter was operating at a different scale than Benedict, with an eye to the ordering of wider society. Augustine himself, the theological giant behind Benedict, would be inspired by

---

118. Benedict, *The Rule of St. Benedict*, 2.2, 21.
119. Ibid., 5.4, 29.
120. Ibid., 2.3, 21; 5.6, 29.

Cicero's political philosophy to describe marriage as the 'seedbed . . . of a city'.[121] However, at this point, and with Baxter, what is doing the formative work in shaping the character of the house is not a distinctively Christian account of kinship, but rather a political philosophical commitment with pre-Christian origins. In Augustine's *Praeceptum*, in Basil's instructions to monks, and in Benedict's *Rule*, there is disclosed a distinctively Christian account of kinship at the heart of the house. In Baxter's work, membership of the house is determined by other factors without Christian origins. Nevertheless, Baxter's vision would profoundly shape contemporary visions of what constitutes a Christian household.

Richard Baxter has been taken as indicative of a particular Puritan tradition of the ethics of family (no such claim could be made that Baxter is representative of other Puritans on doctrinal issues such as justification). His work has been explored both for the internal consistency of what *he* says (for instance, noting his avowed dependence on certain theorists, even to the point of advising their use instead of biblical sources) and as a useful representative of English Puritanism more widely – particularly, as a representative of the tradition that crossed the Atlantic to become New England Puritanism.

As such, if one wished to chart the journey of English Puritanism to the New World, then Baxter's particular idiosyncrasies would not be relevant, but only those indicative of a wider movement of which he is taken as a representative. Max Weber considered Baxter to be *personally* significant in shaping the ordering of life in the New World. For Weber, Baxter stood out not just because of a 'practical and realistic attitude' but also because of the 'universal recognition accorded to his works'.[122]

As has been mentioned earlier, Baxter was eager to fill the life of the household with continuous work and worship, with rest being allowed for the purpose of enhancing these – the previous argument looked at his focus on duties *within the household* and the concentration of energies there. Weber takes a slightly different turn, looking at Baxter's development of labour as 'an approved ascetic technique',[123] that liberates the Christian from the temptations of leisure (with the creation of leisure being the chief temptation of wealth).[124] For Weber, the ascetic discipline of work and concern about idleness that was present in Baxter and other Puritans crossed the Atlantic to colonies in the North East of what is now the United States. Weber distinguishes this carefully from the Southern States, to which a different kind of migrant than the Puritans with their 'middle-class outlook' gravitated.[125] Indeed, he notes the irony of the outworking of his argument – that the 'large

---

121. Augustine, *City of God*, 15.16, 625. Cf. also Augustine, 'The Excellence of Marriage', 1.1, 33; Shaw, 'The Family in Late Antiquity', 11.

122. Max Weber, *The Protestant Ethic and the Spirit of Capitalism*, trans. Talcott Parsons, 2nd edn. (London: George Allen and Unwin, 1978), 155.

123. Ibid., 158.

124. Ibid., 156–8.

125. Ibid., 173–4.

capitalists' in the South created what would become a less capitalist social order than the 'preachers and seminary graduates' of the North East.[126]

Weber's argument is not that Baxter himself was the key architect of this capitalist social order in the north-eastern colonies, but rather that he stands out as a particularly practically minded intellectual and also an influential writer (and one with a reach well beyond English Puritanism) to select to epitomize the social ethics of Puritanism more generally, which influenced the shape of that social order.

Allegiance to Weber's grand argument about the development of capitalism is not necessary for present purposes. It is a humbler claim that is pertinent: the form of the household that Baxter encouraged was exported to the New World. Baxter then becomes a representative Puritan on the matter of the ordering of the household and the particular emphasis on the extended duties of family worship.[127] Even still, this suggestion serves mainly to raise a flag rather than support a grand narrative: the expectations of American kinship, as outlined, say, by David Schneider, with his account of strict roles in the household and the clear division of the domains of house and work,[128] conforms much more closely with Baxter than with Benedict. The historical narrative that is more important theologically is the one that traces Benedict to a radical reading of scripture, and Baxter to a particular trend in contemporary political philosophy that is subsequently read into scripture in the transition from *Holy Commonwealth* to *A Christian Directory*.

Neither the transatlantic journey of Baxter's thought nor, indeed, the representative character of Baxter's theory of the family has been demonstrated. Rather, a narrative has been mooted that demands pause for thought: that a particular political philosophy of the household as the building block of society is revived in the context of the Renaissance, and subsequently exerts an influence over the Puritan intellectuals that would populate the New World, with its enormous growth of power and influence. An attempt has been made

---

126. Ibid., 55–6.

127. For an old but influential and detailed study of the Puritan family in seventeenth-century New England, see Edmund S. Morgan, *The Puritan Family: Religion and Domestic Relations in Seventeenth-Century New England*, rev. edn. (New York: Harper and Row, 1966). Compare, for instance, Baxter on family worship, and the New England Puritan Cotton Mather: 'does not every Society owe Religious Acknowledgements unto GOD? . . . Is not a FAMILY the very First Society, that by the Direction and Providence of GOD is produced among the Children of Men. . . Does not the very Light of Nature teach us, That Families should Glorify God with some Family Worship?' (Cotton Mather, 'Family Religion Urged', in *Dr. Mather's Reasonable Religion*, ed. Daniel Williams (London: Printed for N. Cliff and D. Jackson, 1713), 109–10.)

128. Schneider, *American Kinship*, 46. For an account of the development of the role of Puritanism in separating work from the Victorian home on both sides of the Atlantic, see Rosemary Radford Ruether, *Christianity and the Making of the Modern Family* (London: SCM, 2001), 83–106.

to show that this is plausible, but its main value stands in pushing the Christian thinker – especially those in a Western world heavily influenced by Puritan thought – back onto themselves, to reconsider whether the structures they have always known really do appear consistent with the Christian gospel, or whether it has simply been assumed that such structures are natural, necessary and Christian. At minimum, the sheer difference of Baxter's vision of the household from that of Benedict demands careful reflection on Christian understandings of who one lives with and what that means for relationships beyond the household.

This sort of attention to the ethics of household organization, in the light of a pared-down genealogy of the family, is of course not new. Weber's genealogical approach was motivated by an interest in the origins of capitalism, itself reminiscent of the attention paid to the subject in Engels's *The Origin of the Family, Private Property and the State*, which used Lewis Henry Morgan extensively in exploring the history of the family.[129] Engels was motivated by a particular problem – the unfair distribution of private property, particularly as it related to the structure of families – and he sought to discover its origins. Engel's main thesis concerns the supposed ancient shift (for women only) from promiscuity to monogamy, and he proposes that women are enslaved in marriage as a form of prostitution, with the supremacy of men being protected by bourgeois law.[130] More interesting for this project is Engels's use of genealogy to explore the problem of rampant poverty, seemingly *enhanced* by particular family forms rather than *alleviated* by it.[131] The alternative? Engels proposes that 'the monogamous family as the economic unit of society be abolished'.[132]

Plato stated a similar problem, albeit from a very different perspective.[133] He proposed that 'these women shall be wives in common of all these men' and that children also be cared for in common.[134] Aristotle objected, writing:

> There will be less friendship among them if their children and women are in common. . . . For we think that friendship is the greatest of blessings for the state, since it is the best safeguard against revolution, and the unity of the state, which Socrates praises most highly, both appears to be an is said by him to be the effect of friendship . . . in the state friendship would inevitably become diluted

---

129. Friedrich Engels, *The Origin of the Family, Private Property and the State* (London: Penguin, 2010).

130. Ibid., 132–41.

131. Ibid., 216.

132. Ibid., 105.

133. I owe this reading of Plato and Aristotle to Michael Banner, *Christian Ethics and Contemporary Moral Problems* (Cambridge: Cambridge University Press, 1999), 245–6.

134. Plato, *The Republic*, ed. G. R. F. Ferrari, trans. Tom Griffith (Cambridge: Cambridge University Press, 2000), 457.d, 154.

4. The Christian Household and the Reimagining of Kinship

in consequence of such association, and the expressions 'my father' and 'my son' would quite go out.[135]

Aristotle took to heart Plato's objection to the problem of family loyalties in the just and stable state, and turned Plato's concerns around: without kinship and friendship how can the state be formed? Like Plato, Engels deliberately set out to undermine the necessary form of the family, and made his point clearly: there was something wrong with how family life was conducted in Victorian England. By offering a response that takes Plato's objection seriously while also attending to the apparent need to divide affections and obligations, Aristotle provides a helpful model for any response to Engels.

This excursus on Plato, Aristotle and Engels serves to highlight a key problem raised in the discussion of household, to show how Benedict can respond. There is, in these debates, something of a dichotomy between the requirements of fairness and of intimacy. Plato and Engels were both struck by the problems of particularizing affections and obligations, whereas Aristotle was concerned about the loss of intimacy in the wider opening of affections and obligations. Baxter might satisfy Aristotle's requirements for the organization of affections, resourced as he was by a rich humanist tradition, but it is not clear that he resolves the problem of exclusion – clearly a philosophical problem, given the concerns of Plato and Engels, and also a theological problem, given the universalizing implications of the logic of the Eucharist mentioned in the previous chapter. Benedict, however, satisfies both: on the one hand, he reorganizes the household according to that disruptive Christian social logic, and dispenses with pre-existing social rank or reproductive ties; on the other hand, new hospitable communities are formed that particularize stable relationships of intimacy and accountability, with membership being made available to any celibate man in the body of Christ.[136]

Whereas Baxter's household compares strikingly with the household described in Schneider's *American Kinship*, Benedict has a different inheritance, which is worth exploring now in two sites. The first site will be a modern-day English Benedictine monastery, and the second a L'Arche community for shared living between those with and without intellectual disabilities.

---

135. Aristotle, *Politics*, trans. H. Rackham, Loeb Classical Library 264 (Cambridge, MA: Harvard University Press, 1932), II.i.15–17, 81–3.

136. Issues of gender and celibacy will be discussed in the following chapter, but for now it should be sufficient to say that Benedict's model in Monte Cassino would be emulated by others, including celibate female monastic contexts and that celibacy in the community allowed this universalizing logic to be better honoured, as it excluded special relationships within the monastery on the basis of marriage.

Counter-cultural Christian households today

Richard Irvine, in his ethnography of Downside Abbey, describes the 'everyday life of monks' as determined by a commitment to prayer – it is not an arbitrary social experiment, but has a clear purpose. Indeed, prayer permeates the entire life, challenging the distinction between prayer and secular activity.[137] Nevertheless, the ordinariness of the life is underlined, and when asked in a radio interview whether the monks ever have fun, the Prior (the superior of the Abbey) responds drily, 'Well, occasionally. Most of it of course is penance and suffering.' Having shrugged off the radical nature of the monastery, the Prior then takes a critical step into the supposedly ordinary realms, by adding 'But occasionally we have a really good meal'.[138] This is indicative of an attention to social eating in the Abbey, a classically family activity that the Prior considers to be under threat in the 'normal' household, with snacking and separate eating times – a point reiterated by another monk later.[139] The permeation of prayer into the life of the monk might represent something distinctive about the monastic context. With food, however, Downside can also be seen to represent a critique of social life within local culture, with the weakening of social ties altogether through the loss of shared eating. The call-ins for the radio show reflect a belief that monastic life must be antisocial, hard and unsustainable, but the Prior reveals a life that is not only social but also sustainable through the refreshment and security of shared meals.

The refectory (a term that comes from the Latin word for refreshment, where meals are served) is beside the abbey church, and the two buildings reflect the two kinships of the monks. Irvine notes that the meals are precisely that – 'family' meals – where kinning occurs through the sharing of life in proximity.[140] In the church, there is another meal that is shared – the Eucharist – which is the meal of a different sort of kinship which was explored in the chapter on substance. While the monastery might reflect the kinship implicated by membership of the church, it is clear that the kinship Irvine sees is not universal, but grounded in proximity and shared life. The social structure is certainly disrupted by the logic of kinship within the church, but it nevertheless still bears the hallmark of shared time together. In accordance with this, Benedict's gentle suggestions of a break with old family (derived from a much stronger statement in Basil) does not generate at Downside a breach with old family, who are often visited, and always welcomed, as still sharing special ties with the monks. (It is not made clear how Downside would manage having 'natural' brothers in the monastery, to which Benedict draws attention in

---

137. Richard Irvine, 'The Everyday Life of Monks: English Benedictine Identity and the Performance of Proximity', in *Monasticism in Modern Times*, ed. Isabelle Jonveaux and Stefania Palmisano (London: Routledge, 2016), 191.

138. Ibid., 193.

139. Ibid.

140. Ibid., 196.

forbidding any kind of special treatment.[141]) Irvine reveals how the practice of granting a set number of days away allows a continuity in the English Benedictine between the old family and the new, which nevertheless supports both as real households and as real families.

Irvine contrasts this with life within a Mexican convent described by Rebecca Lester, in which 'rupture and discontinuity' are valued.[142] Even there, though, one finds a similar way of finding continuity between the *ideas* of a family. Lester records the language of family in a Mexican convent being used by Mother Anabel, the 'mother general', who uses it in a protective way, saying, 'you wouldn't want someone coming into your living room, sitting on your couch and taking notes about everything you do' to advise Lester not to interfere with the sense of family in the course of her fieldwork.[143] This disruptive use of the idea of family, coupled with a recourse to a traditional sense of the need for privacy in family life, reveals how the monastery balances contextualization and critique. In a cultural context in which the time spent alone with others is necessary for intimacy, placing limits on the openness of the house might allow the fostering of deeper mutual understanding and care between residents.

The Benedictine example generates a helpful principle: the construction of the household can reflect radically the reality of Christian kinship, with the re-ascription of concepts of siblinghood, without destroying pre-existing relationships that might be positive, whether or not those relationships were defined as kin according to worldly terms.

This continuity also manifests itself in the sharing of the monastic life with those outside, most strikingly in the performance of marriage ceremonies, with Irvine making it clear that these marriages are held up as a good, while remaining a good the monks do not seek for themselves.[144] This is not hospitality to the spiritually immature, but a clear endorsement of a practice – marriage – which might prompt different ways of structuring the house, but which will obviously preclude taking the monastic vow of celibacy. Benedictine monasticism might well offer new modes of thinking about kinship as a Christian, but it does not stand in opposition to the goods of marriage and procreation, which will be discussed in a later chapter on gender.

Downside Abbey presents both an alternative life for some and a challenge to wider norms in Christian kinship. This is a sociable existence, in which brothers in Christ (in the case of Downside) and sisters in Christ (in the case of the Mexican convent) support one another, and regard one another as kin, even if wider society would not have described them as such. Usual kinship ties are not dispensed with

---

141. Benedict, *The Rule of St. Benedict*, 69.1–4, 92–3.
142. Rebecca J. Lester, *Jesus in Our Wombs: Embodying Modernity in a Mexican Convent* (Berkeley: University of California Press, 2005), 211. Cited in Irvine, 'Everyday Life of Monks', 197.
143. Lester, *Jesus in Our Wombs*, 50–1.
144. Irvine, 'Everyday Life of Monks', 198.

altogether but opened to a wider range than would otherwise be possible, so that fellow monks at Downside are brothers (or father).[145] Hospitality is emphasized, but kinship within the monastery and with original families is nevertheless fostered through shared time. These create ties that are recognizably, to the anthropological observers, kinship ties.

Patrick McKearney describes quite a different response to the culturally standard household, in an ethnography of a L'Arche community. His ethnography focuses on one member of a federation of 149 communities worldwide, set in a large British town called, pseudonymously, 'Endsleigh'.[146] L'Arche Endsleigh is a community of assistants and intellectually disabled members living in a reciprocal relationship. Most notably, the intellectually disabled teach the assistants who might be raised in a culture that values status and achievement to prize 'love, acceptance and relationships'.[147] The intellectually disabled are at the core of the community, taking the role of mysterious agents, whose communication can be disorienting to the assistant – in a way that ordinary life might be disorienting to the intellectually disabled.

There is something profoundly Christian about the subversion of worldly power in the L'Arche house. It emerges from a care for those with intellectual disabilities, who might otherwise miss out on this rich social life, and it also relies upon an implicit critique of the narcissistic pursuit of status through economic and political means. It is not a patronizing fiction; the intellectually disabled really do stand at the centre of the community as those who offer both example and means for a better life for the assistants, while the assistants support the intellectually disabled. It is reminiscent of the subverting values of the beatitudes in Matt. 5, and Paul's declaration that 'whenever I am weak, then I am strong' (2 Cor. 12.10), in recognition of his utter dependence on Christ, and the reconfiguration of his life in response to what Christ has done vicariously. The monastic house goes to great lengths to cultivate this recognition of dependence on God in prayer, and in L'Arche it is learned from the subjectivity of the intellectually disabled, which is recognized in the power to surprise those who might otherwise doubt the subjectivity of the person with intellectual disabilities. The assistants are prepared for this by a disorienting practice in which they learn to recognize the subjectivity of the intellectually disabled members of the community in unexpected places.[148] This is strikingly contrasted by McKearney with a non-L'Arche community, in which an intellectually disabled man grabs McKearney, and the care worker apologizes: 'Sorry, Watch out. He grabs people.' The embarrassment and violation are placed on the man with intellectual disabilities, and McKearney's sense of his own normal-ness is reaffirmed by the carer. This does not happen at L'Arche, but the

---

145. Ibid., 197.
146. Patrick McKearney, 'Enabling Ethics: L'Arche, Learning Disability, and the Possibilities of Moral Agency', (PhD, Cambridge, University of Cambridge, 2016), 22.
147. Ibid., 23.
148. Ibid., 90.

assistants are coached through submersion in a world in which the intellectually disabled are coherent agents and it is the assistant who is lacking in their capacity to understand.[149]

L'Arche Endsleigh cultivates a strong interior life. However, it does so for the benefit of those who otherwise would have little or no participation in social life, barred from entry by a society that construes meaningful social interaction in ways that exclude those with intellectual disabilities. L'Arche Endsleigh demonstrates, then, a sort of inverted interiority, creating a relatively exclusive community which recognizes and seeks the gifts of the excluded. It fulfils powerfully a mission of hospitality, but it does so in a strongly internal way that might not be optimal for a community in which there happened to be no members with intellectual disabilities. Even alongside this, it continues to cultivate a wide circle of hospitality inside the house – for evening meals and for large special occasions such as birthdays and Christmas – and enables visits outside the house of those with intellectual disability.[150] In the process, the state-care systems that view the intellectually disabled as clients and the assistants as carers are replaced with family membership, grown in a '"family" home' that is full of memories, stories and shared living.[151]

Perhaps the Puritan household would have made space for those with intellectual disabilities within the homes of their birth families, but little space was made available for the abandoned, bereaved or otherwise in need of support. L'Arche creates a distinctive home that genuinely regards those with intellectual disabilities as having unique gifts and experiences from which assistants can learn, and thus creates ties that are strengthened by reciprocity. Hospitality outside the household is key, but most of all, L'Arche houses stand as houses of hospitality in themselves, investing in rich interior lives for those ill-equipped for participation in societies where inclusion is granted through economic and political exchanges. Members of households where no one has intellectual disabilities might be challenged to become members or friends, or they might find other ways to create spaces of belonging within their walls or be prompted to create ties outside the walls.

L'Arche Endsleigh and Downside Abbey represent different responses to the challenge of forming Christian households. Downside Abbey is structured around services and prayer, with a heavy emphasis on hospitality to outsiders and service in the surrounding area. L'Arche Endsleigh still offers prayers and services, but they do not shape life to the same degree, and the emphasis is on the forging of relationships within the household that might not be possible in another context. Both highly value mealtimes as necessary to human flourishing in social life, and neither is structured according to ties of procreation, but rather according to ties of time and commitment. In both, kinship flourishes, offering plausible alternatives to Baxter's vision of the Christian house, shaped as it was by political concerns,

---

149. Ibid., 87–8.
150. Ibid., 35.
151. Ibid., 42–3.

and each reflects more easily the logic of kinship implicit in Benedict's *Rule*. This is obvious for Downside Abbey – a Benedictine monastery – but it is also the case of L'Arche Endsleigh, which views kinship with strangers as a joyful possibility.

Conclusion

This chapter has examined alternatives to the organization of the household in *American Kinship*, which is reminiscent of the social ordering prescribed by Richard Baxter in seventeenth-century England. Benedict's *Rule* was taken as epitomizing a tradition that already had deep theological roots, through Augustine, Basil, Cassian and others, in Christian scriptures. It revealed a practical outworking of the social logic of the Eucharist described in the previous chapter, and a radical attempt to live in such a way that the teaching of Jesus penetrated deeply into every sphere of life. However, it is not monasticism, but the relationship between kinship and the house in Christian thought and practice that is the focus of this chapter.

The logic of Benedict's account of kinship can be 'scaled', as it were, to non-monastic settings. The reimagining of the household that Richard Baxter seeks to offer has Christ at its centre and the warmth of hospitality at its edges. These two might more thoroughly inform the Christian house if the exclusiveness of its membership and the inwardly focused nature of many of its tasks were to give way to something more like what Benedict offers. Why? Benedict, in rethinking the house, rethought what it means to be kin, and this can inform less radical contexts – encouraging adoption and fostering, taking the sting out of the need for biological kin that (in part) underpins new reproductive technologies, lessening the pressure to leave inheritances and liberating conscientious parents to greater generosity to charities. Benedict is no arch-legalist but unburdens his hearers of the myth that it is untouchable human nature that is behind contemporary kinship practices. Does he abolish kinship? By no means! Rather, he *reimagines* it and in so doing opens the house to the stranger, not as servant or colleague, but as sister or brother.

Chapter 5

GENDERED RELATEDNESS

Introduction: Gendered relations and relative gender

While gender will be the focus of this chapter, it has clearly already been a major topic in the previous chapter on the house. This illustrates the point that in the history of European and American kinship the idea of gendered realms and roles has played a central role in determining the shape of the household. The fact that, in Schneider's *American Kinship*, one can be related by blood or by marriage testifies to the intertwining of kinship and gender.[1] Notions of gendered differences, roles and authority, and the related issues of sexual ethics, have played a huge role in informing the meaning of relatedness in the West and therefore require theological scrutiny if a deep engagement with a theological logic of kinship is to be articulated.

In *American Kinship*, marriage creates an important, but disputed, form of kinship. Schneider records a woman's answer to his enquiry as to whether her husband was a 'relative', to which she responded: 'My husband? A lover, Yes! A relative, No!'[2] So, even though large groups of people related according to the 'natural order of things' can become related through marriage according to the 'order of law', the married couple themselves are related in a paradoxical sort of way.[3] The horror in the woman's response is almost certainly fed by prohibitions of incest ('the gravest wrong'[4]) that carefully distinguish the partly erotic 'conjugal', from the entirely non-erotic 'cognatic' love.[5] Conjugal love unites opposites together as kin according to the order of law, whereas cognatic love reflects the pre-existing unity of material substance and includes as its epitome the love of parents for children.[6] The relatedness of the married couple is problematic because kinship according to the order of law finds its meaning in kinship according to

---

1. Schneider, *American Kinship*, 21.
2. Ibid., 38.
3. Ibid., 26–7.
4. Ibid., 40.
5. Ibid., 39.
6. Ibid., 38–9.

the order of nature. Being related by the order of law means honouring 'the laws of man, which are of human invention' and therefore treating others *as if* they were related by nature.⁷ When asking the woman, though, whether she was related to her husband, it suggests being *really* related, according to the order of nature, which confuses conjugal and cognatic love, and is forbidden. Clearly, the marriage has created kinship between her and her in-laws, or her husband and his in-laws, but when it comes to their own marriage, to treat one another *as if* they were related by nature is shocking. There is love, but not that sort of love.

Integral to the separation of the orders of nature and of law that make a paradox of the kinship of spouses is volition. Those who are related by nature are related by fact, whereas those who are related by law are related by a construct that emerges from human will.⁸ Accordingly, however, divorce is greeted in American kinship, is it nevertheless coherent, on this formula, to speak of no longer being related according to the order of law, in a way that it is not coherent to speak of no longer being related according to the order of nature. One can be an ex-spouse, but not an ex-parent, ex-sibling and so on.⁹

This brief picture of American kinship raises the first key question, then: What does it mean to be related by marriage, for Christians? The second key question can be drawn from the anthropology of gender and kinship.

In the 1980s, Collier and Yanagisako took Schneider's idea that biology was a 'native cultural system' through to its conclusion with respect to gender: neither the perceptions of male and female bodies nor the social imagining of sexual procreation can be assumed to map directly onto the natural.¹⁰ They argued, then, that it is *culture* that makes natural facts of sexual difference more socially significant than, say, the natural fact of the colour of one's eyes.

The idea that gender is not a necessary entailment of natural sexual differences is important and coheres with trends in gender theory outside of social anthropology. In 1949, Simone de Beauvoir famously wrote, 'One is not born, but rather becomes, a woman. No biological, psychological, or economic fate determines the figure that the human female presents in society; it is civilization as a whole that produces this creature, intermediate between male and eunuch, which is described as feminine.'¹¹ Collier and Yanagisako's essay contributes to the

---

7. Ibid., 37.
8. Ibid., 39.
9. Ibid., 23–4, 46–7.
10. Carsten, *After Kinship*, 58–9. Collier and Yanagisako are arguing 'against the notion that cross-cultural variations in gender categories and inequalities are merely diverse elaborations and extensions of the same natural fact'. (Jane Fishburne Collier and Sylvia Junko Yanagisako, 'Toward a Unified Analysis of Gender and Kinship', in *Gender and Kinship: Essays Toward a Unified Analysis*, ed. Jane Fishburne Collier and Sylvia Junko Yanagisako (Stanford: Stanford University Press, 1987), 15.)
11. Simone de Beauvoir, *The Second Sex*, ed. H. M. Parshley (London: Penguin, 1972), 295.

combined anthropological study of gender and kinship, and Carsten challenges the way in which nature and culture relate in this unified analysis.

Carsten recognizes that a 'starting premise for the study of gender is that we need to be careful to distinguish the apparently natural differences between men and women from the cultural meanings that are attached to them'. Nevertheless, she is concerned that other sites of anthropological interest (e.g. birth and death) do not generate the same 'persistence or anxiety' in distinguishing *given* from *made*.[12] She proposes a closer dialogue between studies of nature and culture. Something is lost if theory stays too close to this starting point of gender studies and fails to explore the 'context and ideas and practices' – with this context tending to be kinship.[13]

In other words, Collier and Yanagisako recommend a 'unified analysis' of gender and kinship, as 'a single field that has not succeeded in freeing itself from notions about natural differences between people'.[14] Carsten, however, recommends an even more unified analysis. She places kinship and gender alongside each other as two disciplines that have been hindered by folk conceptions of the natural order of things. She also places them alongside one another in a unified analysis of nature and culture, by not taking the dichotomy for granted. Thus, she chooses to study the various shared sites of kinship and gender in a more normal anthropological way. She essentially endorses the Schneiderian turn of Collier and Yanagisako, which has challenged the idea that gender differences are a self-evident entailment of sexual difference, but she also bids anthropologists to study the physical context in which kinship and gender play out not just for the sake of distinguishing nature from culture.[15]

While Collier and Yanagisako have seen anthropological endeavours hindered by presumptions about the relationship between gender and certain natural facts, there has also been a certain constriction of anthropological reflection from the other side of the spectrum. Carsten cites Jane Atkinson as a particularly helpful guide in seeing the problematic nature of the distinction. In a 'constructionist depiction of Wana beliefs about the similarity of men's and women's bodies' that seeks to show just how culturally constructed perceptions of gender differences are, Atkinson was quite candid in reporting 'unease' because of a natural fact that clearly informed local ideas of gender: high rates of maternal mortality in childbirth.[16] The fact that this generated unease reflects a fault within the discipline whereby natural facts have been ruled as irrelevant to the construction of gender,

---

12. Carsten, *After Kinship*, 59–60.

13. Ibid., 75.

14. Collier and Yanagisako, 'Toward a Unified Analysis of Gender and Kinship', 15. The use of Collier and Yanagisako's term, itself borrowed from Schneider, *A Critique*.

15. Carsten, *After Kinship*, 75.

16. Ibid., 78–9. Citing Jane Atkinson, 'Quizzing the Sphinx: Reflections on Mortality in Central Sulawesi', in *Fantasizing the Feminine in Indonesia*, ed. Laurie J. Sears (Durham: Duke University Press, 1996).

either because of wider political commitments of anthropologists or dominant trends within the theory.

In the case of the Wana, one sees a natural state of affairs that can only affect women – dying in childbirth – playing a role in determining the local construction of gender. The determining factor is not entirely local, but its effects *were* local. This reflects a distinction important to kinship theory as well – natural facts *do matter*, but they do not matter in the same way in every place. Therefore, while it is not that certain cultural practices and understandings are necessarily entailments of universal natural facts, one might nevertheless expect certain cultural practices to occur more frequently than others. Take, for instance, the fact that roughly half of the world's population is capable of bearing children, with the added risks this imposes, and the fact that for a large share of the world's population breastfeeding will be required for the survival of these children, with the mother being the most plausible candidate. Or take the fact that roughly half of the world's population can be forcibly impregnated – all these facts conspire to make some ways of constructing gender and desire more likely than others. It should not seem strange that the materiality of body and world will inform the way in which human beings live. Carsten makes the point well: 'Bodily transformations entail social obligations, and vice versa.'[17]

If the *theologian* were to take Carsten's advice then they would consider the construction of gender and kinship, and the natural facts associated with them, as a shared topic. Accordingly, it is necessary to add to the question raised earlier – about how Christians have thought about relatedness by marriage – the further question: How have Christians conceived of the relationship between gender and natural facts in the construction of gendered relatedness?

Augustine's theology of marriage set the standard for Western Christian practice to come. Alternative Christian perspectives on marriage and its gendering will be discussed later in this chapter, but for now Augustine's theology of marriage will be taken as descriptive of an important and dominant strand in the Christian ethics of marriage. Additionally, Augustine's treatment of celibacy alongside the goods of marriage brings out an important feature of New Testament witness on the gendering of relatedness. Following this, Karl Barth's similar and highly detailed dogmatic account of human gendering as it relates to marriage will be discussed, introducing, to Augustine's notion of the sociability of the sexes, Barth's method for interpreting creation in the light of the concept of covenant.

Christianity and gendered kinship: Augustine

'If there had been no sin, marriage would have been worthy of the happiness of paradise.'[18] Augustine was adamant, not just against Manichees but also against

---

17. Carsten, *After Kinship*, 81.
18. Augustine, *City of God*, 14.23, 585.

more orthodox Christian figures like Jerome,[19] that marriage was good. However, he sought to interpret the goods of marriage in the light of salvation history, with different justifications at different stages. This notion that salvation history had different stages with different implications for the justification of marriage would recur throughout Christian history, as the church sought to understand, among other things, the implications of the arrival of Jesus (viewed with the assistance of key Pauline teaching) for marriage.

Paul Ramsey has done seminal work tracing this theme in Augustine, and finds four stages: (1) before the Fall, when marriage was required to make up the number of the saints, (2) after the Fall, when marriage took on the extra requirement of bringing about the birth of the Redeemer, (3) after redemption, when marriage retained its natural goodness but when the *telos* of Christ had been fulfilled and a great number of people born (though Augustine is careful not to state that the number of the saints has now been filled up) and finally (4) eschatologically, when there will be neither marriage nor procreation.[20] In short, kinship changes

---

19. Jerome wrote in a letter against Jovinian's suggestion that married couples were equal to consecrated virgins, 'before the fall they [Adam and Eve] were virgins in Paradise: but after they sinned . . . they were immediately married'. (Jerome, 'Against Jovinianus', in *Jerome: Letters and Select Works*, ed. Philip Schaff and Henry Wace, trans. W. H. Fremantle, vol. 6, Nicene and Post-Nicene Fathers: Second Series (New York: The Christian Literature Company, 1893), 1.16, 359.) To quote Peter Brown, 'The pamphlet was a disaster'. At the time it stood against popular opinion, but it nevertheless tapped into a pre-existing and widespread theological tradition. (Brown, *The Body and Society*, 377.)

20. Paul Ramsey, 'Human Sexuality in the History of Redemption', *Journal of Religious Ethics* 16, no. 1 (Spring 1988): 56–86. Bennett engages critically with Ramsey's account at a number of points, but as this principally serves to introduce those major themes in Augustine's theology of marriage that are relevant to the relationship between gender and kinship, it should be sufficient simply to add that Bennett finds, in Augustine, a postlapsarian good for Adam and Eve: obedience to God in their procreative union, which enables them to share in God's ordering of creation even after the Fall. This good of obedience, though, is available after Jesus's obedience through the non-procreative means of the sacraments. Indeed, 'holy child-bearing' becomes a dual act of cooperation, not only involving the physical bearing but also bringing the children to become members of Christ in baptism, and in that way becoming related to them in a higher, spiritual way. (Bennett, *Water Is Thicker Than Blood*, 70–3. For this development of holy child-bearing, Bennett draws on Augustine, 'Holy Virginity', in *Marriage and Virginity*, ed. John E. Rotelle and David G. Hunter, trans. Ray Kearney, The Works of Saint Augustine: A Translation for the 21st Century, I/9 (Brooklyn: New City Press, 1999), 3.3, 69; 6.6–7.7, 70–1.) Bennett also argues persuasively that Augustine was not, in the end, confident of the status of marriage in the final resurrection, though he remains confident, in the light of Mt. 22.30 that, if present, marriage will be a radically altered relationship between men and women, whose bodies will remain sexed. (Bennett, *Water Is Thicker Than Blood*, 76–7. Cf. Augustine, *City of God*, 22.17, cited in Bennett, *Water Is Thicker Than Blood*, 77.)

with Christ, as the motive to marry and have children gives way and other social units centred less on reproduction become a live possibility. The question now is whether there might be a religious rationale for bearing new children. In other words, what – if any – are God's purposes for reproduction, and how might this bear on a Christian understanding of kinship?

For Augustine, during the era of salvation history before the birth of Christ, marriage had a very specific purpose and that was obedience to the command in Gen. 1.28: 'be fruitful and multiply'.[21] This, however, Augustine sees as being fulfilled in Christ and that people prior to Christ 'looked to have children from their marriages because of Christ. . . . This was so that it could be the special bearer of prophecy concerning him, in particular by foretelling what race and what nation he would come from in the flesh'.[22] Everything is in place, in Christ, for the inauguration of a new era in which members of the body of Christ will neither marry nor be given in marriage (Lk. 20.35), so Christians are no longer under the command to multiply. This is the grounds on which Augustine understands Paul's encouragement of celibacy in 1 Cor. 7, in which celibacy is described as the greater good. Nevertheless, the purpose of marriage remains the fulfilment of the good of procreation, along with the fulfilment of the other well-known goods of fidelity (honouring one's marriage vows) and of the sacramental character of marriage (in which marriage provides a symbol of Christ's commitment to the church).[23] Jana Marguerite Bennett adds to that friendship, arguing persuasively that *De bono coniugali* introduces it.[24] Augustine is devoted to keeping the goods of marriage together, so that a marriage is good only if it is aimed towards the fulfilment of all those goods together, and not just at pleasure.

So, for Augustine, marriage now must have the same purposes as before, including procreation, even if the command to multiply has been fulfilled in Christ. The fulfilment of that command in the birth of Christ means that committed celibacy becomes a greater good than marriage.[25] Marriage, though good, is a concession to those who might otherwise be tempted to engage in sexual intercourse that is not directed to the goods ordained it and ordered in marriage (for instance, sex outside of marriage).[26] As such, the connection between reproduction and marriage is complex. Marriage is still ordered towards

---

21. Augustine, *City of God*, 14.22, 584.
22. Augustine, 'The Excellence of Marriage', 19.22, 50.
23. Ibid., 24.32, 56–7.
24. Bennett, *Water Is Thicker Than Blood*, 61.
25. Bennett distinguishes, in Augustine's work, between committed virginity as a vowed state (rather than physical status) and celibacy as an abstinence unmarked by a vowed state. (Bennett, *Water Is Thicker Than Blood*, 207n61.) This is a welcome challenge to the notion of virginity, but given these usual connotations, celibacy will be used both generally and for Augustine's work, to refer to any intentional avoidance of sex and marriage, with a qualifier added to clarify, if necessary, that this is a vowed state.
26. Augustine, 'The Excellence of Marriage', 11.12, 43.

procreation, and so the hope for procreation must remain alive even in situations where it is highly unlikely, such as in the case of the elderly.[27] Seeking the goods of procreation, faithfulness, sacramental reflection of Christ's love for the church and friendship dignifies the marriage partner in the sexual act, prohibiting the mere search for pleasure to eclipse the other person in the disordering of desire. For Augustine, the goods must be held together as before Christ was born. Paul Ramsey disputes this, arguing that the spontaneous quality of sexual love can provide a space where the couple can be 'accessible to one another from the heart' and thus can honour the good of fellowship without at the same time honouring the good of procreation.[28]

However, this does not matter greatly for present purposes. While Augustine holds that marriage can still be good, the fact that Christ has now been born means that, in general, celibacy is to be preferred to marriage. Marriage is, however, better than failed celibacy.

Marriage, then, remains good in Augustine's eyes, but he allows the concerns of 1 Cor. 7 to speak to the present age as a new era of salvation history in the light of the coming of Christ. Given the pressure – now and in Augustine's time – to marry and bear offspring, Augustine's perspective on the relative importance of marriage is strikingly counter-cultural. Marriage is good, but Augustine provides very limited grounds to choose it: the avoidance of sexual sin for those who do not consider themselves equipped for the greater good of celibacy. The Christian can learn from Augustine to consider carefully the root of all those other social and economic pressures to marry and procreate and see if these are indeed compatible with call to single-minded devotion to Christ in 1 Cor. 7. The pressures may in fact arise from secular demands that are not compatible with the Christian faith, or religious demands that are no longer in force (but which might have been co-opted for non-religious purposes).

Augustine's criticism of the theological rationale for marriage and offspring would have challenged the 'silent majority' of Christians, who Carol Harrison argues were very much in sync with Greco-Roman norms.[29] Peter Brown corroborates this, writing that the churches at Rome and Carthage were a 'confederation of believing households, in which married persons predominated'.[30] Marriage was economically significant, not least for producing heirs. Augustan marriage laws encouraged marriage because the Roman Empire needed more children.[31] Brent Shaw characterizes Roman law as 'conceiv[ing] of a series of steps leading from the "copulation" of man and woman, through children, then the *domus*, to the

---

27. Ibid., 3.3, 34–5.
28. Ramsey, 'Human Sexuality in the History of Redemption', 60.
29. Carol Harrison, 'The Silent Majority: The Family in Patristic Thought', in *The Family in Theological Perspective*, ed. Stephen C. Barton (Edinburgh: T&T Clark, 1996), 87–105.
30. Brown, *The Body and Society*, 79.
31. Treggiari, 'Marriage and Family in Roman Society', 150.

state'.[32] From the point of view of political theory, Cicero described marriage as the foundation of the state.[33]

This is echoed by Augustine when he writes that marriage is the 'seedbed . . . of a city', but he then clarifies this by adding, 'as far as the race of mortals is concerned'.[34] Economic and political pressures might create social pressures to marry and have children, but, for Augustine, these influences on the majority of Christians do not have theological backing. Rather, while Augustine is certain to highlight the *goodness* of marriage, he relativizes its importance by pointing to the goodness of celibacy. Augustine calls on Christians to consider celibacy as a genuine possibility that might not fit easily into a culture shaped by political and economic pressures to marry and reproduce, but which might reflect better the reality of this age in salvation history as described in 1 Cor. 7.

In endorsing celibacy, and indeed in endorsing the value of sexual difference, Augustine's theology of the body impacted the practices of kinship. Dispensing with his earlier claim of the inferiority of women,[35] Augustine's reflection that there was 'natural sociability' between the sexes (and therefore that sexual differentiation was to be valued),[36] constituted a minor disruption of the Greco-Roman family, which was structured around the *paterfamilias*, as an individual. A more significant disruption was Augustine's endorsement of celibacy, in which the dominance of the *paterfamilias* and his ownership of the bodies of the family passed to God. This protected women who, instead of being pressed into service for family allegiances or the production of heirs, could be lauded for recognizing that the true owner of their body was God alone, as they submitted to the church as consecrated virgins. In these two ways, Augustine promotes a theology of marriage, three features of which are significant and representative of a dominant Christian view of marriage: first, that marriage creates a permanent tie of relatedness; second, that this relatedness is gendered, making reference to socially significant natural differences; third, that this permanent gendered relatedness is, after Christ, voluntary and – generally – not the best choice, even if it opens up a range of goods to be enjoyed.

---

32. Shaw, 'The Family in Late Antiquity', 11n16.

33. Cicero, *De Officiis*, n.d., 1.54.

34. Augustine, *City of God*, 15.16, 625. Cf. also Augustine, 'The Excellence of Marriage', 1.1, 33.

35. Augustine, 'Continence', 9.23, 207.

36. Augustine, 'The Excellence of Marriage', 3.3, 34. This is particularly significant, given Aristotle's notorious claim that 'the female is, as it were, a mutilated male', which is contradicted in Augustine's words, in *City of God*, 'now a woman's sex is not a defect'. (Aristotle, *De Generatione Animalium*, ed. J. A. Smith, trans. A. Platt, The Works of Aristotle Translated into English (Oxford: Clarendon, 1910), 2.3; Augustine, *City of God*, 22.17, 1057.)

Christianity and gendered kinship: Karl Barth

Marriage is, for Augustine, a voluntary, permanent and gendered form of relatedness. Given the enormous influence of Augustine's theology of marriage, his account has been taken as indicative of general Christian teaching on marriage in the West. However, to explore further how gender informs relatedness in Christian thought and practice, the notion of gender itself needs to be explored alongside kinship, as Carsten proposed. Related questions, concerning issues in gender and sexuality, have come to prominence in recent decades. Accordingly, Karl Barth, an enormously influential twentieth-century theologian, stands as an obvious dialogue partner for a deeper investigation into the notion of natural sociability between the sexes. Subsequently, issues raised in this discussion will be discussed with various theologians critical of the gendering of marriage. The main aim will remain, however, exploring the extent to which gender provides insight into Christian modes of relatedness.

An additional reason Karl Barth is an obvious interlocutor is his commitment to drawing theology solely from revelation. Accordingly, he ought to be ideally placed to inform an investigation into, as it were, a *Christian culture* of gender as it bears on kinship, free from culturally contingent perceptions of the natural order of things.

The defining concept of Karl Barth's doctrine of creation is that creation is the 'external basis of the covenant' and, correspondingly, covenant is the 'internal basis of creation'.[37] The logic is relatively simple: the purpose and dignity of creation are to be found in God's creative purposes – which are for covenant – and not within the creature itself as something inherent to its particular constitution.[38] This ties together creation and covenant, so one can expect neither that the meaning and purpose of the created order will be ascertained by observing it nor that God's creative purposes are going to cut across the grain of creation.

This relationship between creation and covenant structures his interpretation of the image of God mentioned in Gen. 1.27. The phrase 'male and female he created them' completes a parallelism with the *imago Dei* reference that precedes it: 'So God created humankind [*adam*] in his image, in the image of God he created them.' Humanity was, for Barth, created to bear God's image, and be distinguished in no other significant ways than the one mentioned, between male and female. In this way, humanity is not divided into 'groups and species' like animals (Gen. 1.25), or into 'races and people' as the National Socialist ideology Barth so hated might have claimed.[39]

---

37. Karl Barth, *Church Dogmatics: The Doctrine of Creation*, ed. G. W. Bromiley and T. F. Torrance, trans. J. W. Edwards, O. Bussey, and H. Knight, vol. III/1 (Edinburgh: T&T Clark, 1958), 94ff, 228ff.
38. Ibid., III/1, 94–5.
39. Ibid., III/1, 186.

In parsing the notions of female and male Barth uses this category of relationship derived from his account of the *imago Dei*. He writes that in this relationship is found a kind of 'created freedom' that is played out in the 'conjunction and inter-relatedness of man as male and female', and further that the meaning of the notions of female and male are comprehended in this context of active relationship rather than 'an existing quality or intrinsic capacity'.[40] Barth sees the *imago Dei* as not held by female or male, but female *and* male, which he calls 'existence in confrontation'.[41]

Sexual difference is still shared 'formally' with non-human animals, but in the case of humanity it reflects something of the *imago Dei*, pointing to God as 'One' but not 'solitary'.[42] Principally, this imitates God's own being in Triune relationship, but it also creates a 'type of the history of the covenant and salvation'. Precisely the division between female and male reflects something of the relationship between Creator and creation; hence, the New Testament symbolism of Christ as the bridegroom of His Church, the bride.[43] The human being stands before God as one differentiated *from* God *for* covenant fellowship, and this differentiation for fellowship suggests that to bear the image of God in being created female and male is to be created for fellowship in differentiation.

Does this mean that 'male and female he created them' indicates simply that humanity was created for relationship? For Barth, one also learns that man is 'the head of the woman, and the woman is his δόξα [glory] as he himself is the δόξα of God'.[44] Barth cites 1 Cor. 11 and Eph. 5 in support.[45] The former claims, 'But I want you to understand that Christ is the head of every man, and the husband is the head of the wife, and God is the head of Christ. . . . For a man ought not to have his head veiled, since he is the image and reflection [or glory, δόξα] of God; but woman is the reflection [or glory, δόξα] of man' (1 Cor. 11.3 and 6). The latter restates the idea of the head: 'For the husband is the head of the wife just as Christ is the head of the church, the body of which he is the Savior' (Eph. 5.22). The former appears in the context of a discussion of head coverings and the latter in a household code, and neither is exegetically uncontroversial (particularly the former, with its notoriously confusing claim that 'a woman ought to have a symbol of authority on her head, because of the angels').[46]

Barth picks up the issue again in his exegesis of Gen. 2.18-25, which he takes to have a single theme: 'the completion of the creation of man by the adding to

---

40. Ibid., III/1, 195.
41. Ibid.
42. Ibid., III/1, 186.
43. Ibid., III/1, 186-7.
44. Ibid., III/1, 205.
45. Both English and German texts cite Eph. 3, but the context suggests Eph. 5 was intended. Cf. Karl Barth, *Die Kirchliche Dogmatik: Die Lehre von Der Schöpfung*, 3rd edn., vol. III/1 (Zürich: Evangelischer Verlag, 1957), 231.
46. Barth, *Church Dogmatics*, 1958, III/1, 205.

the male of the female'.⁴⁷ Humanity is found in 'the unequal duality of male and female'.⁴⁸ This, of course, raises a whole new problem – where does this notion of inequality come from, what does it mean and how could it possibly be justifiable? Barth is careful about difference but is happy with it insofar as it makes possible – as a natural basis – the gracious use to which it should be put; in this case, as a 'type' of the relationship established in the covenant.⁴⁹ The *fact* of the helpmeet (or partner) difference is necessitated by the I-Thou distinction which Barth finds in the creation of female and male. Barth follows a 'Goldilocks' recipe for making the man 'not alone': the other must be neither so similar as to be a copy that does not confront the man's 'I' by evoking a 'Thou' nor so different as to be just like other creatures and failing to provide the solidarity that is required.⁵⁰

This sense of incompleteness is further elaborated in Barth's exegesis of the man's speech: 'This is at last the bone of my bones and flesh of my flesh.' He is related to the newly created woman 'as to another part or member of his own body'. Therefore, she also 'fulfils something which he himself ought to fulfil in this special part or member but cannot, so that it awaits fulfilment in her existence'.⁵¹ The narrative reflects God's own intentions for the inherent relationality in humanity; the man does not create the woman, but rather the woman and man are taken to share the same flesh in a manner that maintains the difference sufficient for the I-Thou relationship. Similarly, the man does not search for a partner but is presented with one as he names the animals, only retrospectively declaring, 'at last', when he sees the woman.⁵² The name chosen is unique, signifying a special relationship: *ishshah* from *ish*, woman from man.⁵³ In the very creation of woman, then, God brought about something distinctive about the relationship, as previously man was alone with creatures unsuitable for covenant relationship, and now, at the very moment of the completion of the creation of humanity, there is the fellowship that was the internal basis of creation.⁵⁴

Barth appears, in this exegesis, to be uncertain about the 'unequal duality' he expressed before. He takes the account of woman by man as reflecting *not* that she is 'mannish', 'man's property', 'not a human being in the full sense', but rather that 'in her being and existence she belongs to him', and she is 'helpmeet', 'without detriment to her independence she is part of him', 'beside him', and 'surpasses it [man's humanity] in a definite and decisive respect, although she surrenders and forfeits it if she tries to exchange it for that of man'.⁵⁵ However, he then

---

47. Ibid., 288.
48. Ibid.
49. Ibid., III/1, 290.
50. Ibid.
51. Ibid., III/1, 296.
52. Ibid., III/1, 294.
53. Cf. Ibid., III/1, 292.
54. Ibid., III/1, 300.
55. Ibid., III/1, 301.

reasserts, over and above the language of difference, the language of inequality – 'the relationship is not one of reciprocity and equality' – but with extensive qualifications: it is not 'a question of value, dignity or honour, but of order', it does not bestow a 'higher humanity' on man, it is not to the 'shame' of woman, but indeed is an 'acknowledgement of her glory, which in a particular and decisive respect is greater even than that of man'.[56]

Graham Ward writes as a receptive critic of Barth at this juncture. He approves of the idea of humanity being created for fellowship, but finds in Barth an inconsistency beyond that mentioned earlier. Barth, he claims, 'returns to a natural theology his whole theological system is set up to refute'.[57] He is referring particularly to the issue of sexual difference that is necessary even to make sense of the concept of homosexuality in Barth's writing. Ward admires Barth's rejection of 'stereotyped roles for "male" and "female"', but takes Barth to be determining his account of female and male in III/4 'in terms of their biology alone'.[58]

Ward is relatively consistent with Barth when he writes that God 'sees human being in partnership, in covenantal relationships of I and Thou, One and the Other reflecting His own Triune nature'.[59] However, he departs from Barth when he claims that 'God does not see male and female. . . . He sees the couple as human being, not male and female'.[60] The crucial difference is, as Christopher Roberts puts it so eloquently, 'Ward would have the significance of the person's physical body disappear under so much symbolism, as if human materiality were indifferent to God's theological purposes, as if Barth had never argued for a connection between creation and covenant'.[61] It is this last criticism that particularly hits home – Barth is not inconsistent in claiming a physical distinction between women and man precisely because he considered God to have created it for the purpose of covenant. In other words, God made physical reality in such a way that it could correspond well to His purposes for fellowship. This is simply not natural theology, because Barth is deriving this from Gen. 1 and 2, Song of Songs and their New Testament interpreters. He is not observing differences and thinking they must be theological significant. Rather, he observes a theologically significant difference but remains very reticent indeed about defining where the physical differences might lie that correspond to God's covenant purposes.

Ward seeks, in the first place, to take Barth to task for assuming certain gender differences uncritically. While Barth has been defended earlier, he is not wholly

---

56. Ibid., III/1, 301–2.
57. Graham Ward, 'The Erotics of Redemption – After Karl Barth', *Theology and Sexuality* 8 (1998): 65.
58. Ibid.
59. Ibid., 62.
60. Ibid.
61. Christopher Roberts, *Creation and Covenant: The Significance of Sexual Difference in the Moral Theology of Marriage* (London: T&T Clark, 2007), 194.

innocent of Ward's charges.[62] This contributes, however, to a larger project, which is, in the second place, to deploy Barth's concept of the significance of sexual difference in a different way, troubling the usual distinction between homosexual and heterosexual. Ward writes: 'True desire, that is, God-ordained desires can only be heterosexual.'[63] The heterosexuality that Ward speaks of does not cross genders but crosses some other form of difference. He wants the alterity that Barth considers to be built into properly ordered fellowship precisely in the design of creation. Ward is quite happy to borrow from Barth and develop him, accepting that there is a 'call to difference mediated by the Spirit', that there is 'sexual difference, a difference mediated by desire' and that 'Christian life partnerships' are marked by a 'narrative of performance and operation of the divine kenotic and human erotic giving.' However, these are borrowed from Barth's exegesis of Genesis, Song of Songs and the New Testament, which themselves generate the idea that there is an intrinsic relationship between how God has ordered things and the covenant relationships that He wishes to see. By all means, the difference in female and male points towards 'a density of signification above and beyond their anatomical specifications' insofar as they act as typologies of the relationship between Christ and His Church, but anatomical difference is important for Barth's theological reflection on the created ordering of things.[64] Moreover, Barth's eventual conclusion that bodily difference marks a gendered relationality that forms the basis for gendered relatedness has considerable support in the tradition, and indeed, in scripture – when he rejects the possibility of homosexual unions, he cites Paul in Romans 1.[65] Nevertheless, that only serves as confirmation of a constructive account of gender that Barth offers in dialogue with Gen. 1 and 2.

Barth turns to the language of shared substance in considering the treatment of marriage in Gen. 2. The woman is made from a rib, and the woman is bone of man's bones and flesh of man's flesh. Therefore, when the man leaves his parents and 'clings to his wife' they become one flesh. The completion of the flesh in fellowship is preceded by man being made physically incomplete as his rib is removed.[66] While Barth does not explicitly state that the man was incomplete before seeing the woman, it is implicit in his connection between the imagery of the rib on the one hand, with the imagery of the one flesh that explains the 'Therefore' (Gen. 2.24) on the other.[67] Barth parallels all marriages with this first marriage, in which there is a breach from leaving the old 'nearest' (the parents) that makes ways way for the new 'nearest' (the wife), to become, together, 'an absolutely integrated

---

62. For instance, Ward questions whether male-led seeking really explains the 'Therefore' of Gen. 2.24. (Ward, 'Erotics of Redemption', 67.)

63. Ward, 'Erotics of Redemption', 71.

64. Ibid., 69.

65. Barth, *Church Dogmatics*, 1961, III/4, 166.

66. It is striking that Barth ignores the possibility that the removed rib changes the man, so that it is not just the female but also the male that is derived from the man.

67. Barth, *Church Dogmatics*, 1958, III/1, 296.

whole'.[68] The language of physical incompleteness is deployed for the social leaving and cleaving of marriage.

The use of physical imagery to describe this union is important for the connection between kinship and gender. On the one hand, Barth does not concede the idea of incompleteness without a member of the opposite gender (though his use of imagery suggests it), and on the other hand, Barth establishes the idea of a deep kinship between the genders in marriage, which mirrors the ties to parents left behind. The new tie is one of substance: the married couple are one flesh, which emerges from the symbolism of the lost rib, and the creation of the other who is 'bone of my bones and flesh of my flesh'. There is, then, a bodily relationality that provides the basis for the Christian kinship of marriage.

Barth introduces a second angle on which to look at the text, which explores the notion of a duality that is unequal. Again, he seeks to explain the 'Therefore' that connects the meeting of woman and man with the following section on marriage. The passage describes the man leaving the family and clinging to a wife and, in this, Barth finds in man a 'supremacy' (as the one who seeks) but also has as its goal the 'subordination' that man experiences in the context of marriage, 'the unity in which alone man and woman can be together, twice man, in love and the marriage based upon it'.[69]

Barth is trying to work out what can be said about human duality based on Gen. 2.18-25. Barth seeks to diffuse the problem of inequality by casting the man as responsive to a divinely ordained *lack*, rather than casting him as the active partner to the passive woman. He belabours the point that man was asleep in the making of woman, in order to describe the man's role as seeker as disclosive of both 'supremacy' and 'subordination'.[70]

Is the point of the passage really that man is the seeker, though? Could it not simply be suggesting, first, that God created in humanity the capacity for fellowship, and second, that the marriage bond is serious? After all, Jesus uses Gen. 2 to answer negatively the Pharisees's question about the permissibility of divorce.[71] This is not to say that Jesus exhausts the meaning of the passage, but surely it is problematic to postulate (as Barth recognized) any kind of supremacy, and also problematic to postulate that there is a lack prior to marriage (as Barth does, in trying to deal with the problem of supremacy). After all, the New Testament ascribes dignity to celibacy. Certainly, one *might* interpret Gen. 2 in those ways, but as always it raises the question of over-interpretation: Does the passage, by taking the contemporary notion that it is the male that seeks the female, really seek to endorse that arrangement, especially given it seems that the passage can be rich with significance without resorting to this interpretation?

---

68. Ibid., III/1, 305.
69. Ibid., III/1, 306.
70. Ibid.
71. Mt. 19.4-6. Cf. 1 Cor. 6.16; Eph. 5. 28-33.

Barth addresses the issue of celibacy in a later volume, again referring back to Gen. 2.24. He interprets the passage again as implying a 'correspondence' between female and male, in the light of which it must be said that marriage is the *telos* of the relationship between female and male, so that those who are celibate 'are human, even without individual and concrete partnership, even without the contraction of marriage, only in so far as in their own way they share in the fellow-humanity which is implicit in the dualism of male and female and has its goal in marriage'.[72] This is a strong statement, but the strength of it comes from Barth's perspective on the importance of the typological character of the Gen. 2 passage: the relationship between man and woman points towards that between Christ and the church.[73] In light of the fact that Christ has come – who 'had no other beloved, bride or wife, no other family or domestic sphere but this community [His Church]'[74] – it is possible to live in the light of the future reality in which no one marries (Mk 12.25). The fellowship is complete. Additionally, there is not the same need to procreate now that Christ has been born, though Barth clearly still sees it as an option that has 'status, necessity and dignity' not least in the fact that marriage and procreation can both still represent the fellowship for which humanity was made which is found in the first instance in Genesis between female and male and in the fullest sense between Christ and the church.[75]

The notion of incompleteness, then, is important for Barth's theology of gender. He is open to the possibility of celibacy, by all means, but only when it is required by circumstances.[76] In that case, completeness comes through Christ as the celibate Christian waits for Christ without the distractions of married life (1 Cor. 7).[77] How, then, does this satisfy Barth's claim that 'there is no abstract manhood, there is no abstract womanhood' with its logical conclusion that humanity 'for the woman consists in being the wife of a male and therefore the wife of a man' (as also the opposite)?[78]

The masculine and feminine, for Barth, are found in relationship with the other sex, and in this instance, it might reasonably be assumed that the celibate man, for instance, is gendered male only potentially (to the extent that it is possible that he might marry) and female prospectively (if one were to literalize the metaphor of the marriage between Christ and the church) in relation to the coming of the bridegroom. After all, whichever place a member of the church might occupy in human marriage, they will always occupy the place of following Christ, and never of preceding Him.

---

72. Barth, *Church Dogmatics*, 1961, III/4, 142.
73. Ibid., III/4, 143.
74. Barth, *Church Dogmatics*, 1958, III/1, 144.
75. Ibid., 1961, III/4, 143.
76. Ibid., III/4, 144.
77. Ibid., III/4, 147.
78. Barth, *Church Dogmatics*, 1958, III/1, 309.

This is clearly not the only distinction Barth draws between man and woman, insofar as he regards there to be a created difference that marks each from the other, though the only social significance he is willing to grant the man-woman relationship is this complex notion of preceding and following. He justifies the prohibition of homosexual unions (following Rom. 1.26-7 in particular[79]), because he regards something about creation as the external basis of the covenant fellowship of the married fellowship. God built into bodies the distinctions that were to be animated in this fellowship. When Barth claims that he wishes to avoid 'an existing quality or intrinsic capacity, possibility or structure of his being' as the marker of sexual difference[80] he simply means to avoid the idea that femininity and masculinity can be found in isolation from the other, not that no material created differences confront either woman or man as a sign of the difference that incites fellowship.[81]

This need not bring him into conflict with the social anthropology that demonstrates the cultural contingency of notions of gender. Barth is not making an anthropological claim but a theological claim. He describes, theologically, a worldview in which certain bodily differences that distinguish men and women are theologically significant as part of the created order of things which is teleologically ordered towards covenant fellowship. It is not arbitrary to identify those particular natural facts that make possible procreation given the connection in Gen. 1 between vv. 27 and 28: 'male and female he created them. God blessed them, and God said to them, "Be fruitful and multiply."' This does not mean that it is *procreation* which distinguishes female and male, and Barth certainly does not wish to argue that, but it gives a clear basis on which to identify the natural differences that are significant in marking out man and woman, ordered as they are for fellowship.

Barth, however, does not subscribe to the position that celibacy is forbidden, even if he takes men and women necessarily to be oriented to the other. He regards either marriage or celibacy as a 'vocation'[82] so that marriage is required neither

---

79. Ibid., 1961, III/4, 166.
80. Ibid., 1958, III/1, 195.
81. Ibid., III/1, 186.
82. Ibid., 1961, III/4, 183. This use of vocation, combined with the incompleteness Barth implicates in the unmarried, suggests a reticence about celibacy traceable to Luther. Luther, following Matthew 19, concedes that there might be 'eunuchs for the sake of the kingdom' who are physically 'equipped for marriage' but 'bridled by the grace of God' and thus voluntarily celibate, but he considers them to be rare, and meanwhile considers 'priests, monks, and nuns' to be 'duty-bound to forsake their vows' when their desire for marriage is strong. (Martin Luther, 'The Estate of Marriage (1522)', in *The Christian in Society II*, ed. Walther I. Brandt, Luther's Works 45 (Philadelphia: Muhlenberg Press, 1962), 18–21.) Cf. also Martin Luther, 'A Sermon on the Estate of Marriage (1519)', in *The Christian in Society I*, ed. James Atkinson, Luther's Works 44 (Philadelphia: Fortress Press, 1966), 9–14.

by nature nor general divine law.[83] Indeed, he charges those who marry because of cultural custom or because they think marriage reflects 'biological maturity' with 'human caprice'. Marriage should be based on the calling of the Holy Spirit, a call to a practice that God made good, and thus can express the freedom of the gospel.[84]

Responding to the matter of procreation, Barth dismisses any possibility that procreation is the chief end of marriage. First, as has already been discussed, the absolute priority of procreation is no longer in force now that Christ has been born,[85] and second, marriage is an end in itself for the union that it brings about.[86]

What, then, does Barth wish to communicate about gender that might be relevant to kinship? First, marriage, which creates an indissoluble tie of kinship, is justified theologically. Second, Barth rejects the idea that procreation is necessary to marriage, even if it too is good. Third, when Barth practices caution, he advises scepticism about attempts to claim, from scripture, knowledge of the differences that mark out woman from man beyond respective roles in procreation (which need not have necessarily have further social implications), and he certainly forbids any attempt to infer different roles from observations about the natural order. Fourth, he considers that there is a difference of substance between woman and man that God intended for fellowship between the two, and that creates a kind of incompleteness without marriage even if that incompleteness might be satisfied through living in such a way that looks towards the ultimate consummation of God's purposes for humanity found in union between Christ and the church, a purpose which might lead to some being called to celibacy. Fifth, when it comes to the ordering of the household, Barth implies that there might be gendered realms and roles, though the case is unpersuasive, and certainly not defended with any vigour. Indeed, he interprets Christologically the scriptural grounds that might have been used in making such a case, instead of using them to support a conclusion about gender roles in marriage.

Barth, therefore, connects gender and kinship with substance, personhood and household, offering ample material with which to investigate the close relationship Carsten describes between cultures of kinship and cultures of gender. In doing this, he supports the idea that there is, in marriage, a theologically justified mode of special kinship (that is, with obligations and affections that are not due to other recipients of the kinship made available in Christ) in the present age. The tie is established by choice, in a marriage covenant, but refers – in making sense of the nature of the tie – to a gendered relationality not dissimilar to the natural sociability between the sexes that Augustine described.

---

83. Barth, *Church Dogmatics*, 1961, III/4, 183.
84. Ibid., III/4, 184.
85. Ibid., III/4, 143–4.
86. Ibid., III/4, 188, 266.

Initial theological conclusions

What difference does this make for the overarching question of the relationship between gender and kinship in the Christian moral imagination? Barth offered a theory of sexual differentiation in which the telltale signs are procreative capacity but in which the *telos* is communion between God and His people, for which God has equipped humanity by building a correspondence to the other into humanity itself. In so doing, he could make sense of the goodness of marriage and procreation, but he was left offering a slightly weak account of the goodness of celibacy, under the threat of the incompleteness of male or female without the other.

Augustine offers a vision of celibacy as a high calling without denigrating marriage as his patristic peers, and indeed as philosophical precursors, did. Marriage was a good but only insofar as it generated offspring, that being the purpose to which it was originally put. At that point, Ramsey offers a valuable critique of Augustine, pointing to the possibility that, in an era of salvation history in which procreation is no longer required, marriage might still involve rightly ordered loves without the orientation towards procreation, provided the traditional 'unitive good' of covenant relationship is seen as served by sexual intercourse, so that it is not merely remedial but oriented towards the covenant relationship that Barth so prized in his theological thought between wife and husband. On the issue of celibacy as a high calling, though, Augustine's argument stands, as a simple exegesis of 1 Cor. 7, and on that point Barth – and even Luther – concede that there might be a special calling for some, whereas Augustine envisages a worthwhile celibate life which Luther and Barth struggle to imagine.

To establish the value of celibacy, in opposition to the vestiges of Barth's suggestion of an in-built need to marry that goes beyond the need for covenant fellowship, one can look to the monastic tradition, to which Augustine was an important contributor. This approach to monasticism will be conditioned by Sarah Coakley's treatment of how Christianity might reconstrue gender in ways that call into question the suggestions implicit in Barth's account that ordering of gender towards fellowship implies something incomplete about an unmarried state.

Practising marriage, practising celibacy

Sarah Coakley argues, with great clarity, that it is theology, and not social science, that must ground attempts to describe whether, and what, natural facts ought to be considered socially significant. In doing so, she turns deconstruction against the gender theorists. She writes that desire is 'more fundamental than gender' and she seeks to work out what an appropriate Christian understanding of desire might be.[87] Her account is reminiscent of Barth: 'gender "matters" primarily because it

---

87. Sarah Coakley, *God, Sexuality, and the Self: An Essay 'On the Trinity'* (Cambridge: Cambridge University Press, 2013), 52.

is about *differentiated, embodied relationship* – first and foremost to God, but also to others. Its meaning is therefore fundamentally given in relation to the human's place as one made in the "image of God".[88]

The theological ideas that Coakley brings into dialogue with secular gender theory are as follows: first, concerning the hopes and despairs of gender theorists, she points to the story of creation, Fall and redemption as 'plac[ing] the performances of gender in a spectrum of existential possibilities *between* despair and hope'; second, she grounds this hope in the past 'event of Christ's incarnation and resurrection'; third, responding to Judith Butler's call to trouble gender, described in terms of performativity, Coakley suggests that the repressive forces in the world are destabilized by 'performances' of contemplation, but which find their end in 'submission' to God.[89] Using these ideas, she attempts to respond to the gender theorist's rejection of repressive gender norms with a theological account of desire. Coakley accepts that gender is not a necessary entailment of certain bodily realities, and also accepts that gender norms can be destabilized through counter-performance, but she sees the proper site for this in contemplative response to God, through which gender is made 'redemptively labile'.[90]

The typological character of gender that appeared in Barth is brought to the fore by Coakley. Coakley rebuts the gender trouble of Judith Butler and other gender theorists, who lack the 'final point of reference' in God in the light of which the Christian theologian can construct some positive account of desire and its proper use beyond that of critical response to norms regarded as oppressive.[91] She proposes instead a 'contemporary trinitarian *ontology of desire*' in which 'divine desire can be seen as the ultimate progenitor of human desire, and the very means of its transformation' as 'God the "Father", in and through the Spirit . . . forges them . . . into the likeness of his Son'.[92] She finds in Christian worship a fluidity to gender that mimics the fluidity of gender in Eph. 5 and 1 Cor. 11, which each take the familiar contemporary power dynamics of marriage and play with the power and submission therein: 'Christ is the head of every man, and the husband is the head of his wife, and God is the head of Christ.'[93] Coakley's account may appear overly optimistic about the transformative potential of contemplation. However, Benedict's *Rule* takes contemplative prayer and study to be a vital part of daily life, and once placed within a comprehensively reimagined life, it becomes easier to see how the work of contemplation might transform everyday desire. Coakley's

---

88. Ibid., 53.
89. Ibid., 53–4.
90. Ibid., 59.
91. Ibid., 10.
92. Ibid., 7.
93. 1 Cor. 11.3. Cf. Sarah Coakley, '"In Persona Christi": Who, or Where, Is Christ at the Altar?', in *A Man of Many Parts: Essays in Honor of John Westerdale Bowker on the Occasion of His Eightieth Birthday*, ed. Eugene E. Lemcio (Eugene: Wipf and Stock Publishers, 2015), 95–112.

reconfiguring of desire and gender offers the backdrop against which a celibate life can more easily be taken to enjoy the human freedom for fellowship which Barth describes. While Coakley's account of desire serves chiefly to make sense out of a celibate life as plausibly good in the Christian moral imagination, it has broader implications, not just for those who are committedly celibate.

Sarah Coakley brings a deconstruction of gender through the category of desire, pointing to its *telos* in the Triune economy of desire in which the Christian is drawn to completeness in Christ, enacted now through contemplative prayer, which disrupts the Fallen norms of power and submission. Indeed, the very scriptural depiction of fulfilment in Christ takes up and reworks the power dynamics of first-century gender norms. Most importantly for present purposes, though, it troubles the notion of the incompleteness of male without female and vice versa that appears in Barth.

This theological revision of gender is apparent in monastic practice, where the structure of life would come to challenge prevailing idioms of gender. Clearly, the gendering of roles within many houses could not occur in single-sex monasteries. Still, gender shaped the kinship structures of the monastery in this separation, and in the prescription of celibacy. This separation was clearly intentional, though Benedict never explains it (indeed, the most explicit requirement of celibacy is found in his call for monks to 'treasure chastity'[94]). It is unlikely that it needed to be explained, though the *Rule* requests that Cassian's *Conferences* be read regularly,[95] and it also recommends other works at the end of the *Rule*,[96] which together offer plenty of information about this call to chastity. Celibacy, and the accompanying separate accommodation of men and women in the monastic life, was a matter of this treasuring of chastity. It was certainly not, for either Cassian or Augustine, that marriage was wrong,[97] but the monastic life called for the kind of single-minded devotion to God that is implied by Paul's endorsement of celibacy in 1 Cor. 7.32-4.

As such, in offering an assessment of the understanding of Christian kinship evident in the monastery, one cannot ignore the call to celibacy. The monastery was significant not just for creating a family not bound by blood (and therefore not regarded as sharing the same substance), but also one not bound by marriage,

---

94. Benedict, *The Rule of St. Benedict*, 4.64, 28. Earlier in that same chapter, Benedict calls monks 'not to commit adultery', but given this is placed between the prohibition of murder and of theft, it is reasonable to assume that this indicates nothing distinctive about the monastic life!

95. Benedict, *The Rule of St. Benedict*, 42.5, 64.

96. Ibid., 73.5, 95.

97. John Cassian, *The Conferences*, trans. Boniface Ramsey, Ancient Christian Writers (Mahwah: Newman Press, 1997), 21.4.2, 721. Also, Cassian, 21.10.1, 727. There are many affirmations of marriage in the works of Augustine, but none so celebratory (and, indeed, radical) as his claim that 'If there had been no sin, marriage would have been worthy of the happiness of paradise'. (Augustine, *City of God*, 14.23, 585.)

and also lacking in the dynamic of power between men and women.[98] Robert Song describes the theological influence that makes this possible: 'Human flourishing has been given a profound reorientation: full humanity, full participation in the imaging of God, is possible without marriage, without procreation, indeed without being sexually active. Celibacy, in other words, has become an appropriate stance for those who wish to live in the new age.'[99] Song connects this reorientation explicitly to the new identity received in sharing Jesus's blood, providing a basis of covenant membership and identity not linked with the procreative ties that bind membership of the old covenant.[100] This endorsement of celibacy is not simply responsive to scriptural proof texts gone rogue from their original context, but rather is rooted in an overarching New Testament message about covenant membership through Christ, which has profound implications in practice. Accordingly, Song and others do not rely on texts like Lk. 20.35-36. Rather, they rely on the reschematizing of social relations that this discloses, the basis of which is found in the coming of Jesus Christ.[101]

As monasticism grew in social importance historically, the call to celibacy would alter concepts of gender, undermining the social requirement to marry. Specifically, it would erode contemporary definitions of masculinity. J. L. Nelson argues that a problem of masculinity was created by the celibacy of professional churchmen, as the removal of marriage as a possibility also removed the context in which 'gendered difference' was made 'visible'. This created an anxiety about 'the needs of the body, the attractions of sex, the social requirement of procreation' (exacerbated by the refusal of monks to take up arms).[102] Writing about the Carolingians around the turn of the ninth to tenth century, Nelson records a degree of obsessive anxiety about sexuality as illustrated by the dying words of a boy (who likely committed suicide) that 'however wicked I was in other ways, I never slept with a woman'.[103] Diet was gendered – the might of men was aligned with hunting and eating meat as well as with sex with women, whereas the abstinence of monks and nuns could be compared with pigs eating vegetables – as seen in the rant of a monk's angry

---

98. Convents presenting a rare instance where male headship has not applied historically, with the exception of occasional Episcopal oversight.

99. Robert Song, *Covenant and Calling: Towards a Theology of Same-Sex Relationships* (London: SCM, 2014), 18.

100. Ibid.

101. Candida Moss proposes that the call to celibacy in 1 Corinthians 7 and the call to unity in the church in the remainder of the epistle are conceptually connected, and provide evidence of Paul's belief in this reschematizing of social relations. (Candida R. Moss and Joel S. Baden, *Reconceiving Infertility: Biblical Perspectives on Procreation and Childlessness* (Princeton: Princeton University Press, 2015), 189–92.)

102. J. L. Nelson, 'Monks, Secular Men and Masculinity, c. 900', in *Masculinity in Medieval Europe*, ed. Dawn Hadley (London: Routledge, 2014), 122.

103. Ekkehard IV, *Casus Sancti Galli* c. 43, ed. H. F. Haefele (Darmstadt, 1980), 96–9, cited in Nelson, 132–3.

uncle: 'how could you prefer the life of pigs in a vegetable-garden? what about the joys of hunting? what about the voluptuous touch of women?'[104] The practices of monasticism for men conflicted with cultural perceptions of masculinity across the board, and these combined potently with the rejection of 'carnal intercourse' in the case of Charles, then a prince and later emperor, who cast off royal clothing and sword belt in the same declaration.[105] Not just in the attributes but also in the duty to continue the family line, it was challenging for a monk to remain a man.[106]

These anxieties need to be set in a wider context of strategies for the consolidation of power and property, particularly for the nobility, that could create further anxieties through shifting responsibilities to have or not to have children, to marry or not to marry, to be sent to a monastery or not. This was crucial to the renegotiation of masculinity. The church offered a service through which the powerful connect with the work of the monastery, which was incentivized by the way it helped with strategies of inheritance and the management of power conflicts. The role of the powerful was then reshaped, with "masculine' justice' accommodating '"feminine" mercy and gentleness', and with the powerful observing the pursuit of Christian holiness in their oblated sons. Within the monastery, young men had to reconceive their own masculinity stripped of its usual features, and outside the monastery close ties with the elite reshaped masculinity in the upper echelons of society.[107]

The monastic call to celibacy did not just reshape concepts of masculinity, but relationships between persons of the same gender. In Aelred's famous work on spiritual friendship, one sees the practical outworking of theological commitments to both celibacy and fellowship. For Aelred, 'in human affairs there is no goal that is holier than friendship, nothing more useful, nothing more difficult to find, nothing that is sweeter to experience, nothing more enjoyable to maintain. For friendship bears fruit in this life as well as in the life to come.'[108] He celebrates the profound fellowship for which humanity was created, but not in the context of sexual relationships only scripturally endorsed for the marital relationships that crossed the sexes. By all means there might be some kind of 'natural sociability' between the sexes, as Augustine had it,[109] that God had ordained for marriage with its procreative purpose pre-Christ, but in the context of the higher calling of celibacy after Christ, there is a better ordering to be had, as the Christian is called to God, in Christ, by the Spirit, as Coakley described in her endorsement of contemplative prayer.

---

104. *Narratio de monacho Cenomanensi ad canonicam vitam et habitum converso*, PL 129:1263-8, cited in Nelson, 'Monks, Secular Men and Masculinity, *c.* 900', 133.

105. Nelson, 'Monks, Secular Men and Masculinity, *c.* 900', 133–5.

106. Ibid., 138.

107. Ibid., 139–42.

108. Aelred of Rievaulx, *Spiritual Friendship*, trans. Mark F. Williams (Scranton: University of Scranton Press, 1994), 2.9, 44.

109. Augustine, 'The Excellence of Marriage', 3.3, 34.

Friendship was a powerful product of the monastic movement, as the new economic reality and living arrangements, uncomplicated by contemporary views of gender, allowed for celibate fellowship within the body of Christ that fulfilled in part the sociability for which God had created humanity. Not an easy fellowship – Aelred warns that 'friendship is not able to endure except among the good'[110] – but one that fills a lack.[111]

Here, then, is a Christian insight that defies a culture that seeks self-fulfilment in procreation and marriage. Instead, Christ figures as the highest object of properly ordered human love, but at the same time as human beings are called together to form the body of Christ this takes place in fellowship. There is retained within Christian thought a notion of sexual difference, which is crucial to marriage and the economy of sexual desire. It creates the conditions in which the appropriate Christian setting for the conception of children is marriage, which suggests a relationship with a father and a mother, though beyond that the household might be troubled from other quarters of Christian theology, as seen in the earlier chapter. However, there is a Christian tradition, playing off 1 Cor. 7, that does not see marriage and procreation as necessary, because kinship can be found in the celibate (indeed single-sex) monastery. Here one finds what can only be called, following the logic Paul's language in 1 Cor. 11 and Eph. 5, a feminizing of the Christian. Monasteries are places of submission in which the fullness of humanity is found in fellowship with Christ, as part of a multi-personal body (the church) marked by fellowship. The monastery can honour the special affections and indeed obligations of intimate friendships, making them appear to be nothing other than relationships of kinship.[112]

---

110. Aelred of Rievaulx, *Spiritual Friendship*, 2.41–3, 50.

111. Jana Marguerite Bennett writes conversely that modern 'loss of respect for nonsexual relationships' like friendship 'fuels a desire for sexual relationships, whether that is seen in terms of marriage and family or in terms of a free-swinging single life that is distinct from marriage and family'. (Jana Marguerite Bennett, *Singleness and the Church: A New Theology of the Single Life* (Oxford: Oxford University Press, 2017), 38.) Bennett's observation helps us not just protect friendship but properly protect marriage. When marriage is seen as the default and, perhaps, the only way to seek the social goods of intimacy, faithfulness and fellowship, that is surely a load too heavy to bear; marriage becomes a one-stop shop for human fulfilment, which will surely only disappoint, while leaving other relationships neglected. By downplaying nonsexual relationships and idealizing (or idolizing) marriage, Bennett observes later that it becomes difficult to live out kinship in Christ. (Bennett, *Singleness and the Church*, 127–8.)

112. Recent work by Robert Song deserves mention, though it falls just outside the scope of further investigation. He distinguishes his proposal for same-sex covenant partnership (as well as marriage) from friendship as the latter does not imply a 'formally celebrated and publicly recognized undertaking . . . indicat[ing] entry into a set of commitments that is different in kind and brings with it definable and perhaps legally enforceable rights and obligations'. (Song, *Covenant and Calling*, 53.) It is difficult, here, to do Song's argument

Conclusion

This chapter started with the recognition that the ideas and practices surrounding gender vary so widely from culture to culture that natural facts alone cannot be taken self-evidently as having particular social consequences for the construction of gender. Furthermore, the ideas and practices that have come to be associated with gender are certainly not drawn ineluctably from natural differences. Foucault argues that not just gender, but even desire itself, on which theories of sexuality are readily built, is constructed not on the basis of natural facts but on the basis of power relationships within society: 'For the Greek moralists of the classical epoch, moderation was prescribed to both partners in matrimony; but it depended on two distinct modes of relation to self, corresponding to the two individuals. The wife's virtue constituted the correlative and the proof of a submissive behavior; the man's austerity was part of an ethics of self-delimiting domination.'[113] What Foucault found in the Greek moralists, recent gender theorists have found more generally, and thus called into question the very basis of ideas about gender, sex and sexuality in their respective cultures.

This is not, however, to say that there is nothing morally significant about sexual difference, even if human biology does not itself require a particular practice of gender to be recognized. Coakley argued that these secular gender theorists are

justice, because the core of his proposal enters the territory of sexual ethics. Here, the gendering of marriage is only discussed insofar as a natural affinity is taken theologically to provide grounds for relatedness. Indeed, Song upholds something like the gendering of marriage described here, on the grounds that it is 'unavoidably linked to procreation' and proposes a separate category for non-procreative covenant partnerships, with a sexual component, that are not gendered (Song, *Covenant and Calling*, 54.). Accordingly, he affirms more for these covenant partnerships than is being claimed here for friendship within the monastic household. Nevertheless, covenanted friendships, for want of a better word, could display the good of faithfulness in such a way as to enrich monastic kinship. However, the theological justification offered here for monastic kinship was the need for mutual accountability, intimacy and obligation within the context of a limited social life, marked by co-residence. Covenanted non-marital unions (setting aside the question of intercourse) certainly could be justified on similar grounds, but further argumentation would be needed to define these as exclusive pairings, given that monastic kinship responds to the expanding influence of the sacraments on the practice of kinship. Song's suggestion that non-procreative covenant partnerships could 'function as a kind of eschatological witness' gaining 'their ultimate intelligibility from being a witness to God's covenant love to human beings' could provide those grounds. However, further justification would need to be offered to counter the pressure of eschatological witness towards expanding kinship (Song, *Covenant and Calling*, 28.). Song's proposal that these partnerships have a sexual component could certainly offer the basis for this further investigation, but would bring this discussion onto matters of sexual ethics beyond the scope of this book.

113. Michel Foucault, *The Use of Pleasure*, trans. Robert Hurley, The History of Sexuality 2 (London: Penguins, 1985), 184.

cut adrift, operating against oppressive political forces, but lacking the resources to provide a constructive moral account of the proper uses of desire and power.

Accordingly, Barth and Augustine have been drawn on, as key historical interpreters of scripture, to provide a basis on which such a constructive account of gendered relatedness can be offered to the Christian. They present accounts of gender that do not (at their best) depend on natural observations about bodily differences to generate their ideas about gender. Instead, their teleological framework is not the critique of power found in Foucault and Butler, but a theological account of the world and its relation to its Creator. On this basis, they offer a theory of bodily differences that is grounded on revelation rather than nature, and yet which can make reference to nature in the context of doctrines of creation also grounded in revelation. That is to say, they do not ignore nature, but rather they allow God to disclose in scripture the meaning in creation.

What might a Christian account of the relationship between gender and kinship look like then? Human beings were created for fellowship, with bodily differences being oriented to that fellowship. In the era before Christ, these bodily differences served two purposes. First, these bodily differences fit with God's revealed purposes for human beings, that they be ordered towards fellowship. Second, they serve as the basis for procreation as human beings at the time operated under an ordinance to multiply, teleologically ordered towards the birth of Christ. The first of those, the sociability, finds its ultimate fulfilment not in ordinary marriage but in the union between Christ and the church as human beings live out the covenant relationship with God for which they were made, with a capacity for fellowship built into their very earliest origins. Bodily differences are ultimately signs of the fellowship for which human beings were created. After the birth of Christ, it is no longer necessary to procreate, though the longing for fellowship is still proper to human being, and marriage is an appropriate response to that, acting as a sign of the relationship between God and His people. Marriage serves as a context for the honouring of a covenant in joyful fellowship and bringing into the world children. These children no longer have that same purpose of populating the holy generations that culminated in Christ, but they remain every bit as much a blessing to be welcomed.

There is a still higher calling: celibacy. This claim defies the idea that ultimate fulfilment is found in earthly marriage, but celibacy so conceived is not merely a form of cultural defiance, but a sociable state in itself, lending itself to the practice of kinship. Special affections are nursed and obligations are honoured to those with whom the celibate Christian lives, even as they form a house hospitable to the isolated and alone. In this state there is no procreation, as sex is intended only for marriage.

Where it is not possible to refrain from sexual sin then marriage is precisely the calling that Paul expects, as a good and honourable concession in a Fallen world, even if it presents itself as a challenge and calling of its own. Where children are born they remain with the adults to which they are proximate – ideally at least the mother and her covenanted husband – but where this is not possible and a sad breach is necessary they can find kinship elsewhere, just as the celibate Christian knows themselves to be created for modes of fellowship that are not limited to the ties of marriage, even if that is the only place for sex. The act of reproduction, then, properly takes place within a form of gendered relatedness –marriage – and it is wholly appropriate that the bearer of the child and her covenanted husband should be among those to receive that child as their kin. However, should events transpire in which one or both of them cannot be present to parent the child (death and displacement being the most obvious circumstances), then another might become just as much the parent of the child – or, rather, almost as much, because the proximity of gestation (to be discussed more in the next chapter) is such that there is always at that point a lost kinship tie to be mourned along with whatever tragedy caused the parting. There is, then, to be found in gender a basis for relatedness – marriage. Yet Christianity is distinctive in relativizing even the importance of marriage, as celibacy is presented as an even higher calling to those who wish to seek the God's kingdom above all.

While this chapter has taken a parsimonious stance on the place of nature in constructing gender, and gender in constructing kinship, it has nevertheless identified a form of gendered relatedness as a properly Christian practice: marriage. By way of a coda, then, how can that endorsement of gendered marriage as a Christian practice be defended against the critiques of Foucault, Butler and others, that it is built on illicit use of power?

Clearly, marriage is often used to inscribe patterns of subjugation and domination. This was clearly evident to Paul in the first century, and so he goes out of his way to reject the wider culture of gendered power in which he lives, pointing his readers instead towards Christ when identifying a proper model for the use of power. The unlimited power differential between Creator and creation is expressed in Christ giving Himself up for the church because 'Christ loved the church' (Eph. 5.25). Sacrifice, not domination. And so, when Paul speaks into the first-century power differential between husbands and wives, he asks husbands to pattern their love for their wives after Christ's love for the church. Even, then, if marriage were meant to contain a power differential, it cannot justifiably look like subjugation and domination. But Paul does not recommend a power differential; he recommends mutual submission: 'Be subject to one another out of reverence for Christ' (Eph. 5.21). Marriage is a gendered form of kinship, organizing affections, obligations and accountability. This gives opportunities for the grasping of power, as does any relationship. When granted power, though, the Christian is called to place it at the service of the other, out of reverence for Christ.

So far, this book has argued that blood is an adequate basis for kinship – but the blood of Christ offered to all in the Eucharist rather than the blood of genetics – but also that special kinship ties can be shared within that wider body of Christ with those with whom one shares a house or to whom one is married. In this way, the assumption that reproductive ties organise all possible kinship was firmly rejected. The book now turns to its final theme – personhood – and will argue that kinship in Christ is the true basis of earthly kinship, while at the same time identifying further bases for special ties as an expression of that wider kinship, especially as relating to the care of children.

Chapter 6

PERSONS IN CHRIST

KINSHIP BY BAPTISM

Introduction: The anthropology of personhood and kinship

Prince Andrei, in *War and Peace*, illustrates two important points for this chapter in a discussion with Pierre:

> 'But how can you live for yourself alone?' asked Pierre, becoming heated. 'What about your son, your sister, your father?'
> 'But they're the same as myself, they're not *others*', said Prince Andrei.[1]

The first way this illustrates the relationship between kinship and personhood is that human persons are at least perceived to be constituted in some sense by the communities of which they are a part, and all the more so when these are communities of kinship. Marshall Sahlins calls this 'mutuality of being', by which he means that 'kinfolk are persons who participate intrinsically in each other's existence; they are members of one another'.[2] The second is that kinship creates new ways of living 'for yourself alone', as is Prince Andrei's initial aim after the death of his wife and his return from the war.[3]

Personhood is the last of the four topics, Janet Carsten suggests, that needs to be explored to make sense of kinship. In a sense, this is obvious: claims about relatedness suggest an underlying account of what human beings are, in themselves and in their relation to one another. This is not to say that certain

---

1. Leo Tolstoy, *War and Peace*, trans. Richard Pevear and Larissa Volokhonsky (London: Vintage, 2009), 2.2.11, 384.

2. Marshall Sahlins, *What Kinship Is – And Is Not* (Chicago: University of Chicago Press, 2013), ix.

3. Or, to return to the anthropologists, and Carsten's (broadly appreciative) response to Sahlins: while this mutuality of being might evoke a 'warm, fuzzy glow', kinship is a double-edged sword that also enables '[d]ifferentiation, hierarchy, exclusion and abuse'. (Janet Carsten, 'What Kinship Does – and How', *HAU: Journal of Ethnographic Theory* 3, no. 2 (2013): 245–6.)

ideas of the person are necessarily connected with certain ideas of kinship. That would be to give the terms of reference a predictive rather than merely descriptive quality. Instead, the introduction of the concept of person into this exploration of Christianity and kinship widens the range of questions asked theologically, on the basis that such a widening has been useful for describing the breadth of human practices in anthropology, and that this experience might suggest some relevant questions to ask theologically.

Marilyn Strathern characterized Euro-American norms of kinship in this way: '*Kinship*, though, is where Westerners think about connections between bodies themselves.'[4] It has been argued that this Euro-American idea has very dubious theological origins and, indeed, that the Eucharist, which contributed historically to this notion of physical relatedness, serves to *critique* this way of thinking about kinship. This raises the question, then, as to what theological ground there might be for relatedness, if the basis in logical relations between bodies is dispensed with. After all, in Schneider's *American Kinship*, kinship according to the 'natural order of things' provides the basis for kinship according to the 'order of law' in which some people are treated *as though* they have this logical relation between their bodies.[5] As such, 'A relative is a person who is related by blood or marriage.'[6] These two forms of relatedness 'provide for relationships of diffuse, enduring solidarity' which is implied by the unity of substance (under the order of nature) and practised in the context of marriage (under the order of law).[7] This unity of substance, then, or relationship between bodies, not only has social significance but also implicates a way of thinking about persons. To put it Prince Andrei's way, kin are 'the same as myself, they're not *others*'.

In the chapter on substance, the blood of Jesus was presented as binding Christians together in the Christian imagination. In this chapter, the case will be made with greater depth, chiming with a tradition of high theological explanation of the Christian life to suggest that Christians can view themselves as properly constituted as persons *in Christ*. Accordingly, Christians should profess a logic of relations between persons, which is analogous to the one Schneider and Strathern find in Euro-American kinship, but based instead in the unity of the body of Christ. Before entering this dogmatic tradition, however, another vital Christian ritual will be discussed, to show how – at the level of ordinary practice – baptism supports professions of union with Christ. This generates a self-perception, and attendant understanding of personhood, that is neatly summarized by Paul in Gal. 2.20: 'it is no longer I who live, but it is Christ who lives in me.' It will be argued

---

4. Strathern, *Kinship, Law and the Unexpected*, 26.
5. Schneider, *American Kinship*, 26–7.
6. Ibid., 37.
7. David M. Schneider, 'Kinship, Nationality, and Religion in American Culture: Toward a Definition of Kinship', in *Symbolic Anthropology: A Reader in the Study of Symbols and Meanings*, ed. Janet L. Dolgin, D. S. Kemnitzer, and David M. Schneider (New York: Columbia University Press, 1977), 67.

that this comes to be determinative of kinship practices, in the form of the practice of spiritual, or baptismal, kinship.

This theology of personhood in Christ will be made explicit with the help of theologians, but it will be proposed that this conceptuality supports and alters everyday Christian practice, serving, as it were, like the rules of grammar. There are many more rules than most competent speakers of any language could articulate in the way that an expert in grammar might, but they demonstrate tacit knowledge of them by following them in their speech. Similarly, what is being made explicit here are theological conceptualities that most Christians may not articulate in the ways that theologians seek to, but still demonstrate tacit – and approximate – knowledge of them by observing them in practice.[8]

It will be argued, then, that the basis for Christian relatedness is this unity in the body of Christ. Special affections and obligations might, in the present age, have explicit theological justification in organizing the body – for instance, within houses, or within marriage, as described earlier – but they find their theological basis not in the idea of shared bodies but in union with Christ. This union with Christ can provide justification for the organization of affections in order that they might be deepened, in anticipation of the intimacy that might be universalized in the sanctified reality of resurrection life. However, it still exerts an outwards pressure, towards hospitality and inclusion, as it recognizes all people as recipients of welcome into the body of Christ.

Christian personhood

One of the areas of investigation into kinship and personhood that Carsten identifies concerns the nature of human relationships. While Carsten rejects as simplistic the dichotomy between 'a Western individualized person and a non-Western "joined-up" person', which was discussed earlier, she still advises the ethnographer to attend particularly to local practices to see the extent to which persons are thought of as constituted individually, relationally, or as parts of a whole, with this leading for Carsten into the issue of how a sense of personhood can be compromised by a lack of parent, child, spouse and so on.[9] This provides a useful entry point into the cross-cultural variation of understandings of personhood. It serves this book well that some of the most compelling research on this topic concerns the dissemination of Christian concepts of the person.

Joel Robbins offers an anthropological illustration, both of how understandings of personhood can vary cross-culturally, and how Christianity can shape understandings of the person. In Urapmin culture a person never eats the food they grow, but always gives it to others, who have an obligation to give them food in return. When Robbins asks why they don't eat from their own garden, he is

8. Cf. Banner, *The Ethics of Everyday Life*, 201.
9. Carsten, *After Kinship*, 84.

told that that would be to 'eat nothing', because you may fill your belly, but you won't form any social ties.[10] Robbins describes the shift with a story about Rom, an Urapmin man trying to make sense of his village's conversion to the Christian faith. Rom is reading the Parable of the Ten Young Women in Matthew and he draws out one thing in particular: 'Then they [the foolish women] want oil, but the other women say we only have enough for ourselves. The Bible says each person has their own belief. My wife can't break off part of her belief and give it to me.' Here the way in which *persons are thought of* had to adapt in order to accommodate a theological idea, which Joel Robbins summarizes: 'The individual alone is the unit of salvation.'[11]

This theory that Christianity promotes individualism will be returned to shortly, but before moving into that discussion, this serves as a perfect example to illustrate how conflicting cultures of exchange can shape the construction of interpersonal relations. Marilyn Strathern summarizes the idea (developed by Chris Gregory, following after Mauss[12]) neatly: 'In a commodity oriented economy, people . . . experience their interest in commodities as a desire to appropriate goods; in a gift oriented economy, the desire is to expand social relations.'[13] This is of course a generalization, and this is not to say that there is no notion of the individual in gift economies. Rather, Strathern adopts the distinction between gift and commodity for analytic purposes, recognizing that most cultures will sit between these two poles.[14]

How, then, does this perception of persons economically inform relatedness? An example is, once again, available from the Urapmin: in their gift economy, the elite – called, 'big men' – cannot draw on kinship idioms in asserting obligations, but rather must embellish with stories of all they have done for someone.[15] Their society is powerfully structured by gift exchange, whereas societies that use commodity exchange need a separate logic on which to base the structuring of society, and so one might expect the language of kinship to become especially significant. The way society is structured economically both reflects local perceptions of personhood and shapes local perceptions of personhood, with implications for the construction of relations generally and kinship specifically.

---

10. Joel Robbins, *Becoming Sinners: Christianity and Moral Torment In a Papua New Guinea Society* (Berkeley: University of California Press, 2004), 292.

11. Ibid., 295.

12. See Mauss' famous essay, 'Essai sur le don: Forme et raison de l'échange dans les sociétés archaïques', originally published in 1923–24 in *Année Sociologique*. English translation: Marcel Mauss, *The Gift: The Form and Reason for Exchange in Archaic Societies*, trans. W. D. Halls (London: Routledge, 2002).

13. Marilyn Strathern, *The Gender of the Gift: Problems with Women and Problems with Society in Melanesia* (Berkeley: University of California Press, 1988), 143.

14. Ibid., 7–8.

15. Robbins, *Becoming Sinners*, 203.

To choose an example from the Western world, one might think that the notion of the Roman *paterfamilias* who owns the household and everyone in it is long forgotten. However, Viviana Zelizer, in a history of the perceptions of children, points out that while children might not be regarded as economic assets in the Western world, they can still be thought of as having an *emotional* value, so that they are regarded as a must-have item in the heavily marketed perfect family.[16] This example points to two connecting ideas about the person that are significant for kinship. First, the way in which ownership is conceptualized informs the concept of a person, thereby transforming how persons are thought of, which feeds into the idea. Second, such a notion of the person might also structure the relationship between parents and children, whereas in a culture in which the idea of ownership is alien (or, moving away from one extreme, less important, or navigated in a different way), other social forces might structure the relationship in a way that is more consistent with a theological account of kinship.

The notions of self-ownership and other-ownership are disrupted by the very idea of Christ as a gift that changes the recipient. This translates poorly into commodity-type ways of thinking economically, and the division of the world into individuals. It is curious that the anthropologist Joel Robbins records his Urapmin informant individuating human persons so clearly, on a *Christian* basis. Clearly, the concept of faith can exert pressure in distinguishing persons. However, the most famous theorist of justification by faith alone – Martin Luther – draws his readers away from a preoccupation with the individual, seeing *sin* as that which is profoundly individuating, rather than faith. While it is a scriptural account of the nature of the sin that is exerting theological pressure at this juncture, rather than the need for an account of personhood for the doctrines of the Trinity or of the Incarnation, the same logic is evident in his use of orthodox trinitarian formulae in his 'Confession Concerning Christ's Supper': he writes about the self-giving of the Father, of the Son and of the Spirit.[17] This description of God's movement towards sinful human beings suggests that Luther is much less interested in the individual than Rom is.

Recent work by John Barclay on Paul's theology of grace utilizes the anthropological terminology of the gift, and describes Christ as an '*incongruous gift*'.[18] Barclay traces Paul's re-reading of scripture, searching selectively for the incongruous grace of God to Israel, in order to show how precisely that same grace – that 'root that has created and sustained Israel from its beginning'[19] – is available

---

16. Viviana Zelizer, *Pricing the Priceless Child: The Changing Social Value of Children* (Princeton: Princeton University Press, 1985), 209. Cf. Banner, *The Ethics of Everyday Life*, 64.

17. Martin Luther, 'Confession Concerning Christ's Supper (1528)', in *Word and Sacrament, Volume Three*, ed. Robert H. Fisher, trans. Robert H. Fischer, Luther's Works 37 (Philadelphia: Fortress Press, 1961).

18. John M. G. Barclay, *Paul and the Gift* (Grand Rapids: Eerdmans, 2015), 566.

19. Ibid., 568.

also to the Gentile. Barclay pairs this with Paul's account of human sin to show how, from the sinful human side (regardless of membership of Israel), one finds the unworthy recipients of incongruous grace. This leads Barclay to conclude, at the end of the book, that '[b]y starting from the Christ-event, and by clarifying with radical sharpness the unconditioned grace that was given in Christ, Paul provides resources for the dissolution of pre-formed assumptions and for the construction of boundary-erasing communities'.[20] This, he argues, was precisely the context in which Paul was operating, and was the context in which the language of grace was deployed – as a disruptive force that reshaped the identity of the communities addressed.

Still, even as Barclay concludes his book, he uses the language of the individual: 'The drama of their movement from death to life, from flesh to Spirit, and from sin to righteousness is encapsulated in baptism, whose "newness of life", derived from Christ, is experienced in new social relations and in the reconstitution of each individual self (Gal. 2.19-20).'[21] The passage he cites from Galatians seems to warrant it: 'For through the law I died to the law, so that I might live to God. I have been crucified with Christ; and it is no longer I who live, but it is Christ who lives in me. And the life I now life in the flesh by faith in the Son of God, who loved me and gave himself for me.' The recurrence of the language of 'I' warrants the language of the individual, but every way that 'I' is described militates against the separation of the individual. This 'I' is radically reconceived as being part of another – Christ – that prompts a theological question which Colin Gunton formulates thus: Are human beings properly understood individually, relationally or collectively?[22] Gunton opts for the second of these, but at the very least Paul's strong language of union with Christ, or Athanasius's soteriological account of the Incarnation, or the frequent language of the church as a body (Rom. 12.5 or 1 Cor. 12.12, for instance) might provoke a pause for thought to ask: Might it indeed be appropriate to think of human beings collectively – as collectively part of Christ – in the light of scriptural and early Christian Christology?

In this way, a further theological pressure on the notion of the person is brought to light, with respect to which Lewis Ayres insightfully points out: 'The mystery of the incarnation includes the mystery by which members of the Christian community are united to the person of Christ and purified toward the vision of God.'[23] As Christians have sought to affirm how their fates intertwine with Christ's, this has decreased the plausibility of certain more individualistic accounts of the human person. Such accounts appear less compatible with the strange notion that the human being is conjoined with Christ and shares in His body in the church.

20. Ibid., 573.
21. Ibid., 568.
22. Colin Gunton, 'Persons', in *Dictionary of Ethics, Theology and Society*, ed. Paul Barry Clarke and Andrew Linzey (London: Routledge, 1996), 638.
23. Lewis Ayres, *Nicaea and Its Legacy: An Approach to Fourth-Century Trinitarian Theology* (Oxford: Oxford University Press, 2004), 36.

In light of this supposedly 'dividual' logic of Christian personhood, Joel Robbins's discovery that the conversion of the Urapmin led to a newfound individualism should surprise the theologian. While it might be tempting simply to put the effect immediately down to the cultural baggage of missionaries to the Urapmin and other Melanesian communities, or to the reality of a Fallen world that renders Christians inconsistent with their faith, it should at least send the theologian back to their own tradition to see if their own cultural horizon has caused something to be missed.

Rom is not the only example of the convert perplexed by individualism, but his story is part of a trend that has generated an important debate in the anthropology of Christianity. In a recent article, Robbins notes that, from the beginning of the invigoration of the anthropology of Christianity in the 1990s, scholars emphasized that Christianity, especially evangelical Christianity, 'introduce[d] individualism among its converts'.[24] This individualism manifested itself, in the descriptions of anthropologists, as breaches with kin, the challenging of local traditions, simply speaking one's mind unrestrained by usual norms, or regarding the individual as the 'unit of salvation'.[25]

Robbins also records the voice of Mark Mosko, one of the more radical in a small number of dissenting voices. In his 2010 article, Mosko examines a set of Melanesian Christian communities. Melanesian cultures have been a particular focus for anthropologists interested in partible personhood, and as such it has also sustained the work of anthropologists of Christianity like Robbins who find an individualizing tendency in Christianity. Mosko begs to differ, instead finding a Christianity that sustains the partibility of personhood. In one specific instance, that of the North Mekeo, he finds that the introduction of Christianity brought not a break with partibility but rather a Christian partibility of the person.[26]

Might there be a certain degree of individualism in Christianity, perhaps found in talk of faith, repentance and, most of all, souls, which might individualize Melanesians, or others far more profoundly dividual than Western theologians are able to easily imagine?

The challenge for Rom emerged from dreams within the community about few being saved, which coheres with Rom's worries reading the Parable of the Ten Young Women, in which he sees the responsibility for salvation cast back on the individual person. What, though, should the theologian make of such a claim? On the one hand, they might wish to point out that the pastor really does save – in this case, Jesus, the High Priest, who 'nourishes and tenderly cares' for the church, 'because we are members of his body' (Eph. 5.29-30). On the other hand,

---

24. Joel Robbins, 'Dumont's Hierarchical Dynamism: Christianity and Individualism Revisited', *HAU: Journal of Ethnographic Theory* 5, no. 1 (June 2015): 176–7.

25. Ibid., 177.

26. Mark Mosko, 'Partible Penitents: Dividual Personhood and Christian Practice in Melanesia and the West', *Journal of the Royal Anthropological Institute* 16, no. 2 (1 June 2010): 231–2.

they might also recognize that seeing oneself as constituted in Christ might set up a new dividualism, patterning life in a way set apart from traditional culture, and thus seen as individualistic from the perspective of traditional Urapmin culture, as indeed appears to be the case in the parable that troubled Rom (Mt. 25.1-13), because the new Christian worldview may not recognize the old form of dividualism.

At this point, the pertinent question does not concern what the best anthropology says about individualism and Christianity, but rather what the best theology says. In light of that, the supposed theological dividualism of Christians in North Mekeo, and incipient individualism of Urapmin Christians, can be received theologically. Take the features of individualism mentioned earlier: breaches with kin, the challenging of local traditions, simply speaking one's mind unrestrained by usual norms, or regarding the individual as the unit of salvation. Certainly there is potential for theological challenges, but the character of all of them is *transitional* between the old and the new. The Christian faith might bring the value of individualism, but only in the particularization of the Christian person in transition from membership of and old culture to a new – ultimately in the transition from the old creation to the new creation, but in the present age this might be visible in the rejection of old practices, channelled through the particular human being by their newfound faith. This is entirely consonant with the new dividualism of Christianity that Mosko notes, for instance, the rendering of ideas about personal connections with God or the Devil in North Mekeo.[27] This need not worry Robbins terribly, and he is clear in a dialogue with another anthropologist, Werbner, that 'the lives of Christians are not wholly dominated by individualism'.[28]

It reveals a tension for the Christian life, situated as it is between heaven, earth and the Resurrection – united now with the ascended Christ, but looking towards the fulfilment of this union in the Eschaton. One side of this tension is evident in the public response by Justin Welby, the Archbishop of Canterbury, to the recent discovery that his biological father was not who he thought it was. While confessing that this came as a great surprise, he was emphatic that it did not change who he considered himself to be: 'I know that I find who I am in Jesus Christ, not in genetics, and my identity in him never changes.' He illustrated this with a story from his inauguration, in which the incoming Archbishop traditionally knocks at the door and waits to be received. 'Evangeline Kanagasooriam, a young member of the Canterbury Cathedral congregation, said, "We greet you in the name of Christ. Who are you, and why do you request entry?" To which I responded: "I am Justin, a servant of Jesus Christ, and I come as one seeking the grace of God to travel with you in His service together." What has changed? Nothing!'[29]

27. Ibid., 230.
28. Robbins, 'Dumont's Hierarchical Dynamism', 179.
29. Justin Welby, 'A Personal Statement from the Archbishop of Canterbury', available online: http://www.archbishopofcanterbury.org//articles.php/5704/a-personal-statement-from-the-archbishop-of-canterbury (accessed 14 April 2016).

Towards a theology of personhood for the ethics of kinship

Justin Welby's claim of identity in Christ blurs the boundaries between persons, but, at the same time, this also entails particularization, as he is removed by this participation in Christ from certain kinds of union with the world. There is a transfer, then, of God's beloved child from communion with a world that shapes their experience and action, to communion with the Triune God, who shapes their experience and action in place of the context of the old self. In his wrestling with human freedom, Barth writes – in a Pauline tradition – that freedom is only freedom if 'lived out and exercised in the act of responsibility before God'.[30] This might appear to be a strange form of compatibilism, but the hermeneutical key is to be found in the assumption of a new status in Jesus Christ, so that it is meaningful for the freedom of God to become the freedom of the human being in Christ. There is a wrestling between the old and new selves (cf. for instance Eph. 4.22-24) that is necessary for the anthropologist to make sense of Christian self-understanding, but at the same time the new self is conferred through union with Christ, whose true identity is not revealed by 'flesh or blood' (Mt. 16.17).

Kathryn Tanner makes a similar point, arguing that human nature cannot be understood in itself, precisely because human faculties 'were made to operate as they should, to operate well, only when incorporating what remains alien to them, the very perfection of Word and Spirit themselves'.[31] The 'I' the anthropologist observes may not be the 'I' that guides their actions (to the extent that they are in Christ by the Spirit in the sense, say, of Rom. 8.9-10), nor indeed the 'I' to which the Christian aspires. The logic of the latter is expressed in Barth's thought, well summarized by McKenny: 'The human subject is ontologically constituted by the summons to appropriate the grace of election, that is, to determine oneself, by one's own choice or decision, in accordance with one's divine determination.'[32] The outworking of this is a process of particularization, as the original culture ceases to provide the context for new Christian identity. Among other changes, the orientation towards old kinship norms is troubled by new kinship norms, made comprehensible in the church's teaching about the person of Jesus Christ.

John Zizioulas describes the implications of this Christian reconceiving of personhood for kinship, drawing attention to the moral theological problem of the exclusivity of affections.[33] In so doing, his work provides a helpful starting point for entering a high tradition of theological development of the concept of the 'person'.

---

30. Karl Barth, *Church Dogmatics: The Doctrine of Creation*, ed. G. W. Bromiley and T. F. Torrance, trans. H. Knight et al., vol. III/2 (Edinburgh: T&T Clark, 1960), 196.

31. Kathryn Tanner, *Christ the Key*, Current Issues in Theology 7 (Cambridge: Cambridge University Press, 2009), 28.

32. McKenny, *The Analogy of Grace*, 194-5.

33. John Zizioulas, *Being as Communion: Studies in Personhood and the Church* (Crestwood: St. Vladimir's Seminary Press, 1997), 57.

A pared-down version of his account will provide the basis for articulating the implicit logic of widespread Christian kinship practice, as it relates to personhood.

Zizioulas distinguishes three human hypostases:[34] biological, ecclesial and Eucharistic. The biological hypostasis is determined by natural necessity and therefore lacks ontological freedom, and the body that was made to be the tool for communion is repurposed as the tool for separation.[35] The ecclesial hypostasis is the one most dramatically contrasted with the biological. Freed from simple obedience to natural instincts,[36] it is revealed in Christ that human nature can be both assumed and 'hypostasized in a manner free from the ontological necessity of his biological hypostasis'.[37] This new hypostatization, in which actions are determined by love of the kind not motivated by biological instinct, is played out in the church – hence, *ecclesial* hypostasis. However, this ecclesial hypostasis is not fully realized in the present age, but rather human beings continued to be born and die as one would expect of biological hypostases, and so Zizioulas suggests an additional category: the Eucharistic hypostasis. This Eucharistic hypostasis has 'roots in the future and . . . branches in the present'.[38] While the Eucharistic hypostasis continues to operate as a biological hypostasis, their actions are determined in the light of their future reality as an ecclesial hypostasis.

Relating this to kinship, Zizioulas writes that the ecclesial hypostasis is thus oriented by this sharing in divine love towards an alternative network of relationships that transcends the exclusiveness of biological kinship.[39] Accordingly, the church's commandeering of kinship language for relations within the body fits better with the ecclesial reality to which Christians look forward, and which they are drawn to participate by God, as Eucharistic hypostases.[40]

Undergirding this account is the idea that, theologically, it is the ecclesial hypostasis that has true personhood. His argument proceeds thus: the ancient Greeks affirmed the logical priority of substance over personhood, but the doctrine of the Trinity demands the reversal of this. Indeed, for the Father to be free, His action cannot be determined by prior substance which He did not Himself determine.[41] In His freedom, the Father causes the Son and the Holy Spirit,[42] placing Himself in communion and thereby also determining His being

---

34. Hypostasis here means, approximately, 'person', though the insufficiency of this approximation will become clear in the course of the argument.

35. Zizioulas, *Being as Communion*, 52–3.

36. Ibid., 53.

37. Ibid., 56.

38. Ibid., 58–9.

39. Ibid., 57.

40. Ibid., 60.

41. Ibid., 43.

42. John Zizioulas, *Lectures in Christian Dogmatics*, ed. Douglas Knight (London: T&T Clark, 2008), 79. Cf. Zizioulas, *Being as Communion*, 44.

which, Zizioulas explains, is 'the personal existence of God'.[43] To say that 'God is love' (1 Jn 4.16), for Zizioulas, is to say that love '*constitutes* His being' as it is love that makes God what He is. God's ontological freedom is to be identified with this love, and that ontological freedom also gives hope to human beings of becoming 'an authentic person'.[44] In love, God determines His own being, and therefore He can be said to be exercising real freedom, as He is not constrained by a prior nature that He did *not* determine. The human person can then share in this ontological freedom of God by sharing in this love, thereby receiving a mode of being not determined by nature but shared with the Father, by participation in His freedom. The human being, then, is free – and therefore also authentically a person – to the extent that they participate in the freedom of the Father, with their actions being oriented in love towards communion with God and the church.[45]

Clearly, this account of Christian theological anthropology is particular to Zizioulas. However, Zizioulas properly lays claim here to a deep tradition of Christian construction of the person. He sees himself as an expositor of Cappadocian Trinitarian theology and adopts Gregory of Nyssa's language of causation within the Trinity in order to describe human personhood and its relation with freedom.

For Gregory of Nyssa, God has no source, but the Father is the uncaused cause (*aition*) of Son and Spirit.[46] Gregory explains this with cautious Greek, translated so as to show the tortured precision, 'We do not deny the difference between the cause and the caused, in which alone we grasp that one is separated from the other, but believe there to be, one which is the cause, and another which is of the cause, and we consider there to be another difference in the one being from the cause. For one, directly from the first [cause], the other, through the one from the first [cause].'[47] In order to describe the causality between Father and Son, Gregory uses the term '*Monogenes*' – 'Only Begotten'[48] – grounded in descriptions, like Jn 1.18, of Jesus as 'God the Only Begotten' (*monogenēs Theos*). Gregory distinguishes Father, Son and Spirit in their relation to one another, described in terms of causation. McPartlan summarizes the Cappadocian tradition thus, in a way informed by Zizioulas's own reading of the tradition: 'The Cappadocians thus identified, at the origin of being, the person of the Father, characterized by absolute freedom in

---

43. Zizioulas, *Being as Communion*, 41.
44. Ibid., 44.
45. Ibid., 50.
46. Paul McPartlan, 'Person', in *Encyclopedia of Christian Theology*, ed. Jean-Yves Lacoste (London: Routledge, 2005), 1228.
47. *tēn kata to aition kai aitiaton diaphoran ouk arnoumetha, en hō monō diakrinesthai to heteron tou heterou katalambanomen, tō to men aition pisteuein einai, to de ek tou aitiou. kai tou ex aitias ontos, palin allēn diaphoran ennooumen. To men gar prosechōs ek tou prōtou, to de dia tou prosechōs ek tou prōtou* . . . (Gregory of Nyssa, *To Ablabius, On Not Three Gods* (PG 45:133b)).
48. Gregory of Nyssa (PG 45:133b-c).

communion with the Son and Spirit. This is the pattern of true personhood; and, in so far as humanity is made in the image of God, this pattern also has relevance for anthropology.'[49]

Gregory's development of the conceptuality of intra-trinitarian relations reveals the context in which the very idea of the person, as spoken about today, came about. Indeed, the anthropology of the person testifies to this. Marcel Mauss's seminal anthropological lecture on the subject, *A Category of the Human Mind: The Notion of Person; the Notion of Self*, offers a genealogy of the 'subject', *personne*, and with it a history of the notion of the person in which Christian doctrinal debates play a key role in the development of the notion of the person.[50] Two historical episodes are determinedly Christian: first, there is the episode of 'The Christian "person" (*personne*)', which explores a range of patristic doctrinal discussions, and second, there is the final episode, 'The 'person' (*personne*): a psychological being', in which the Pietists, Puritans, Wesleyans and Moravian Brothers play roles.[51] Mauss identifies an array of theological debates to be informing the development of the idea, which he neatly sums up as the unity of person, Church and God. It is perhaps a little simplistic to say, as he does, that 'It was resolved after many discussions', but he is spot on when he writes that, in order to record the role of Christianity in informing the notion of the person, 'It is the entire history of the Church that would have here to be retraced'.[52]

While the word 'person' has had its meaning expanded by theology, its ultimate origins are pre-Christian. Paul McPartlan traces the ancient origins of the word 'person' to a Roman adaption of *phersu*, meaning 'mask', to *persona*, from '*personare*, "to speak through"', referring to a mask used ritually by the Etruscan cult of 'P(h)ersephone'.[53] In the Roman world, the word '*persona*' would come to be used to refer to 'persons' in grammar in the third century BC, and to refer to social and legal roles in the first century BC.[54] While that might be the origin of the English word 'person', its meaning has been deeply informed by its roots in Greece, where the word '*prosopon*' referred to a face as well as a mask, but was

---

49. McPartlan, 'Person', 1228. This last point, McPartlan supports with reference to Gregory of Nyssa, *Great Catechism*, 5 (PG 45:24c-d).

50. Marcel Mauss, 'A Category of the Human Mind: The Notion of Person; the Notion of Self', in *The Category of the Person: Anthropology, Philosophy, History*, ed. Michael Carrithers, Steven Collins, and Steven Lukes, trans. W. D. Halls (Cambridge: Cambridge University Press, 1985). Translating his 1938 *Huxley Memorial Lecture*, published as 'Une Catégorie de l'esprit humain: la notion de personne celle de "moi"', *Journal of the Royal Anthropological Institute* 68 (1938): 263–81.

51. Mauss, 'A Category of the Human Mind', 19–22.

52. Ibid., 19.

53. McPartlan, 'Person', 1227. McPartlan's overview of the history of the theology of the person will form the basis for this brief account, but primary sources will be investigated directly, and the chapter will depart from his account at a few points.

54. McPartlan, 'Person', 1228.

given its philosophical depth both by its theatrical origins and by its use by both Plato and Aristotle.

The movement from the human individual – which is to say an instance in a set, or a member of a species – to the notion of the human *person* was driven theologically, and in part by accident, being influenced by theological debates about *divine* persons, as will be seen. The term 'person' and its etymological forebears convey meaning that the language of the individual did not convey, and some of that meaning has rubbed off on human beings from the study of the divine. The key intellectual turn came with debates about the nature of God and the status of Jesus Christ.

Theologically, the origins of the use of the Greek word '*prosopon*' with respect to the Trinity are found in Hippolytus, who lived from around AD 170 to 236.[55] However, Hippolytus showed himself to be uncertain about the word, using it only for Father and Son, and not for the Holy Spirit. He would contrive other ways of describing the Spirit, in one place saying, 'There are not two gods but one, and *two persons*, and a third *oikonomian*.'[56]

Tertullian, writing in Latin between 197 and 217,[57] would use the language of *persona* in the context of both the doctrine of the Trinity and the doctrine of the Incarnation. He used the language of *persona* to describe God as one substance but three persons, and Jesus as both God and Man, one person with both divine and human 'substance' (*substantiam*), later in the same work.[58] Tertullian thereby formalized the chief challenge in the ensuing debates: How does one affirm that Jesus Christ was one person with two natures, and that the divine nature was unitary (so that God could be called one) but at the same time tri-personal?

In his opposition to Arianism in the fourth century, Athanasius articulated the otherness of the Son from the Father while still affirming that they shared in the being or substance of God.[59] At this time, the language of *ousia* and *hupostasis* were not yet distinguished in the way that they would be soon after.[60] Hebrews 1.3, for instance, uses *hupostaseōs* to describe that which the Son shares as the imprint

---

55. Ibid.

56. Hippolytus of Rome, *Against Noetus* 14 (PG 10:821a). The date and authorship have also been challenged, cf. Ronald E. Heine, 'Hippolytus, Ps-Hippolytus and the Early Canons', in *The Cambridge History of Early Christian Literature*, ed. Frances Young, Lewis Ayres, and Andrew Louth (Cambridge: Cambridge University Press, 2004), 142–51. For a less detailed, but more recent treatment, see Riemer Roukema, *Jesus, Gnosis and Dogma* (London: T&T Clark, 2010), 175–6.

57. Ronald E. Heine, 'The Beginnings of Latin Christian Literature', in *The Cambridge History of Early Christian Literature*, ed. Frances Young, Lewis Ayres, and Andrew Louth (Cambridge: Cambridge University Press, 2004), 133.

58. Tertullian, *Against Praxeas* 11–12 (PL 2:167c–178c); 27 (PL 2:191b).

59. *To de idion tēs ousias tou Patro (hōmologētai gar ēdē touto einai ho Huios)* (Athanasius of Alexandria, *Orations against the Arians* 20 (PG 26:53a).)

60. McPartlan, 'Person', 1228.

(*charaktēr*) of the Father and so was using it to describe substance or being, and certainly not the individuation of persons. The language of three *hupostaseis* was not yet developed in the manner that would later be considered orthodox. Indeed Athanasius uses precisely that expression in order to describe the theology of his enemy, Arius.[61] The 342 Synod of Sardica characterized the Arians much the same as affirming the 'hypostases of the Father, Son and Holy Spirit to be various and separate'.[62] The Synod itself affirmed there 'to be one hypostasis, which the heretics call "being [*ousian*]", of Father and of Son and of Holy Spirit'.[63] In other words, the Synod strongly affirmed an anti-Arian position using the language of God as one *hupostasis* that would appear heretical only a little later in ecclesiastical history.

The Cappadocians – Basil of Caesarea, Gregory of Nyssa and Gregory of Nazianzus – brought about the key pivot in the meaning of *hupostasis* in the latter half of the fourth century. Sabellian modalism came into focus and the word '*prosopon*', given its association with theatrical masks, suggested a modalist reduction of Father, Son and Spirit to three ways of being. As such, they invested the term with 'ontological weight'[64] by identifying *prosopon* with *hupostasis*, which previously meant 'substance', and carefully distinguished *hupostasis* (for the three-ness) from *ousia* (for the one-ness). Basil was scathing of any who failed to distinguish *ousia* and *hupostasis*, which was consistent with the Synod of Sardica, but had an eye beyond simply affirming divine unity towards defining terms for both one-ness and three-ness.[65] With a rhetorical flourish, he declared even Sabellius was better than those who identified *ousian* with *hupostasin*; Sabellius may have been muddled, but at least he divided the persons in some way when claiming the *hupostasin* needed to change form when passing from Father, to Son, to Spirit.[66]

This reflected a shift in Basil's own writing. For instance, in his major work *Against Eunomius*, Basil uses the phrase *treis hupostaseis* to indicate the three persons, but this is the only instance of such a use of *hupostasis* in that major

---

61. *Hōste treis eisin hupostaseis* (Athanasius of Alexandria, *Letter Concerning the Councils of Ariminum and Seleucia* 16 (PG 26:709b).)

62. *diaphorous einai tas hupostaseis tou Patros, kai tou Huiou, kai tou hagiou Pneumatos, kai einai kechōrismenas.* (Theodoret of Cyrus, *Ecclesiastical History* 2.6 (PG 82:1012c).)

63. *mian einai hupostasin ēn autoi hoi hairetikoi ousian prosagoreuousi, tou Patros, kai tou Huios, kai tou hagiou Pneumatos.* (Theodoret of Cyrus, 2.6 (PG 82:1012c–d).)

64. McPartlan, 'Person', 1228.

65. *Hoi de tauton legontes ousian kai hupostasin anagkazontai prosopa monon homologein diaphora, kai en tō periistasthai legein treis hupostaseis, heuriskontai me pheugontes to tou Sabelliou kakon . . .* (Basil of Caesarea, *Letters* 236.6 (PG 32:884c).)

66. *. . . hos kai autos, pollachou sugcheon ten ennoian, epicheirei diairein ta prosopa, ten autēn hupostasin legōn pros ten ekastote parempiptousan chreian metaschēmatizesthai.* (Basil of Caesarea, 236.6 (PG 32:884c).)

text.⁶⁷ It is later, in *Epistle 236*, that the use of *hupostasis* as 'person' is presented as standard. There, the distinction between *hupostasis* and *ousia* allows the word *hupostasis* to be deployed to the persons of the Trinity to grant that 'ontological weight' that McPartlan mentions.⁶⁸ Lucian Turcescu argues that it can offer that weight because of an analogy between 'generic' (*ousia*) and the 'particular' (*hupostasis*).⁶⁹ The usual sense of *hupostasis* as a particular instantiation of a generic *ousia* can convey that God does not just have three difference masks. However, this is one analogy among others, and it does not serve to affirm, for instance, that the Son is simply a particular instantiation of a divine genus. Basil borrowed the generic-particular analogy in order to substantiate the notion of the person as applied to the Trinity, but this separated the meaning of *hupostasis* from any sense of a particular instantiation of a *genus*.

The identification of *hupostasis* with *prosopon* generated semantic cross-pollination, and with it the new meaning to the word *hupostasis*, which would later become *persona* and, from there, 'person'. This entailed the easier separation of persons and the greater salience of relation over the uniting power of the *genus*. In this way, the context is provided for Gregory's discussion of intra-trinitarian relations that Zizioulas develops.

So what does this historical background to Gregory of Nyssa have to do with personhood and kinship? In charting the history of the concept of the person, Mauss looks to later modern developments for the psychologizing of the category of the person as it applies to the human person. The earlier patristic era that Mauss charts is what feeds Zizioulas's account of both divine and human personhood. He reaches back to an earlier Christian conceptuality of personhood, in the light of which he can offer an account of human personhood that is conceived together with divine personhood, implicating some sort of human participation in divine personhood. Zizioulas offers an account of human personhood apart from this participation, certainly – as biological hypostasis – but he distinguishes this from the personhood that the Christian receives by the grace of God, and in the light of which the Christian lives and orients their lives. This personhood is marked by communion, and for Zizioulas a person can participate in that communion by the practice of the sacraments. Accordingly, might it not be possible as well for this Eucharistic hypostasis (which is the biological hypostasis animated in conformity to their ecclesial future⁷⁰) to have other practices beyond the sacraments that are properly conformed to this ecclesial future? In the next section, it will be proposed that the practice of spiritual kinship provides an example of kinship practice

---

67. Lucian Turcescu, 'Prosōpon and Hypostasis in Basil of Caesarea's "Against Eunomius" and the Epistles Author(s)', *Vigiliae Christianae* 51, no. 4 (November 1997): 379.

68. McPartlan, 'Person', 1228.

69. Turcescu, 'Prosōpon and Hypostasis in Basil', 389.

70. Described as 'roots in the future and . . . branches in the present'. (Zizioulas, *Being as Communion*, 58–9.)

properly conformed to this new identity, as Paul describes it: 'it is no longer I who live, but it is Christ who lives in me' (Gal. 2.20).

This new identity that Christians have *in Christ* is made available by the Spirit, who satisfies the conditions by which the human being realizes now the reality of the adoption to which Paul looked forward eagerly (Rom. 8.23). After all, 'When we cry, "Abba! Father!" it is that very Spirit bearing witness within our spirit that we are children of God' (Rom. 8.15-16, cf. also Gal. 4.6). J. Todd Billings points out that in the writings of Paul, there is a trinitarian grammar to this adoption: 'initiated by the Father, mediated by the Spirit, and grounded in the person and work of Jesus Christ'.[71]

Accordingly, Tanner proposes that 'There is no general relationship of sonship which includes both Christ and us, but a unique relationship between the two of them which we come to share in virtue of our connection with this one Son (1 Cor. 1.9; Rom. 8.29)'.[72] Janet Martin Soskice makes a similar argument in her account of the divine names: 'We are jaded now by sloppy eighteenth-century rhetoric of the "fatherhood of God and the brotherhood of man", a noble aspiration perhaps, but not the New Testament message. In Christian teaching, it is because Jesus is "Son" that God is "Father".'[73] So too, it is because Jesus is Son that the Christian meaningfully calls another Christian 'brother' or 'sister'. The relation between human persons cannot be understood apart from the mediation of God. Accordingly, Jesus commands His hearers to 'call no one your father on earth, for you have one Father – the one in heaven' (Mt. 23.9). This is implicit in Barth's challenge to parents and children to recognize only Father and Son as truly fulfilling the responsibilities that attend each.[74] The Trinity need not (and should not) be said to expand to include other newly divine persons, but rather the Christian can hope to receive through participation in the baptism of the Incarnate Son the description 'This is my Son, the Beloved, with whom I am well pleased' (Mt. 3.17). This new identity that the Christian is granted is rooted in Christ's personhood, and accordingly, also Christ's Sonship, which has implications not just for the relation of the Christian to their God but also for the Christian to their fellow participant, with whom they share in one body.

---

71. J. Todd Billings, *Union with Christ: Reframing Theology and Ministry for the Church* (Grand Rapids: Baker, 2011), 19. Burke reiterates this trinitarian dynamic, affirming that the Spirit and Son are intertwined in adoption. (Trevor J. Burke, *Adopted into God's Family: Exploring a Pauline Metaphor*, New Studies in Biblical Theology (Downers Grove: IVP, 2006), 143.)

72. Tanner, *Christ the Key*, 151–2.

73. Janet Martin Soskice, *The Kindness of God* (Oxford: Oxford University Press, 2007), 83.

74. Barth, *Church Dogmatics*, 1961, III/4:279. Cf. also Karl Barth, *Church Dogmatics: The Doctrine of the Word of God*, ed. G. W. Bromiley and T. F. Torrance, trans. A. T. Mackay et al., 2nd edn., vol. I/1 (Edinburgh: T&T Clark, 1975), 458

Needless to say, the account just offered draws on a tradition of high explanation, and certainly not a comprehensive account of that tradition. Indeed, it is not intended that Zizioulas's account be taken uncritically.[75] It is simply contended that something like this is evident in the grammar of Christian cultural thinking about personhood and kinship, which is visible in the shaping of distinctive practices, such as that of spiritual kinship.

---

75. There are two main problems. First, Turcescu critiques his account as superimposing the categories of philosophical personalism on theology. Zizioulas emphatically denies the charge, and clarifies that his engagement amounts to a critique of their concern about the 'impasse of human personhood' and presentation of a distinctly theological resolution. Papanikolaou summarizes Zizioulas: 'only a trinitarian theology that affirms the monarchy of the Father can ground and justify the philosophical notions of person in terms of freedom, uniqueness, and relationality'. (Lucian Turcescu, ' "Person" versus "Individual", and Other Modern Misreadings of Gregory of Nyssa', *Modern Theology* 18, no. 4 (1 October 2002): 527–39; John Zizioulas, *Communion and Otherness: Further Studies in Personhood and the Church*, ed. Paul McPartlan (London: T&T Clark, 2006), 140–1; Aristotle Papanikolaou, 'Is John Zizioulas an Existentialist in Disguise? Response to Lucian Turcescu', *Modern Theology* 20, no. 4 (October 2004): 605.) Second, key to Zizioulas' argument is the claim that for the Father to be free, His action cannot be determined by prior substance He did not determine. The problem can be shown by re-naming the two horns of a dilemma Peter van Inwagen presents for freedom generally: first, if the act of the Father is determined by some prior substance over which God had no decision, then God is not free and the argument is struck by the horn of determinism; on the other side, if the act of the Father is entirely undetermined (and what would there be to determine the decision of the Father if His very being is still to be determined?) then the argument is struck by the horn of *in*determinism: 'an undetermined action is simply a matter of chance'. (Peter van Inwagen, 'Free Will Remains a Mystery: The Eighth Philosophical Perspectives Lecture', *Philosophical Perspectives* 14 (2000): 15.) If it is simply a matter of chance, then it cannot properly be called the free decision *of the Father*, as the causing of the Son and the Spirit are determined not by the nature of the Father, but by chance. If so, Zizioulas' account of the priority of the Father does not attain the theological *desideratum* of divine freedom and risk subordinationism. Alan Torrance has proposed that the *ousia* of God could still be identified with primordial communion of the three persons, which avoids the danger of differentiating the personhood of the Father from that of the Son, or indeed, the Spirit. The persons are then said to be free to the extent that there exists unconstrained orientation towards the other in full recognition of the worth of the other. In other words, freedom is found in the loving recognition of the other as the proper recipient of love (Alan Torrance, *Persons in Communion: Trinitarian Description and Human Participation* (Edinburgh: T&T Clark, 1996), 290–1.) This retains what is needed here, for offering a Christian account of the nature of personhood, that also makes sense of Christian adoption as participation in the Sonship of Christ.

Practising baptism: Spiritual kinship

The recognition of baptismal kinship emerges from the coincidence of ideas that, first, the community of believers must develop practices of mutual upbuilding and accountability, and second, that baptism disrupts the culturally prescribed limits to affections and obligations. Its origins are found in sponsorship, with the sponsor acting as a guarantor of the reality of the faith of the one being baptized. In the Roman liturgy, the infant was asked, 'Do you believe . . .' and the sponsor responded, 'I believe . . .'; in North Africa, the sponsor was addressed, 'Does he believe . . .', and they responded 'He believes . . .'[76]

Lynch claims sponsorship emerged in response to two problems the Christian church faced from the middle of the second century. First, a large number of adult converts were expected to have a Christian to vouch for their sincerity. Second, Christians were having children who were coming forward for baptism, and so the question of the participation of infants and young children in the liturgy was raised.[77] Derrick Bailey finds no evidence for sponsorship prior to a brief reference by Tertullian around the years 198–200 (baptism itself is a separate matter).[78] From the third to the fourth centuries, however, elaborate procedures for the preparation and baptism of adults and children emerged.

Originally, parents or other family would sponsor the child, and involved no additional responsibility.[79] Even still, Tertullian, writing around 200–206, expressed fear about the nature of the risk guarantors at an infant baptism took upon themselves.[80] With risk came risk-mitigating strategies: prayer, encouragement and instruction of the child. In the early Middle Ages, when the switch was made from parental to non-kin sponsorship, sponsorship's obligations and risks would evolve into a close, personal bond: *spiritual* kinship.

Prior to this shift, Augustine proposed its theological presupposition. Writing to Boniface, Augustine claims that the whole of the church is involved in offering the child, and so the parent-sponsor stands for the whole church at baptism. He did not challenge the role of the parent-sponsor by advocating non-kin sponsorship,

---

76. Joseph H. Lynch, *Godparents and Kinship in Early Medieval Europe* (Princeton: Princeton University Press, 1986), 120–1.

77. Ibid., 83.

78. Bailey also dismisses any comparison to the one who brings forward the neophyte in Judaism as superficial, the claim that Justin Martyr refers to sponsorship as a misreading of the evidence, and he sharply sees off any comparison to the *ba'al berit* at circumcision as this, he claims, does not appear until the tenth century. (Derrick S. Bailey, *Sponsors at Baptism and Confirmation: An Historical Introduction to Anglican Practice* (London: SPCK, 1952), 1–4.)

79. See Hippolytus' description of baptism in the early third century, and Augustine's assumption that sponsors would be parents in the early fifth century in Letter 98.2, discussed in Lynch, *Godparents and Kinship in Early Medieval Europe*, 122, 125.

80. Lynch, *Godparents and Kinship in Early Medieval Europe*, 123–4.

but he still undermined their significance through emphasis on representation.[81] With baptism came membership, sealed by the sacrament, of the community of the church, 'our mother'.[82]

Though Pseudo-Dionysius mentions non-kin sponsors, and speaks of a *theios pater* – a 'god father'[83] – evidence for the development from sponsorship to spiritual kinship comes with Caesarius of Arles. Caesarius 'abandoned this fiction' of prebaptismal fitness that had previously attended baptismal liturgy, and focused on 'postbaptismal duties'.[84] On these, Caesarius was emphatic: 'admonish and discipline those whom you have received from the font just as you do those who are born from you'.[85]

The precedent of banning marriage between spiritual kin emerged in the East with Justinian, and so was unfamiliar in the West when Boniface remarks on the strangeness of such a ban.[86] Jussen remarks that the origins of the incest taboo with spiritual kinship might be found in the expectation that sponsors would educate the sponsored child, thereby taking on a role like parenthood, though he goes on to doubt that the ban was even respected in the West.[87] Nevertheless, the ban indicates the sincerity with which sponsorship was regarded as kinship. By the time of Gregory of Tours' *History*, two generations later, the relationship was no longer described as that of a guarantor, but the language of kinship had replaced it. If baptism was a spiritual rebirth (Jn 3:5-7), it entailed a spiritual re-kinning.[88]

Spiritual kinship subverted kinship norms not just through appropriation but through divergence. Jussen notes its dissimilarity to Roman adoption: spiritual kinship did not create inheritance rights or an heir: 'It was not a corrective to biological chance, nor a fiction.'[89] Further, it demanded no involvement in family feuds, and there were no complex family trees tying spiritual kinship with blood ties, though these emerged later.[90] Still, that is not to say that spiritual kinship was not open to abuse, and Jussen's chronicle of King Gunthcramn provides ample evidence of this. However, spiritual kinship's association not with obligations to

---

81. Augustine, *Letters 1-99*, 98.5, 429.
82. Ibid.
83. Pseudo-Dionysius, 'On The Ecclesiastical Hierarchy', in *Dionysius the Pseudo-Areopagite: The Ecclesiastical Hierarchy*, trans. Thomas L. Campbell (Lanham: University Press of America, 1981), 89. Cited Lynch, *Godparents and Kinship in Early Medieval Europe*, 138.
84. Lynch, *Godparents and Kinship in Early Medieval Europe*, 148.
85. Caesarius of Arles, *Sermons, Volume 1 (1-80)*, 13.2, 75-6. Cited in Bernhard Jussen, *Spiritual Kinship as Social Practice: Godparenthood and Adoption in the Early Middle Ages*, trans. Pamela Selwyn (Newark: University of Delaware Press, 2000), 127.
86. Jussen, *Spiritual Kinship as Social Practice*, 36.
87. Ibid., 40.
88. Lynch, *Godparents and Kinship in Early Medieval Europe*, 170.
89. Jussen, *Spiritual Kinship as Social Practice*, 22.
90. Lynch, *Godparents and Kinship in Early Medieval Europe*, 27.

feuds or inheritance but with 'words such as "friendship" and "love" . . . subject only to rather vague norms', is telling.[91] The font produced a commitment similar to blood or marriage, with love and education and responsibility attending it, but without the binding power of property in the form of inheritance. Existing kinship norms were not duplicated, but commandeered and subverted, creating a parallel social system. Spiritual kinship interwove with ordinary kinship, creating relationships of *compaternitas* – 'coparenthood' between sponsor and natural parent.[92] Adrian Thatcher describes spiritual kinship as making 'porous' the usual boundaries of kin and non-kin, with the child at the centre.[93]

Sponsorship grew in responsibility and the number of sponsors per child increased in the high and late Middle Ages.[94] Family trees became complicated, with godparenthood, coparenthood, spiritual fatherhood (baptizing priest to child) and spiritual siblinghood (baptized child to non-spiritual children of the godparent).[95] These ties connected differently with blood and marriage, so there were no spiritual nephews or nieces, or godchildren-in-law. The purpose of this smaller spiritual kinship group was to welcome the child into a much larger family, and to teach them the household rules, as it were, of their much larger family: the church. This membership of two families is an excellent example of what Wayne Meeks termed the 'amphibian life' of the average Christian.[96]

Spiritual kinship grew organically, sometimes under attack.[97] It has appropriated and subverted kinship norms, putting them to the service of the establishment of communities of accountability that reflect membership of Christ's body, and thereby 'troubling', as Michael Banner calls it, kinship.[98] Spiritual kinship would be a reality of Zizioulas's Eucharistic hypostasis, re-patterning present reality in conformity to resurrection reality, in the likeness of Christ.

The radical disruption of baptism to prevailing kinship norms is strikingly revealed in Juliet du Boulay's ethnography of life in the Greek Orthodox village of

---

91. Jussen, *Spiritual Kinship as Social Practice*, 215.

92. Lynch, *Godparents and Kinship in Early Medieval Europe*, 165.

93. Adrian Thatcher, *Theology and Families* (Oxford: Blackwell, 2007), 202.

94. Joseph H. Lynch, *Christianizing Kinship: Ritual Sponsorship in Anglo-Saxon England* (Ithaca: Cornell, 1998), 123.

95. Ibid., 165.

96. Wayne A. Meeks, *The Origins of Christian Morality: The First Two Centuries* (New Haven: Yale University Press, 1993), 109.

97. Luther saw it as indicative of the growth of the power of 'clerical tyrants' even though his criticism reveals agreement with the basic principle: 'They have in common the sacraments, the Spirit, faith, and spiritual gifts and blessings, by reason of which they are more closely related in Spirit than through the outward act of sponsorship.' (Martin Luther, 'The Persons Related by Consanguinity and Affinity Who Are Forbidden to Marry According to the Scriptures, Leviticus 18 (1522)', in *The Christian in Society II*, ed. Walther I. Brandt, Luther's Works 45 (Philadelphia: Muhlenberg Press, 1962), 8.)

98. Banner, *The Ethics of Everyday Life*, 60.

Ambeli, as first noticed by Banner. In Ambeli, blood is much used as a metaphor, so that in marriage, blood is said to mix and conjoin to form a new relatedness. This forms the basis of organization into a tight union of kinship, with high degrees of obligation within the household. This tight-knit sharing of obligations is counteracted, however, by baptism, with the anointing oil also being said to change the blood, so that marriage between any spiritual kin is forbidden.[99] Indeed, most striking of all is the tradition (now extinct[100]) of excluding the parents from the ritual of baptism, with the mother kneeling to the godparents afterwards, to ask for the return of their child.[101] This testifies to the thoroughgoing way in which baptism is taken to have disruptive social significance. In one place, it is partially absorbed into the culture of kinship, extending incest prohibitions and being thought to change the blood, and in another place it displaces the pre-existing tie during the course of the ritual of baptism. Dying and rising with Christ entails, in Ambeli, new kinship within the church that is not to be confused with kinship normally imagined, even if it comes to possess the same sorts of powers to arrange people that usual idioms of kinship have.

Beginning and ending kinship

Spiritual kinship has been identified as one way in which kinship in Christ might be honoured in smaller groups, just as the house and marriage were mentioned in previous chapters. How, then, might a Christian vision of personhood impact on when and how kinship is endowed, and whether it is permanent?

In Schneider's *American Kinship*, persons were conceived of as constituted by static, transmittable substance. Not all people imagine themselves to be constituted statically. Barbara Bodenhorn notes that the Iñupiat in northern Alaska

> seemed to assign relatively little significance to what bodies 'are' and to give rather a lot of weight to what they 'do'. Iñupiaq kinship relations are central to social life; according to many people, they allow you to survive in difficult situations. However... the relations are so potentially transformative that there is virtually no immutable basis for putting forward a claim of kin-related resources.[102]

---

99. Du Boulay, *Cosmos, Life, and Liturgy in a Greek Orthodox Village*, 210ff.
100. Ibid., 424.
101. Ibid., 210–11.
102. Barbara Bodenhorn, '"He Used to Be My Relative": Exploring the Bases of Relatedness among Iñupiat of Northern Alaska', in *Cultures of Relatedness: New Approaches to the Study of Kinship*, ed. Janet Carsten (Cambridge: Cambridge University Press, 2000), 128. 'Iñupiat' is the collective noun for the people, whereas Iñupiaq is singular, or refers to the language or culture.

If one identifies with acts more readily than the constitution of the body, that is likely to impact relatedness, as bodily idioms are likely to give way to others in making sense of social connections. In this instance, '"labour" does for Iñupiaq kinship what "biology" does for many other systems'.[103] Bodenhorn finds that for a relation to be 'real' depends not on biological constitution or some other permanent basis, but rather on the constant 'hard work' of re-establishing social ties through action.[104] Consequently, '"kinship" does not act as a controlling element in the property system. Individuals are free to move within families as well as across space, preventing interdependent actors from becoming dependent relatives'.[105] This requires the context of an earlier claim: 'natal bonds are recognised but given virtually no *determining* character whatsoever. It is not somehow what makes kinship "real"'.[106] In another place 'Giving birth thus does not necessarily create "rights" ... Biological kinship is rarely denied, but the *primary* relationships, both in affect and in moral weight, are formed with those who brought you up.'[107]

The trajectory of Bodenhorn's argument suggests that while birth is socially significant, it does not create permanent connections. The difference appears in the interpretation of personhood – even if the Iñupiat subscribed to the idea that the child and birth mother shared substance, it would make little difference, as relationships are constituted by time, effort and work. This is kinship by sweat, not blood, and to any detractors who consider this implausible, Bodenhorn underlines the point: 'And it is hard work. Having to construct and reconstruct one's social world virtually on a daily basis can be stressful stuff. People develop ulcers wondering whether they are "getting it right".'[108] For a theology of kinship, this raises an important question about personhood that connects closely with the chapter on shared substance: In what ways are relationships between persons constituted, and where, if at all, is permanence to be found, both in relationships and in self-perception?

The stability provided by notions of biological relatedness is captured by Jem in *To Kill a Mockingbird*: 'Atticus says you can choose your friends but you sho' can't choose your family, an' they're still kin to you no matter whether you acknowledge 'em or not, and it makes you look right silly when you don't.'[109] It looks silly not to recognize your kin because it is so obvious, whereas for an Iñupiaq person, kinship

---

103. Bodenhorn, 'He Used to Be My Relative', 128.
104. Ibid., 143.
105. Ibid., 146.
106. Ibid., 141.
107. Ibid. The term '[b]iological' clouds the picture, but is offered as a re-expression of the concept of 'Giving birth', and connects with the idea of 'natal bonds'. Given Bodenhorn's careful rejection of the importance of bodily constitution to Iñupiaq personhood, '[b]iological' is most likely to indicate emergence from a person, rather than implicating shared substance.
108. Bodenhorn, 'He Used to Be My Relative', 143.
109. Harper Lee, *To Kill a Mockingbird* (London: Heinemann, 2015), 248.

is in the recognition. Consider again Strathern's comment: '*Kinship*, though, is where Westerners think about connections between bodies themselves.'[110] The body does not just individuate but also connects. This conceptual use of the body grants meaning to the 'constitutive rule[s]'[111] in which the body becomes the basis of the theory of relatedness to another person, which means that where the story is complicated by egg/sperm/mitochondrial donations, surrogacy, adoption or divorce, relatedness tends then to be described in the terms of discovery which 'once known cannot be laid aside'.[112] In the descriptions of Western kinship practices offered by Strathern and Bestard, negotiation of kinship is grounded in the body, whereas among the Iñupiat it is grounded in work. Now in the case of the Iñupiat, this kinship by sweat emerges from a perception of personhood that 'assign[s] relatively little value to what bodies "are" and to give rather a lot of weight to what they "do"'.[113]

What stability might attend an account of kinship that denies the social significance of the relationship 'between bodies'? Marriage provides a straightforward starting point: Augustine's defence of the unconditionality of marriage vows reflected the unconditionality of the covenant that unites Christ and His Bride, the church.[114] Jesus's description of the Old Testament permission to divorce as being for the 'hard-hearted' leads to his declaration that remarriage after divorce is adulterous (Mt. 19.8-9, a charge Jesus widens for all, cf. Mt. 5.28). The ambiguous exception 'except for unchastity [*porneia*]' stops the door from being closed entirely. However, given His emphatic 'what God has joined together, let no one separate' (Mt. 19.6), it seems more likely that Jesus is permitting a first-century woman to remarry after being evicted from her home and replaced than He is to be endorsing a refusal to forgive adultery. Setting aside the reasons for divorce, there are clear grounds for regarding marriage as based in unconditional covenant and thus permanent, as indeed is explicit in the common vow to commit to one another for better or for worse.

Childbirth does not connect intrinsically to a covenant, however, and if it did it could only go in one direction. James Mumford explores the implications of this emerging quality of life, comparing it to 'the contract formulation of encounters'. He finds the latter in Barth's theology of social life and traces it back to seventeenth-century political philosophy. His worry is that such an account of social life denigrates those encounters that demonstrate the 'fortuitousness of life', with persons being thrown together in ways that are not bilateral or equal in their dependence on the other. He focuses on the emergence of babies *in utero*, 'newones', and the issues it raises for abortion, though his description could pertain to the normal emergence of adult relationships. These only very rarely

---

110. Strathern, *Kinship, Law and the Unexpected*, 26.
111. Bestard, 'Knowing and Relating', 22.
112. Strathern, *Property, Substance and Effect*, 79.
113. Bodenhorn, 'He Used to Be My Relative', 128.
114. Augustine, 'The Excellence of Marriage', 18.21, 49.

appear with genuine spontaneity and randomness but have a preceding context that determines the relationship in some way and which is beyond the control of participants.[115]

Mumford examines the helplessness of the beginning that every human being experiences, and the necessity that there be those who care for the child.[116] He argues that 'Human beings stand in need of the fundamental support-network which is kinship'[117]. He does not offer theological justification for the structuring of kinship by procreation, but kinship is not his focus. Rather, he is seeking a positive Christian evaluation of asymmetrical relationships such as those connected with the emergence of newones, and he offers some theological justification, engaging with Augustine and Luther's description of the goodness of procreation after the Fall, tied with Grotius's theory that initial helplessness was deliberately created by God to induce social life.[118]

Let us grant, for the sake of argument, that there has been an idealization of encounter in the recognition of personhood, which ignores the imbalance of many relationships and the gradually emerging nature of relationship, shaped by factors other than individual choices. All his argument implies for kinship is that there needs to be a person capable of providing for the child's needs both before and after birth.[119] One does not learn from the idea that life emerges who cares for the child. Clearly, he is correct that every child born has experienced a necessary period of closeness to the woman who bore them, and likely, though not necessarily, benefited from changes their bearer made to their life to help them, even if she never intended to raise the child after birth. After that, it is possible for that child to be transferred to the care of others, even though this involves the bereavement of that attachment to the one who bore the child, and to those others whose voices were heard during pregnancy, in short to the only people the child has ever known. These restrictions would not apply if artificial wombs became available. (The aim is, clearly, not to endorse the transfer of parental responsibility or the use of artificial wombs, but simply to identify the precise bases of kinship being depended on.) These restrictions already do not apply necessarily to the male progenitor implicated by Mumford's argument as naturally kin to the child. Every child relies upon a sexual union but is only necessary to describe that as 'the union of my parents'[120] if one already accepts that those who procreate are necessarily kin to the child. That is not a straightforward natural fact but requires further philosophical or theological justification.

---

115. James Mumford, *Ethics at the Beginning of Life: A Phenomenological Critique* (Oxford: Oxford University Press, 2013), xiii. Cf. also Mumford, *Ethics at the Beginning of Life*, 94–5.
116. Mumford, *Ethics at the Beginning of Life*, 112.
117. Ibid., 111.
118. Ibid., 113–15.
119. Ibid., 153.
120. Ibid., 104.

Even if Mumford's treatment of kinship relies upon a culturally contingent notion of natural kinship, how can a Christian account of kinship respond to those kinship relationships that seem to emerge, rather than being contracted – or, rather, covenanted? After all, a picture of human persons as independent, contracting individuals is no more attractive, as Mumford shows. Take two different bases for kinship with those at the start of life – responsibility in procreation, and proximity during the child's development – and consider whether there might be situations in which kinship would not be thought automatically to arise. If this were possible, it might suggest that there is an element of covenanting involved, even if in the majority of cases the decision not to welcome the child as kin would be unthinkable.

Even outside of strange hypothetical cases (a man whose sperm was stolen for IVF, for instance), the idea of procreative responsibility is not sufficient to establish the necessity of kinship, even if in most cases it would be highly suggested by coinciding factors. All that procreative responsibility might entail is the arrangement of a welcoming adoptive home.

Kinship in the case of gestation is different, however, given that the child is, by necessity, close by and sustained for around nine months, whether or not conception was intended.[121] After all, if co-residence contributes to kinship within the monastery, that applies par excellence to the nearness of bearing a child. Such nearness is not universally taken as instituting kinship – take, for instance, cases of surrogacy or simply those cases of adoption where a woman bears a child without intending kinship. These cases (whether or not they ought to exist) provide opportunities to explore more deeply the norms of kinship. The processes of relinquishment and adoption are obvious places to start investigating both the forging of kinship, and questions of its permanence.

Judith Modell's study of closed adoption in the United States provides an introduction that leads easily into the next section on identity. At the outset, she notes the peculiarly white 'familiar face' of adoption, compared with the freer movement of children in Native American and African American contexts. This familiar face is as submissive to kinship norms as it is provocative. The apparent fiction of adoptive kinship mimicked 'real' kinship, and secrecy in adoption was required in order to limit the number of parents to the culturally plausible one or two, which went along with name-changes, legal transfer and a process of matching

---

121. Gilbert Meilaender distinguishes ties of 'biology, gestation, and birth'. These distinctions hint at the cultural work being in a Euro-American concept of biological kinship in grouping these discrete bases for the natural ties that Meilaender assumes to be self-evident. This book has argued that, anthropologically speaking, kinship is (at least) largely culturally constructed, meaning that theological work would need to be offered to affirm the existence of natural ties, which Meilaender does not offer. As the title suggests, he offers an excellent study of the adoptive identity of Christians, but this is prevented from permeating the root of relatedness in Meilaender's description, because of his assumption about natural ties. (Cf. Gilbert C. Meilaender, *Not by Nature but by Grace* (Notre Dame: University of Notre Dame Press, 2016), 31, 46.)

that sought the illusion that these children has been procreated and were therefore 'properly' kin. However, inheritance laws might not recognize the adoption, with some state laws excluding adopted children when someone dies intestate.[122] Both the suspicion of adoption in inheritance law and the practices of adoption indicate the continued strength of the procreative tie.

The opening of adoption has resulted in 'the adopted person claim[ing] an adoptive family is *not* just like a biological family . . . adoption is unique, incomparable, and special'. Birth parents are heard, too, claiming substance and birth cannot be forgotten, and adoptive parents complete the 'noise' with attempts at alternative modes for adoption, past 'legal or institutional blocks'.[123] These voices reveal an irony in closed adoption that suppressed the 'natural' tie, thereby emphasizing that it was indeed permanent, and so needed to be forgotten or ignored. There was no cultural script for non-permanent kinship ties.

United States law endorses and seals permanence. This is evident in the decision that kin-care (movement around relatives) and foster care, even in a non-institutional setting, are treated prejudicially. Foster carers are only 'nominally' treated as parents but hugely disenfranchised in decisions about the child, so that they are treated as 'servants of the state'.[124] It is a stigmatized role in which attachment is discouraged, but loving care encouraged.[125]

Like Modell, this book will not make claims about the welfare of children but rather explore the cultural connections between permanence and kinship, for the sake of theological reflection. Fiscal pressures in the United States discouraged investment in social services and foster care in favour of termination of rights and adoption, but here the instability of childcare could reflect funding pressures and the stigmatization of foster care, rather than the non-permanent nature of the situation. In an insightful aside, Modell suggests, 'Perhaps, too, the criticism of foster care reveals a doubt about the endurance of a spontaneous commitment to a child in need.'[126]

Given that fostering is a societal need, one wonders why there is such a great pressure to avoid attaching to a child who might only live with foster-families temporarily? For the purpose of Christian ethics, then, (and avoiding the practical psychological edge to the previous question) it is pertinent to ask whether, for the Christian, fostering creates kinship and whether that kinship comes to an end? Indeed, the question extends more broadly, to include longer-term nannies and lodgers. Relationships rarely have clear starting-points, and while marriage ceremonies, the signing of adoption papers, baptismal or monastic vows and

---

122. Judith S. Modell, *A Sealed and Secret Kinship: The Culture of Policies and Practices in American Adoption*, Public Issues in Anthropological Perspectives 3 (New York: Berghahn Books, 2002), 2–6.

123. Modell, *A Sealed and Secret Kinship*, 9–12.

124. Ibid., 81–4.

125. Ibid., 88–92.

126. Ibid., 106–9.

the like might indicate the clear beginning of kinship among some, why should one expect that relatedness not emerge in a way that friendship does? In which case, there remains the challenge of differentiating kinship from other sorts of relationships, if it is to remain a meaningful term. It does not require a single factor, as discussed earlier, but some *varying* combination of living together, marital connections, promises, shared history and memories and/or being brought into the world by someone seem to conspire to differentiate kinship from other relationships.

Returning to the Iñupiaq 'kinship by effort', this does not sit easily with Christian social thinking. God makes a covenant with His people – 'I shall be your God and you shall be my people'[127] – which is not conditioned by the later addition of the law, as Paul makes clear.[128] Marriage is traditionally taken to reflect the marriage between Jesus and the church in its unconditionality. There is an aspiration towards committed relationships, even if this need not extend to passing acquaintances. There are competing pressures – on the one hand, deep relationships should be honoured, on the other hand, it is better for 'affection [to] stretch over a greater number' – the reason Augustine endorses exogamy over endogamy (while resolving an exegetical puzzle).[129] Augustine's logic suggests kinship may be useful for showing love, but that love forbids kinship from being a tool for exclusion.

The cultural pressure to think of friends as chosen and kin as unchosen and permanent gains strength from the idea that kinship describes the relationship between bodies. With the rejection of this idea goes some of the force maintaining the permanence of kinship. Nothing more need be offered than the principles that drive Augustine's logic in the section on incest in *City of God*, begging Christians to welcome expansively but love committedly. Some relationships – marriage and the adoption of children – might be marked by clear promises of sorts, but others – siblinghood, bearer of the child – do not of themselves necessarily create kinship in the way that a biogenetic theory of kinship might have it, even though the circumstances (or shared history, shared space, clear dependency) nearly always strongly suggest it.

Perhaps that feels unfaithful to the principle that Christian relationships ought to be committed just as God is committed to His people? If so, a reminder is necessary: no man is to be called father (Mt. 23.9) because God alone is Father, and Jesus Christ binds God's people in the kinship that is reflected in the biblical use of the words 'sister' and 'brother' within the church. Kinship today can only imitate what God might eschatologically realize in full. With respect to the status of foster care, the Christian may celebrate the formation of a stable attachment that lasts beyond the time of the placement, or they may for the relationship to pass on, so that it might be said that they were, for a time, kin.

---

127. Lev. 26.12, Jer. 30.22, Ezek. 36.28. Cf. Gen. 17.8, Rev. 21.3. Also, see Cf. 2 Cor. 6.16.
128. Gal. 3.17.
129. Augustine, *City of God*, 15.16, 623.

Conclusion

The anthropologist opens the moral imagination of the theologian to notice what inflects the expression of kinship in different cultures, pushing the theologian back to their own 'culture' to see how Christians might live. A range of arguments have been offered. Kinship need not be permanent in order to conform to a Christian moral logic, but it certainly should not be unforgiving or rejecting. Conceiving of human persons in terms of encounter might not be helpful for excluding the norm of emerging relationships, but as kinship is not a 'naturally emergent thing' it nevertheless resides at the level of human will, though grounded in welcome and hospitality. The practice of spiritual kinship troubles kinship well, realigning loyalties according to belonging 'in Christ' rather than in blood, property and marriage.

Another thing has been learned, however, which relates to the radical nature of the Christian imagination of the human moral agent. That will be discussed in the conclusion, but this chapter requires a more modest close. There are two main ways in which a Christian account of personhood influences the practices of kinship. First, the idea that the Christian is properly constituted as a person in Jesus Christ, made available by the Spirit to the church, instigates the creation of communities of accountability that reflect the constitution of the church and its mission rather than the structure of the 'family' and its transmission. Second, the basis for recognizing special obligations and affections to some people and not others is certainly not rejected, but its force is significantly weakened by the idea that all are welcomed, and all equally undeserving, of the kinship with God made available in Jesus Christ.

Chapter 7

CONCLUSION

Christian kinship

How, then, should a Christian think about kinship? This book has done two main things: first, it has sought out rich and forgotten parts of the Christian tradition aided by anthropological tools, to bring out how Christians have thought about kinship, and second, it has engaged with these sources to answer the question of how Christians *ought* to think about kinship.

The anthropological voices argued convincingly that kinship is culturally constructed, shaped by a range of factors, none of them being a universal common denominator. It revealed a world of symbols – house, gender, substance and person – which underpin the meaning of the concept of kinship as it translates from Malaysia to the Trobriand Islands to Chicago. These symbols have guided this theological enquiry, prompting a wider range of questions about Christianity than a theologian might otherwise ask, limited by their own particular cultural horizon. Accordingly, this approach identifies a series of avenues into the topic, to test whether the concept of kinship has any legitimate place within a Christian social ethics, and if so, what that might be.

The basic meaning of kinship as a cross-culturally translatable term is this: a mode of organizing society that relies on some of the following symbols – shared substance, house, gender and personhood. These were explored theologically, to see whether a Christian notion of kinship can be offered, and if so, what it might look like.

In Chapter 3, on kinship by substance, the practice of determining kinship on the basis of shared bodily substance (flesh, blood, genes, etc.) was challenged as theologically problematic. It was also argued, contrary to the mythos of the blood tie in Euro-American thought, to be unnecessary. This was not to say that someone thoroughly enculturated to believe that relationships between bodies themselves constitute kinship can simply dispense with all markers of their culture of kinship – it is not realistic to expect that someone can change their culture like they can their coat. That said, the potential for cultural change is evident in an unlikely place, precisely where Euro-American cultural norms are most honoured in the face of adversity. In the case of kinship pursued by ARTs, or made and remade in the context of 'recombinant families' where there has been divorce and remarriage, a remarkable flexibility is demonstrated with respect to the factors that count in enabling a child to be recognized as related (in the case of ARTs, how the various criteria for supposed biological kinship can be met). Constituent kinship-making parts (the proximity of gestation, the formational character of gestation, the responsibility for the procreation of the child, the sharing of different bodily substances) are negotiated according to the desires of the agents involved.

So too, Christians are taught to expect that following Jesus will be costly[1] and that it will entail a God-given transformation of perspective.[2] The Christian expects to re-examine the values of their own culture as a matter of course. Unfortunately, Christian theology – the chapter goes on to argue – has played an unintended role in the development of the practice of determining kinship by bodily substance. Specifically, a genealogy of the concept of the blood tie reveals that a corruption of the theology of the Eucharist created the conditions in which substance-based kinship idioms have flourished in the West. Where idioms of substance-kinship might previously have marked as substandard kinship with the proverbial (and literal!) widow and orphan, how might the social theology of the Eucharist promote that kind of deep hospitality? Existing Christian practices from monasticism to adoption and fostering are examined in later chapters which recognize relatedness in the body of Christ rather than in genetic makeup.

That said, this does not necessarily universalize kinship, diluting affections and obligations, but rather challenges one mode of organizing these ties. The next chapters turn to other modes of organization kinship.

Chapter 4, on kinship by household, compares two very different Christian visions of a household: Benedict's *Rule* and Baxter's *Christian Economics*. Setting Benedict in the context of the households of Roman late antiquity, his vision of monastic living is offered as one possible authentically Christian realization of the Eucharistic social ethics espoused in Chapter 3. Setting Baxter in historical context, the roots of the political structure he endorses are found to be not in the person and teaching of Jesus Christ, but rather in a pre-Christian political philosophy (something, indeed, that he admits in an earlier work, but disguises in *Christian Economics*). Having looked at the way in which Benedict and Baxter critically appraise existing social structures for the organization of the household, it is argued that it is Benedict rather than Baxter who offers the more authentically Christian response to the social norms of his time, in the fundamentals of the composition of the household.

It is then mooted – for the purpose of argument rather than as an independent proposal to be demonstrated – that Baxter's (and other Puritans') crystallization of a pre-Christian political vision of household unity was then exported to the New

---

1. 'If any want to become My followers, let them deny themselves and take up their cross daily and follow Me'. (Lk. 9.23).
2. 'Do not be conformed to this world, but be transformed by the renewing of your minds, so that you may discern what is the will of God – what is good and acceptable and perfect' (Rom. 12.2).

World and, from there, significantly shaped widely accepted contemporary Euro-American idioms of households.

Either way, while both Benedict and Baxter prescribe social forms which can organize obligations and particularize affections, it is Benedict who succeeds in designing a social form that is truly susceptible to the Eucharistic reconfiguring of the Christian's social life to the body of Christ (and, as part of the body of Christ, in welcome to the stranger). This is because the political principle Baxter guards – that the reproductive unit is the building block of society – leads him to create a compulsory social form that structurally excludes, for example, widows and orphans.

Benedict, however, offers a pattern of the household that can be, and has been, readily adapted to organize households of inclusion. A contemporary British monastery, a Mexican convent and a L'Arche community are all critically examined to see how the Eucharistic logic structures those social ties. The social logic of Benedict's *Rule* is then offered as applicable to a wide range of settings – whether it be more radical examples like L'Arche or more culturally normative households that encourage fostering, discourage the protecting of wealth, or in other ways recognize Christ at the centre and practice hospitality at the edges.

The social logic of Baxter's *Christian Economics*, with its dependence on certain political philosophical commitments, is criticized for making the Christian home of his imagining nearly impermeable to the outsider the Christian is called to welcome. That said, a reader will find a healthy degree of genuine piety and nobility in his Christianization of a contemporary norm which he does not critique more deeply (and would not, given his commitment to understanding the household as, at core, a reproductive unit). Baxter's theological basis for endorsing a familiar structure has been criticized. However, many Christian households today – especially in the West – *are* structured as reproductive units, and yet are profoundly hospitable, even if not engaged in adoption, fostering (setting aside the very different structures of the monastery). The contention of Chapter 4 is not that this structure can never be marked by profound welcome. It can certainly be good, and yet there is a popular assumption that the figurative white picket fence demarcates the true Christian household. If that were true, how come other forms are, in their structure, so much more susceptible to hospitality? Instead of buying into Baxter's idea that the household should fundamentally be structured as a reproductive unit, the Christian imagination can be inspired by the witness of the monastery to greater hospitality just as it can be inspired to Eucharist to a more expansive view of relatedness, in the body of Christ.

Clearly, though, a discussion of the household as a reproductive unit is incomplete without an examination of gender: the focus of Chapter 5.

Chapter 5 took as its focus Christian interpretation of relationships between genders and in that context a Christian treatment of sex, with the goal of assessing how kinship and gender interrelate and inform one another in Christian thought. It was argued that just as the cross-cultural variability of kinship norms reveals it to be culturally constructed, so too gender is culturally constructed. This was not at all to say, though, that there is no space for the concept of gender in Christian thought, merely that a certain perception of gender is not strictly determined by human biological make-up (given its cross-cultural variability). Having said that, the 'anxiety'[3] with which Carsten diagnoses the careful distinguishing of cultural from the natural was avoided, on the basis that the materiality of the body does indeed make some gender constructions more likely than others. Accordingly, gender and kinship – and the natural facts associated with *each of* them – are taken as a unified topic of study, in order to avoid both biological determinism and cultural relativism in either.

The project thus proceeds by examining how Christians have conceived of the relationship between gender and natural facts in the construction of gendered relatedness. It did so by examining Augustine, looking at his theory of marriage in historical and theological context, and then turning to Karl Barth, and his study of the relationship between creation and covenant as it pertains to gender and the image of God. The purpose of both was to assess the extent to which some idea of sexual difference is theologically necessary. Then entering into dialogue with more recent treatments of sexual difference, it was argued that there *is* something morally significant about sexual difference, though this is not to say that human biology in any way requires that this be recognized. Taking a lead from Sarah Coakley in her querying of Judith Butler's call for 'gender trouble', a theological basis for the recognition of physical sexual difference was offered. This was done, following Augustine, by the recognition of the goodness of the kinship practice of gendered marriage.

However, while marriage was received as good, it was not presented as necessary. Indeed, the commendation of chaste celibacy for the kingdom, rooted in the teaching of Jesus and, more plainly, of Paul, further relativizes the social significance of sexual difference that was recognized in marriage. The goodness of celibacy forbade any idea that women need men or men need women to be complete. Chapter 4 strongly endorsed the notion that the Christian life is indeed properly social – a theme developed more clearly in Chapter 6, on personhood – but gender is clearly not necessary to the formation of friendship. Aelred's exposition of friendship is one example of a counter-tradition to any trend towards making deep intimacy exclusive to marriage. To be clear, marriage is to be celebrated for covenant love, for the reflection of Christ's commitment to the world, and for the procreation of children. However, in a world in which Christ has already been born, it is no longer required as it once was, and there is a great deal of other satisfying work to be done, that might be more easily achieved without the distractions of marriage, as Paul unromantically puts it in 1 Cor. 7.

However unromantic Paul's words might seem, though, they allow fresh air into a world in which romantic love is glamourized in such a way as to hurt marriage and celibacy alike. Where this ideology of romantic love, in which men and women are incomplete without the other, is affirmed, then the culture drives towards the dispensability of marriage covenants where a particular quality of friendship or

---

3. Carsten, *After Kinship*, 119.

sexual fulfilment is no longer present and makes celibacy seem implausible, a non-starter for the one who seeks the wholeness of *shalom*. Augustine's famous words, 'You stir man to take pleasure in praising you, because you have made us for yourself, and our heart is restless until it rests in you,'[4] are a more fitting and promising reflection on human incompleteness than this romantic vision of an essential encounter between man and woman. To the unwillingly celibate Christian enculturated into this glamourization of romance, and socially isolated in a culture so structured around the reproductive unit, friendship might seem like a poor substitute. That is because it is not a substitute for all that a culture teaches a person is necessary for their fulfilment. Augustine did not write those words coldly, but they express the end of a journey of a man with a chequered sexual past. Similarly, Paul's advice that engaged couples should choose marriage over sexual sin was a concession – one that recognized the goodness of marriage, but nevertheless a concession to a readership which he called to focus on wholehearted service of God. Paul would surely affirm Augustine's words (clearly formed by his reading of Paul) that fulfilment is found neither in marriage nor friendship and that marriage is not the true remedy for that sense of incompleteness so accentuated in the experience of the single person by the structuring of society around the reproductive unit. Neither, indeed, is company itself a remedy, as Bonhoeffer observes, even in a book that sketches the promise of life lived together (and urges people not to be alone): 'Many persons seek community because they are afraid of loneliness . . . Christians too, who cannot cope on their own, and who in their own lives have had some bad experiences, hope to experience help with this in the company of other people. More often than not, they are disappointed.'[5]

In Christian thought, marriage cannot be seen as essential to ultimate fulfilment, even if its joy is recognized in rich metaphors for the relationship between God and His people in *Song of Songs*, and for Christ and church as bride and bridegroom. Marriage, including the companionship it brings and its sexual expression, is good but not to be worshipped, and other parts of social life are elevated. The result is a proposed culture more plausibly good for those who are, for whatever reason, celibate. Turning more directly to kinship, the social logic of this commendation of chaste celibacy further relativizes the importance of the reproductive unit to the structuring of Christian kinship, as against Baxter's dependence on it for his political vision. Aelred's account of friendship is offered as a radical (at the time) experiment in intimacy that honours the social nature of human beings created in the image of God, but which opens the Christian more fully to kinship in Christ than would typically be encouraged by cultural norms around marriage.

Chapter 6 considered how a Christian understanding of personhood might provide an alternative basis of relatedness to that of shared biogenetic substance.

---

4. Augustine, *Confessions*, I.i.1, 3.
5. Dietrich Bonhoeffer, *Life Together and Prayerbook of the Bible*, ed. Geffrey B. Kelly, trans. Daniel W. Bloesch and James H. Burtness, Dietrich Bonhoeffer Works 5 (Minneapolis: Fortress Press, 2005), 65/81.

It did so by retrieving a theological account of personhood, and one found, conveniently enough, in the history of social anthropology. The relationship between ideas about relatedness and ideas of personhood is easily illustrated. It would be simplistic to say that cultures that are more 'collectivist' (with accompanying 'dividualist' understanding of personhood) are less reliant on idioms of kinship to organize themselves socially (as other modes of organization are more salient), and more 'individualist' culture are more reliant on these idioms. However, it illustrates the way ideas about personhood shape ideas about kinship by prompting the question: What is a person, that it can be related to another person?

Tension between dividualism and individualism are not at all alien to Christianity, and these were found in Paul's letters with Barclay and in Melanesian converts with Mosko and Robbins. These were both sites in which the logic of the Christian faith altered perceptions of personhood and connectedness. It was argued that, while it is popular among anthropologists to name Christianity as an individualizing force in cultures to which it is introduced, it in fact merely disrupts existing social structures by introducing new and, in many cases, competing 'dividuality'. This is to say that the social logic of the Christian faith presses the Christian to recognize themselves as fundamentally constituted 'in Christ'. This ought to be as challenging to a European or American tendency to define the personhood in their body as it was to the Melanesian converts who defined themselves according to shifting ledgers of social obligations in village life.

The idea that personhood is found 'in Christ', aside from being a morally powerful idea, provides a helpful bridge into the heart of the anthropological puzzle of how personhood (as an analytic term) should be understood. Marcel Mauss recognized that the concept of the person in the discipline of anthropology was largely shaped by theological debates. In particular, patristic development of the concept 'person' in order to describe divine personhood influenced in large ways current use (both technical and everyday) of the word 'person' and other linked concepts. Of course, this history could be nothing more than that – history – to be cleared up using the terms equivocally: that is divine persons as one thing and human persons as another. However, this genealogy of personhood presents the perfect opportunity to revisit earlier manifestations of the concept of person, to use it as solid ground on which to build a Christian account of human personhood as being constituted by participation in Christ's personhood. The Christian theologian operating in parts of the world directly informed by this history is fortunate to have the concept of the person of the Trinity contained in the shades of meaning of so everyday a word. Whereas social anthropology as a field has struggled with the concept of personhood, precisely because of its highly determined theological content, for the Christian theologian much of the work has already been done in providing a workable concept of personhood 'in Christ', for social ethics.

For John Zizioulas, personhood is constituted in communion. Indeed, when human action is determined by the nature of the human being (merely by their biological constitution) their freedom, and with it their personhood, is called into question. The essence of personhood is found in freedom, available by participation in divine activity, because God alone determines His own being. On such an account of personhood, defining relatedness on the basis of biological constitution would be to build a system of relatedness 'on the sand', as it were, when it can instead be built on personhood 'on the rock', defined in Christ.

Of course, this story of personhood relies on high theological reflection. However, the idea of being constituted in Christ in baptism has historically informed the concept of kinship, as seen in the practice of spiritual kinship. It was argued, from a history of the practice from its early days, through its critique by Luther, to recent practice in a rural Greek Orthodox village, that the concept of personhood in Christ militates to disrupt existing social structures in such a way as to open Christians to kinship in Christ.

Having identified a Christian account of personhood in Christ, evident in practices surrounding baptism, the question was raised: If kinship can begin (rather than simply being a biological fact), then can it also end? The possibility of kinship beginning and ending at different stages in life – easily understood for Westerners when applied to kinship by alliance, but evident in other cultural settings even for kinship by descent – sits uneasily with the idiom that 'you can choose your friends, but you can't choose your family'. However, while biological substance may no longer be available as a basis for the permanence of kinship, the concept of covenant is more than sufficient for making sense of the Christian instinct to consistent faithfulness.

However, that leaves the question: Does that mean every child, for example, must be 'chosen'? Mumford rightly cautioned against understanding human persons as independent, contracting individuals, but his assumption that this means that kinship must be structured around procreation was rejected. Instead, it is accepted that the proximity of gestation and the responsibility of procreation each bring likely obligations to covenant-making. That said, sometimes kinship does end, or begins at another point, such as adoption and fostering. The past patterns of closed adoption in the United States, which used secrecy to mimic cultural norms of biological kinship, was challenged in proposing that the non-permanence of particular kinship relationships must be recognized. This does not mean kinship must be earned, or that is inherently unstable. In place of the unconditionality and stability of kinship based on a theory of kinship as relationships between bodies themselves, the concept of covenant is offered as the basis for unconditionality and faithful stability in kinship, but these concepts allow the existence of temporary kinship (e.g. fostering), provided it expresses hospitable response to the new covenant into which all are welcomed in Christ.

This reconceiving of the person as properly constituted in Christ, evident in the expansion of kinship ties in such practices as adoption, fostering and spiritual kinship, is not incompatible with organization into smaller groups (houses, marriages, godparenthood, etc.). However, this understanding of the person *does* displace the Euro-American idea that kinship is fixed by the unchanging nature of bodily substance. This is just as well, as it makes much better sense of kinship at the margins, between those whose bodily substances have no special relationship to one another, but who are nevertheless not only welcomed but recognized as truly kin in Christ.

This raises the question, though, where this leaves the nuclear family.

What about the nuclear family?

This book is not an attack on the nuclear family. The defenders of the nuclear family may recognize it, with Baxter, as either politically useful (bringing order) or, with numerous popular writers on the family today, as psychologically healthy (creating a healthy environment in which to raise children). The nuclear family has been defended against internal and external threats, whether it be divorce, conflict, marital unfaithfulness, emotionally unhealthy relationships, wider social changes in the use of technology or perspectives on sexual norms, individualism, overt focus on career, rises in violence and gangs, drugs, pornography and so on. There are any number of perceived threats to the traditional nuclear family. By this, it is usually meant the social construction of a married heterosexual couple who have conceived – or possibly adopted – a number of children, whom they raise, living in one house together.

Is the traditional, Western, nuclear family not worth defending? In a way, yes, and many of the threats enumerated in the previous paragraph could damage patterns of intimacy, accountability and responsibility in any system of kinship. The nuclear family will continue, doubtless, to be the normal social construction for many around the world, and especially in the West.

The problem arises when the Christian thinker assumes that family can only be that way. When that happens, it structurally excludes 'the widow and the orphan', to use a common biblical object of concern, from inclusion in family, unless an exception is made (the most recognized of which is adoption, which operates as a corrective to this problem with the nuclear family). This book aims to show that kinship does not belong only to the nuclear family and then, in decreasing intensity, to the extended family. Rather, kinship belongs to us all in Christ, into whose Sonship of the Father we are all invited, and invited in such a way that those who wish to follow Jesus will see their lives change.

In other words, the bedrock of kinship must not be the political unit of the nuclear family defined around reproduction. The bedrock of kinship must be kinship in Christ, so that the Christian recognizes themselves as belonging in Jesus, and through Jesus as belonging to everyone welcomed into His family, that is *everyone*. This deep belonging in Christ makes kinship into a moral question rather than an inarguable natural fact.

Again, though, where does this leave the nuclear family? It is a good thing that people marry, even if in 1 Corinthians 7 it seems that chaste celibacy for the kingdom *can* be the better thing. But if people are called to marry and do so, it is right that they honour their covenants to one another. And, should they conceive, that too is a good thing, and the child is a gift. Who should care for the child? Well, many, of course. The child has only one Father, but will have many Father-figures, from teachers to mentors to family friends, and so on. But of course it is right that the one who carried the child act as mother, after the model of the Father who provides for, nurtures and loves, because quite naturally she has done so for the first nine months of the child's life. And so too her husband will provide for, nurture and love the child after the pattern of the child's true Father. We can rightly call him 'father', even if this title cannot be held in an absolute sense (Mt. 23.9: 'call no one your father on earth, for you have one Father – the one in heaven'). And it will doubtless be a great joy to see the likeness of themselves and their spouse in the child as they grow up – a great gift, but no one's condition for commitment.

Must they live alone in a house together as is common among those with the means in the Euro-American context? Clearly not, and there is such great diversity of living arrangements, but it does confer advantages where it is possible. The most obvious is that the power to choose who enters a domain of vulnerability can guarantee some safety, even if this overlooks the obvious and serious caveat that most abuse happens within the home, away from outside scrutiny. However, for those who wish to honour and love their spouses and their children, living alone in a home together could certainly enable safety and undistracted attention to one another.

Hopefully, this rough-and-ready argumentation demonstrates that there might be an excellent reason for what many will consider the norm. So why bother thinking any more about kinship? One key question is whether one structure (the nuclear family) smuggles with it an assumption about relatedness (that it is based on reproduction – marriage and procreation) that leaves the individual blind to those who are obviously excluded. What happens to the widow with no one close enough in these diminishing networks of reproductive units to call on as their family? What happens to the orphan – whether through death or abandonment – whose care no one takes up other than the state? If they are the kin of Jesus, and so are we, then are they not our kin? And when Christians do take up the case of the widow and the orphan, perhaps to the extent of taking them into their homes or in another sense into their intimacy, why does the myth persist that those taken in are not really family?

This book is not a critique of the nuclear family. Rather, it is a critique of the assumptions that this kind of arrangement has the only claim to kinship, when kinship has been liberally bestowed in Jesus. There are reasons why the nuclear family has become so common as to be considered the norm in the West, and some, though not all, are good reasons. However, if the moral imagination of the Christian has no space for kinship outside of that structure, then it will not be possible to hear the call of God to welcome others into belonging, or indeed to recognize the Triune God Himself as one's most direct kin. Thus, for those who are single, or who are in poverty with or without dependents, or who want to give more generously of themselves in kinship to others but do not think they can, kinship can be a word of inclusive belonging and intimacy, wider accountability, more evenly spread responsibility. The hope or fear that the nuclear norm has a monopoly on kinship is, for the Christian, utterly and obviously unfounded.

This book, though, does not target those who celebrate the nuclear family, when what they are doing is celebrating the goodness of belonging. The nuclear family is a form of permanent belonging, providing all the security that entails and that is rightly honoured. The goodness and security of belonging, though, can be further honoured when it is made more widely available, unshackled from the fear that only one structure of kinship can really work with human nature.

The theology of kinship

So far, this conclusion has summarized the argument of the four central chapters – on substance, house, gender and personhood – in order to make explicit an overarching argument in favour of the idea that Christians are called to recognize kinship in Christ.

What, though, does it actually mean, for the Christian to recognize kinship in Christ amidst the demands of everyday life, enculturated as they are into their own local culture? This book has enabled a glimpse, in some of the practices described earlier, of the shape of an idealized Christian culture with its new loyalties, new affections, new perceptions of self, new living arrangements, new desires and new communities. However, even where it has been glimpsed, it has been glimpsed only in part, always in Christian communities that may have this holiness visible, but are undoubtedly broken in other ways, most obviously Downside Abbey.[6] What good is a select assortment of principles and practices to the Christian immersed in their own culture, in which they experience the ache of childlessness, the painful mystery of an unknown past, the loneliness of old age or orphanhood? How each is experienced may be culturally conditioned, but that doesn't stop them from being powerfully experienced; an American cannot decide simply to wake up tomorrow thinking and behaving like a Trobriand Islander, and neither can the

---

6. Downside Abbey was chosen as an example of monastic kinship simply because an ethnography has been written about it. While it afforded an opportunity to look closely at the lived reality of spiritual kinship in a monastery, it also faced a historic safeguarding scandal involving monks from the abbey who taught at the school, some as abusers and some who did too little to prevent the abuse happening. While the specifics of the Downside Abbey case are beyond the scope of this book, the generic question can be asked: Can such safeguarding scandals implicate monastic kinship? After all, while there was no allegation of abuse within the brotherhood of the abbey, it is all but certain that there has been abuse within monastic communities since their inception. Spaces of trust, without sufficient structures of oversight, can easily be turned into places of abuse, as has happened in many institutions and indeed in many families. Comparing this abuse with abuse in families is not to take a defeatist attitude, but simply to point out that organizing kinship around reproduction does not work as a safeguarding strategy. This book has described kinship as creating relationships of intimacy/affection, obligation and accountability. Any properly structured community will enable not just the experience of intimacy to be fostered alongside the obligation to care for one another but also the mechanisms for accountability which might very well include formal safeguarding structures that many organizations are now learning to create today.

Christian (in their own strength) simply drop their culture and decide to live in an ideally Christian way, even if it were possible to describe what an ideally Christian culture would look like in the present age.

There are strict limits on what a theological ethics of kinship can offer, and the enculturation of all Christians presents only one obstacle (others will be delineated later). It remains the case, however, that the Christian faith changes the lives and outlook of Christians, and it does so in a marked and consistent enough way to start spotting trends – for example, towards restructuring kinship to conform with identity in Christ, in the light of baptism and communion, as seen in the lived examples described earlier.

These trends, once extracted, might look too abstract to be recognizable in everyday life, but they are still there. David Schneider reflected on the problem of describing American kinship in recognizable ways. He came to use the technical, 'diffuse, enduring solidarity' to describe American kinship norms: 'The natives do not use it and although some of them understand it when I explain it to them, it falls like jargon on their ears. Which it should, of course, for that is just what it is.'[7] Similarly, while the average Christian may recognize the language of being persons 'in Christ' from the letters of Paul, it could also sound like theological jargon which is not easy immediately to define. However, say to a Christian that there is an important sense in which the widow or orphan is their sister or brother, and not only would they understand, but they would also likely be able to point to ways in which their Christian community seeks to cultivate this truth in practice. The language of personhood in Christ names the tacit rule underpinning distinctively Christian practices above, just as grammatical rules may explain the speech of a native German even if they could not give a lecture on German grammar.

Just as an ideally Christian culture is not simply 'put on' like a new set of clothes, so too it is not possible to visit a selection of Christian communities and find there – represented in one or patched together from several – an ideally Christian culture. The Christian ethicist cannot, then, be like the anthropologist, writing an ethnography of Christian kinship, as there is no comprehensively Christian community to describe. A Trobriand informant will more readily represent Trobriand culture than any given Christian will represent the kingdom of God, because Christians are always bilingual, working with the symbolic world of their own culture alongside the Christian symbolic world that theologians seek to describe. The only native who can reliably distinguish the kingdom of God from earthly culture is Jesus. That does not mean that the internal logic of the Christian faith does not inform the lives of Christian communities. From a theological perspective it does so because the kingdom really is here. Even from an anthropological perspective, when Christians try to follow Jesus in light of scripture, the result is culture change, and it is reasonable to assume that some of that culture change bears the hallmark of the kingdom. However, the problem of distinguishing the Christian from the other culture in earthly Christian

---

7. Schneider, 'Kinship, Nationality, and Religion in American Culture', 67.

communities is one of the reasons that the Christianity of the anthropologist is not going to be, to the theologian, a reliable guide to the kingdom of God.

To submit Christian ethics to the Christianity of the anthropologist would be to be mastered by the 'general anthropology' Barth rejected.[8] That is to say, it is general anthropology unless such a survey of the present and historic reality of Christian communities is done in the context of constructive dogmatics, which seeks to describe the Christian not as merely as a moral actor, but as one who lives with and under a living and active God. Description of that God as He makes Himself known – Christian dogmatics – thus becomes the grounds for the comprehension of and participation in those practices in a coherently Christian manner. This is why Chapter 6, on personhood, doggedly persisted in seeking to understand the person not simply from the perspective of the anthropologist, but from a theological perspective as one constituted only truly as a person in Christ. The anthropologist *qua* secular academic might be able to report on the reality that Christians believe themselves to be constituted in Christ, but will not be able to report that Christians actually are constituted in Christ. As such, the explanation for Christian behaviour can never be found in the place the theologian will recognize: the supernatural reality that Christians are being brought to participate in Christ, the living 'pioneer and perfecter' of their faith (Heb. 12.2), by the Spirit as He reveals His kingdom in the world. As Christopher Holmes puts it, 'ethics is behaviour that recognizes "the pioneer and perfecter" of our faith . . . ethics is a function of Christ's "continually operative" reconciling and revealing intervention, his perfecting work.'[9] The direction of the pressure of the interpretation must, then, be from the theological to the anthropological, and not the other way round.

Nevertheless, anthropology has a vital methodological role in supporting Christian theological discernment of the kingdom of God.

On the one hand, if the theologian tries to operate in Christian ethics without the critical distance provides by anthropological analysis, then they are susceptible to mere projection of their cultural biases, and the direction of the pressure of interpretation from the divine to the human is lost. On the other hand, if the anthropologist (or Christian ethicists trying to work with anthropology but not dogmatics) used ethnography in order actually to describe the kingdom of God, they would not have access to sufficient information to discern the kingdom from human culture, and so would be lost immediately to mere projection. An anthropologist might suspect that a practice is distinctively Christian, but that suspicion can only reliably come from theology (though perhaps it would be better to say, it can only reliably come from the Word made flesh, present and active in this world by the Spirit). The exposition of the Word is, of course, beyond the disciplinary boundary of what typically constitutes social anthropology.

---

8. Barth, *Church Dogmatics*, 1956, I/2, 782–3.
9. Christopher R. J. Holmes, *Ethics in the Presence of Christ* (London: T&T Clark, 2012), 1.

Ultimately, however, as the concept of kinship in Christ is recognized as regulative in the lives of distinctive Christian practices, it is for Christian dogmatics (resourced by the church's collective witness to Jesus Christ as it interprets scripture) to place that idea in theological context, test it, and in that way to take up the regulative task in order that the ethicist can recognize truly Christian kinship in the practices it describes.

This might go some way to explaining the limits of a Christian theological account of kinship. The modest proposals for properly Christian ideas of kinship neither match entirely with any living Christian practice nor could be taken as a detailed script for an alternative life. There are two factors restricting the descriptive element.

Theological ethics does not displace the role of the Spirit in, first, building, or second, revealing, the kingdom. In both cases, God works as He wills and can particularize His encounter with particular Christians and communities.

However, a theological ethics of kinship can serve this prophetic task of discerning the Spirit's work by calling the disciple's attention to an important moral question – that of kinship – which might be brought prayerfully to God. It does so by organizing a scriptural basis against which Christian communities can test whether an opportunity – such as the planting of a L'Arche community – might be from God, just as it can be used to test those practices already in motion.

The need for caution will be obvious to some but is vital to state when dealing with a phenomenon so powerful, and culturally variable, as kinship. Care must be taken not to overly specify what Christian kinship supposedly must look like, and in so doing make this account of Christian kinship irrelevant to the ordinary Christian life. Janet Martin Soskice, writing about forms of spirituality that emerge from out-of-the-ordinary practices like monasticism, points out the gulf between the experience of the monk and that of ordinary Christians, especially those Christian women who work in the home. They

> do not think, they have not been *taught* to think, of it as spiritual. And here monastic figures who, apparently, found God over the washing up or sweeping the floor will be called to mind; but these are not really to the point, since servile tasks were recommended because they left the mind free to contemplate. What we want is a monk who finds God while cooking a meal with one child clamouring for a drink, another who needs a bottom wiped, and a baby throwing up over his shoulder.[10]

Parsimony in offering principles for the discernment of Christian kinship is premised on the living reality of God revealing His kingdom now, not just in monasteries but presumably also in homes. This is not to forgo any claim to the Christian distinctiveness of the monastery so obviously designed to reflect the

---

10. Soskice, *The Kindness of God*, 22–3.

reality of kinship in Christ, but rather simply to hold back from prescribing such a practice for all people in all places.

The account of the kingdom of God above is premised on the living reality of God who transforms society even now. The question, then, is not of the person already weighed down with present responsibilities being burdened with the world's problems. Rather, the question is whether or not God is inviting them into something different, for which God will provide the means, and which ultimately reflect a lighter burden than the burden a sinful and broken world puts on them – but a burden all the same. For one that may be to participate in a L'Arche community because there is one nearby, for another it might be to start a monastery because they have such a vision and opportunity and for yet another it may simply be to mend their marriage and their relationships with their children.

If such a survey were simply the basis for a blueprint of some imagined and idealized world, then the reality would surely be casting off the 'yoke of slavery' to assume not freedom in Christ (1 Tim. 6.6), but a yoke heavier than the ancestors were supposed to bear (Acts 15.10). It is not the task of Christian ethics to build castles in the sky, but rather to point to Jesus and His kingdom in the real world. Spiritual kinship in Ambeli, by having such continuity with the message of baptism, and such discontinuity with other prevailing cultural priorities, is not simply a wonderful example of a theological principle but a fully realized and workable practice that seems like a visible instance of the kingdom being realized in the midst of this world.

This does not make the recognition of kinship in Christ superficial, as though it were simply a matter of the Christian slightly reorganizing their social circles to make them more inclusive. The recognition of adoption in the ascended Christ, in whom the Christian is sanctified, provides the conditions for life ordered by worship and gratitude as defining features of Christian living construed as life in response to Christ. That recognition also allows Christian practice to be understood as liberating and not burdening. The recognition of the place of the ascended Christ in determining personhood relieves any temptation to treat some human beings as distinctively sub-personal in our practices, but rather discloses them as siblings in Christ, and fellow bearers of adoption.

When Barth writes that all who are 'burdened and afflicted with his own life' will 'explore and exploit all the supposed possibilities by which to shield himself from life which is basically hostile'[11] he is taking a stance against any mode of thinking about life that lives out of the present rather than the future, that denies the resurrection and burdens the hearer with their own flourishing.

In fact, far from a Christian ethics of kinship burdening the Christian with an overly specific practice, not only is the Christian freed by the security they have in Christ to be generous but is also freed from those overly specific cultures of kinship with which they are very likely already be lumbered. What, after all, is stricter and more burdensome than the idea that one can only have the belonging of kinship

---

11. Barth, *Church Dogmatics*, 1961, III/4, 418.

with those to whom one is biogenetically related, so that when confronted by the widow and orphans in their midst, the Christian is placed in the impossible position of fitting Christian hospitality as a duty into an already over-full life? The cultural law of kinship that says reproductive technologies are the only avenue to being parents, or that says care for the widow or orphan is a luxury they cannot afford as they seek to live up to their cultures lifestyle standards or their family, is abolished in order that the Christian can hear the good news of freedom to live as God invites, dependent on His provision. Society can be organized in many different ways, and far from offering a detailed prescription for kinship done right, the purpose of this book is to liberate the Christian from their culture's detailed prescription for kinship done right, so they can truly receive God as their Father and their near or distant neighbour as their sibling.

The freedom of kinship in Christ is expressed in Gal. 4.6-7, 'And because you are children, God has sent the Spirit of His Son into our hearts, crying, "Abba! Father!" So you are no longer a slave but a child, and if a child then also an heir, through God.' Participation in what the Spirit is doing – whether it is simply crying 'Abba! Father!' or radically altering one's social structures – is personal and particular. The law that kinship must be restricted by cultural perceptions of blood, bones, genes, caste and race – whatever – is abolished in favour of the freedom of active participation in the Sonship of Christ by the Spirit who enters 'into our hearts'.

To be specific about a kinship practice from which the Christian is liberated, it has been argued that it is not necessary, inevitable or good that kinship be organized on the basis of shared biogenetic substance. In some circumstances, it leads to the exclusion of orphans from proper care, or motivates the use of those assisted reproductive technologies that involve at least great emotional and financial cost and possibly also loss of life. A word of freedom is offered here, showing that it is not necessary for Christians to organize relatedness in this way and that other options are available that better fit their calling as members of the body of Christ. However, the concept of shared substance – or some other organizational principle – can be deployed well: to decrease exclusion, to increase accountability and to deepen intimacy. The concept of shared substance is deployed par excellence in the language of participation in the body of Christ, as witnessed in different ways in baptism, communion, monasticism and spiritual kinship all display the social logic of the Christian faith. In those practices, all are called to share in a new identity, in Christ, and yet each also recognized a special affection and obligation for others, that the intimacy of kinship in Jesus might be embodied in the day-to-day, but in such a way that the heart is opened to others rather than closed.

A theology of kinship, then, is useful for discernment. It is not a question of sketching a blueprint, but neither is the use of examples from Christian history intended to create a patchwork blueprint, as though the Christian life were simply a matter of looking back to counter-practices like monasticism or high forms of spiritual kinship in order to be faithful. A family organized around ideas of biogenetic relatedness may indeed be disclosive in wonderful ways of the kingdom of God, as the Spirit builds the kingdom in the midst of those people – even if this book warns against nurturing that idea of biogenetic relatedness for the arbitrary exclusion it entails. The theology of kinship ultimately names the idea that relatedness is restricted by biogenetic principles, in other words, as a lie, without making any move to judge those who believe it, or indeed those practices that may in fact have been premised on it even if the Spirit is fostering those practices on the basis that each member of that family is called to one another as a child of God in Jesus Christ. The dissonance for that family, between the cultural idea of biogenetic relatedness and their Christian faith, may come in the sermon of Mt. 12.46-50, or when confronted with the invitation to recognize a neighbour as having a greater belonging in their midst than the doctrine of biogenetic relatedness can recognize.

The Christian, then, is free to try to live out Christian kinship, casting off the cultural notion that they must only care for those who share blood, casting off the need to procreate or marry, casting off the need even to look after themselves, knowing that in doing so they can create communities with more lasting significance beyond the final resurrection. They can start L'Arche communities, learning the secrets at the hearts of those with intellectual disabilities. They can adopt the orphan or the widow into their home instead of feeling it is unnatural to do anything but protect the interests of their genes. They can open their house to the lost, and if like Justin Welby they discover that the origins of their personal history are not what they thought, they can declare their identity to be held securely in Christ. They can do all those things insofar as they discern the leading of the Spirit to their conformity in Christ. This theology of kinship acts as a guide to scriptural witness for the purpose of prophetic discernment, to follow the thread of 1 Thess. 5.20-22: 'Do not despise the words of prophets, but test everything; hold fast to what is good; abstain from every form of evil.' God will lead, but human beings need to exercise discernment in testing what they think they hear against scripture. This theology of kinship aims to organize the witness of scripture for the purpose of such testing of the leading of the Spirit.

Concerning the limitations of the prescriptive element of this account of Christian kinship, anything like a proposed ethnography of Christian culture will always fall short of offering a sufficiently realistic alternative culture, because there simply is not enough information. The picture here is not comprehensive but seeks to articulate the core of Christian kinship – grounded in union with Christ, which makes all whom Jesus welcomes into kin – while showing some ways in which that is practised in the here and now. Monasticism of different varieties, committed celibacy, marriage and spiritual kinship create special obligations within the body, with theological justification. They respond to the implication of membership of the body of Christ, towards opening social groups, reorganized in ways that are less likely to exclude, but still in such a way that they foster intimacy and accountability. These distinctly Christian practices also interact with pre-existing cultures, with transformative effect. Juliet du Boulay's description of life in Ambeli captures this: 'for the most part, the formative influence of the Church has concentrated on building an architecture of Christian meanings which could embrace, unify and transform the fragments of old cultures that live on in Greece wherever they are not directly in contradiction with the

Christian message.'[12] This could, of course, become syncretistic, and one of the key roles that anthropology has played in this book is in flagging up cultural ideas, so that they can be tested theologically rather than simply accepted. What it is intended to show, however, is the limits on moral theological description of Christian relatedness. In the everyday life of the Christian, other forms of social organization will present themselves as reasonable choices, which may not have the hallmark of distinctively Christian practice, but which may not be obviously problematic either.

The idea that all are called to be children of God, and so to receive one another as brothers and sisters, can be realized in the details in a multitude of ways in the small, as Christians balance intimacy and accountability on the one hand, with openness to the stranger on the other hand.

This is just as well, because any decision about life before God is made amidst a range of other factors and existing commitments. Accordingly, there is no problem affirming, with 1 Tim. 5.8, 'whoever does not provide for relatives, and especially for family members, has denied the faith and is worse than an unbeliever'. The husband and father would be quite wrong, on the basis of the argument of this book, to leave his wife and children in order to join a monastery, not just because he is covenanted to his wife, and not just because he is clearly the person responsible (on a number of bases) for the children, *his* children. Both of those reasons would be more than sufficient. He would also be misunderstanding that his life is already committed and that he is not to seek to instantiate in his life the most perfect realization of Christian kinship that he can imagine as though he had no prior commitments. This would be the mistake of the Pharisee declaring as Corban what is owed to his parents in their old age (Mark 7) – there is nothing wrong with an offering to God, provided it is not already committed elsewhere.

But a warning, before that last statement waters down the distinctiveness of the message of this book. A manner of living kinship that is responsive to the social logic of baptism and the Eucharist is going to be marked by hospitable inclusivity, accountability and intimacy. L'Arche communities are, in one sense, exclusive – there are a limited number who live in the community – even if they are remarkably hospitable. But community is formed around a core of those whom wider society does not readily include. As such, the exclusivity of membership is in itself inclusive, enabling the depth of intimacy that finite membership allows while including primarily the otherwise excluded.

However, should that exclusivity be guided by modes of social organization that lead to the exclusion of some from intimate relationships altogether, either because of something intrinsic to the system or because no accommodation has been made for failures in the system, then it bears insufficient likeness to the kinship to come, entrusted to the Christian in Jesus Christ. L'Arche, monasticism, spiritual kinship, fostering and adoption are all examples of counter-cultural practices which repair social perceptions of kinship with a view to full inclusion. They do not offer a

---

12. Du Boulay, *Cosmos, Life, and Liturgy in a Greek Orthodox Village*, 12.

clear answer to how Christian kinship might be lived out in this age, but rather improvise repairs in different ways in a Fallen world. Authentically Christian kinship remains an eschatological reality, but a reality that should circumscribe and shape Christian practice today, as Christians seek to live out the reality of their return to God, in their adoption in Christ, in whom all are fully kin.

Not everyone is given much freedom to decide their future, about who or whether to marry, where to work, whether to have children, who to spend time with, but many do. Where God gives an opportunity to make a decision, the principles of inclusivity (will how I arrange my time further include or further exclude those who are most excluded?), accountability (will I be empowering only myself or will my life be open to accountability to others?) and intimacy (will I form real relationships with people, in which trust and care are shared, or will I spread myself too thin, unable to form any but superficial relationships?) help recognize whether an opportunity is from God or not. It is not the job of a Christian ethicist to identify the possible opportunities a person might face in their life. Even if that were humanly possible, God does not surrender His sole right to call a person.

Final conclusions and further research

How, then, does a theology of kinship inform the Christian life? It describes the context of the Christian more accurately – they are not alone in the world, fit only to look after themselves, but are participants by the Spirit in the life of Christ. As such, they are called to find the kingdom in their midst, living out the freedom of the gospel in which they – and their neighbour – are called to be children of God and siblings of one another. They are not thus burdened with the responsibility of redesigning society – after all, they are not alone, the authors of their own destiny – but are followers of Jesus, the author and perfecter of their faith. They can be free in the security of who they are in Jesus Christ to reject the temptation to treat their neighbour as either fundamentally irrelevant or as an obstacle to their own self-realization. What follows is a question of discernment. Theological ethics of kinship helps with discernment of what God is doing as He leads His family in individual lives as well as in great cultures and nations.

However, to leave the discussion there would be to give the impression that Christians are in a constantly precarious place as they try to discern the leading of God. That is not the case, not just because to be called in Christ is to relativize the ultimate importance of many everyday decisions but also because human life is not composed of an endless series of decisions. Rather, human beings are shaped by practices. Practices fit in between the grand scale of theological ideas, and the small scale of everyday decisions, as middle-scale habits of life that affect many but always instantiated under a specific cultural horizon. On the grand scale, the Christian might be assisted by the theological idea of kinship in Christ. On the small scale they might be assisted in living out that broadening vision to receive all as brothers and sisters in Christ, by looking to form relational spheres that organize their affections, obligations and accountability in a manner marked by inclusion to those otherwise excluded. On the middle scale, Christians will marry, build houses, leave inheritances, have children, go to church, travel, give to the poor, work jobs and do so while following well-worn paths. It is at the middle scale, at the level of these practices, that theological ethics might be most impactful.

One practice that has been singled out for critical attention is the use of ARTs. It has been suggested that the very existence of ARTs as an option might represent and reinscribe an idea of kinship (that it must be biological) that is theologically dubious, unnecessary and possibly harmful. However, that does not in itself forbid the use of ARTs. A full ethical treatment of each ART would require the surveying of a range of other factors from the treatment of embryos, to what constitutes appropriate medical care, to the place of the law in these kinds of choices, all of which are beyond the scope of this book. However, once the restrictive theory of kinship that might motivate the use of ARTs is challenged, then it is a little easier to imagine alternative practices as genuine options, rather than in some sense subpar, not creating the conditions for real kinship.

Similarly, while the practice of adoption is one this book receives warmly, the practice of secrecy in adoption could be taken as representing and reinscribing that same moral idea that makes ARTs seem necessary for those who wish to be parents. Again, a far wider range of moral factors is implicated than just kinship. However, the idea that kinship is fundamentally biological forces those involved in adoption into a protective secrecy that conceals the supposed fiction of the tie of kinship. Here, a restrictive ideology is limiting the imagination of the Christian, and harming a community's ability to generate alternative and better practices to the receiving of children into new families (and, indeed, better practice has started to emerge with the opening of the great secret of adoption in American adoption practice).

Taking each of these practices in turn, and recognizing the place of kinship amidst the other moral factors, presents the greatest area for future research in the light of the conclusion of this book. How an individual spends money, chooses where to work, chooses who to spend time with and chooses how to treat their neighbour or a stranger are in some way influenced by ideas of kinship. And yet balancing different responsibilities will often place Christians into conflict, especially between the duty to care for the poorest on the one hand and their families on the other. In a way, that conflict expresses the heart of the question at hand: How do we organize ourselves as a society, given the radical hospitality and inclusion that Jesus teaches? How can the good news of such a message be realized, so that rather than feeling burdened, the Christian is released from those practices of kinship which only appear to be necessary, inevitable and good? Far from an imposition, that would be a liberation, so that the Christian can embrace the deep calling to kinship in Christ and in that way embrace who they are, even where those practices will often run painfully (but hopefully transformatively) against the stream of society.

A wide range of practices have been surveyed in this book, but the principles are few. In short, the Christian is to understand themselves as properly constituted in Christ by the Spirit, liberated by the security they have in Jesus to receive others as brothers and sisters in Christ. That does not mean the universalizing of their relational sphere but rather invites them to value and share affections, obligations and accountability with their brothers and sisters. The precise limits of their sphere cannot be straightforwardly delineated, but rather is a question of what the Spirit enables. However, in a world in which there is exclusion, examples like the many L'Arche communities prove it is possible to construct small communities with meaningful connection, which represent an inversion of the values around them, because it is formed around a core of those who might otherwise be excluded. That said, the question of kinship is not just about social groups, but appears in any number of practices – those cultural habits that grant a familiar shape to our everyday lives. Kinship profoundly shapes who we think we are, who we welcome into our hearts and how we live our lives. As such, Christians should expect their lives to change as they think through their identity in Christ and the kinship that follows.

BIBLIOGRAPHY

Aelred of Rievaulx. *Spiritual Friendship*. Translated by Mark F. Williams. Scranton, PA: University of Scranton Press, 1994.
Anidjar, Gil. *Blood: A Critique of Christianity*. New York: Columbia University Press, 2014.
Aquinas, Thomas. *Summa Theologiæ*. Translated by Fathers of the English Dominican Province. Vol. 5. Allen, TX: Christian Classics, 1948.
Aquinas, Thomas. *Summa Theologiæ*. Translated by William Barden. Vol. 58. London: Blackfriars, 1965.
Aristotle. *De Generatione Animalium*. Edited by J. A. Smith. Translated by A. Platt. The Works of Aristotle Translated into English. Oxford: Clarendon, 1910.
Aristotle. *Politics*. Translated by H. Rackham. Loeb Classical Library 264. Cambridge, MA: Harvard University Press, 1932.
Athanasius of Alexandria. *Letter Concerning the Councils of Ariminum* in *Patrologia Graeca*, edited by J.-P. Migne, vol. 26. Paris: Imprimerie Catholique, 1857.
Athanasius of Alexandria. *Orations against the Arians* in *Patrologia Graeca*, edited by J.-P. Migne, vol. 26. Paris: Imprimerie Catholique, 1857.
Atkinson, Jane. 'Quizzing the Sphinx: Reflections on Mortality in Central Sulawesi'. In *Fantasizing the Feminine in Indonesia*, edited by Laurie J. Sears, 163–90. Durham, NC: Duke University Press, 1996.
Aubert, Guillaume. 'Kinship, Blood, and the Emergence of the Racial Nation in the French Atlantic World, 1600–1789'. In *Blood and Kinship: Matter for Metaphor from Ancient Rome to the Present*, edited by Christopher H. Johnson, Bernhard Jussen, David Warren Sabean and Simon Teuscher, 175–95. New York: Berghahn Books, 2013.
Augustine. 'Agreement among the Evangelists'. In *New Testament I and II*, translated by Kim Paffenroth, 131–348. The Works of Saint Augustine: A Translation for the 21st Century, I/15 and I/16. Hyde Park, NY: New City Press, 2014.
Augustine. *Answer to Faustus, a Manichean*. Edited by Boniface Ramsey. Translated by Roland Teske. The Works of Saint Augustine: A Translation for the 21st Century, I/20. Hyde Park, NY: New City Press, 2007.
Augustine. *City of God*. Translated by Henry Bettenson. Harmondsworth: Penguin Books, 1984.
Augustine. *Confessions*. Oxford World's Classics. Oxford: Oxford University Press, 2008.
Augustine. 'Continence'. In *Marriage and Virginity*, edited by John E. Rotelle and David G. Hunter, translated by Ray Kearney, 189–216. The Works of Saint Augustine: A Translation for the 21st Century, I/9. Brooklyn, NY: New City Press, 1999.
Augustine. *Expositions of the Psalms 33-50*. Edited by John E. Rotelle. Translated by Maria Boulding. The Works of Saint Augustine: A Translation for the 21st Century, III/16. New York: New City Press, 2000.
Augustine. *Expositions of the Psalms 51-72*. Edited by John E. Rotelle. Translated by Maria Boulding. The Works of Saint Augustine: A Translation for the 21st Century, III/17. New York: New City Press, 2001.

Augustine. *Expositions of the Psalms 73-98*. Edited by John E. Rotelle. Translated by Maria Boulding. The Works of Saint Augustine: A Translation for the 21st Century, III/18. New York: New City Press, 2002.

Augustine. *Expositions of the Psalms 121-150*. Edited by Boniface Ramsey. Translated by Maria Boulding. The Works of Saint Augustine: A Translation for the 21st Century, III/20. New York: New City Press, 2004.

Augustine. 'Holy Virginity'. In *Marriage and Virginity*, edited by John E. Rotelle and David G. Hunter, translated by Ray Kearney, 68–107. The Works of Saint Augustine: A Translation for the 21st Century, I/9. Brooklyn, NY: New City Press, 1999.

Augustine. *Homilies on the Gospel of John 1-40*. Edited by Allan Fitzgerald. Translated by Edmund Hill. The Works of Saint Augustine: A Translation for the 21st Century, I/12. Hyde Park, NY: New City Press, 2009.

Augustine. *Letters 1-99*. Edited by John E. Rotelle. Translated by Roland J. Teske. The Works of Saint Augustine: A Translation for the 21st Century, II/1. Hyde Park, NY: New City Press, 2001.

Augustine. *Letters 211-270, 1*-29* (Epistulae)*. The Works of Saint Augustine: A Translation for the 21st Century, II/4. Hyde Park, NY: New City Press, 2005.

Augustine. 'Praeceptum'. In *Augustine of Hippo and His Monastic Rule*, by George Lawless, 80–103. Oxford: Oxford University Press, 1990.

Augustine. *Sermons (1-19)*. Edited by John E. Rotelle. Translated by Edmund Hill. The Works of Saint Augustine: A Translation for the 21st Century, III/1. Brooklyn, NY: New City Press, 1990.

Augustine. *Sermons (94A-147A)*. Edited by John E. Rotelle. Translated by Edmund Hill. The Works of Saint Augustine: A Translation for the 21st Century, III/4. Brooklyn, NY: New City Press, 1992.

Augustine. *Sermons (184-229Z)*. Edited by John E. Rotelle. Translated by Edmund Hill. The Works of Saint Augustine: A Translation for the 21st Century, III/6. New Rochelle, NY: New City Press, 1993.

Augustine. *Sermons (230-272B)*. Translated by Edmund Hill. The Works of Saint Augustine: A Translation for the 21st Century, III/7. New Rochelle, NY: New City Press, 1993.

Augustine. 'The Excellence of Marriage'. In *Marriage and Virginity*, edited by John E. Rotelle and David G. Hunter, translated by Ray Kearney, 33–61. The Works of Saint Augustine: A Translation for the 21st Century, I/9. Brooklyn, NY: New City Press, 1999.

Augustine. 'The Works of Monks'. In *Treatises on Various Subjects*, edited by Roy Joseph Deferrari. The Fathers of the Church 16. New York: Fathers of the Church, 1952.

Augustine. 'Tractates on the First Epistle of John'. In *Tractates on the Gospel of John 112-24; Tractates on the First Epistle of John*, translated by J. W. Rettig, 97–277. Fathers of the Church 92. Washington, DC: Catholic University of America Press, 1995.

Ayres, Lewis. *Nicaea and Its Legacy: An Approach to Fourth-Century Trinitarian Theology*. Oxford: Oxford University Press, 2004.

Bachofen, J. J. 'Mother Right: An Investigation of the Religious and Juridical Character of Matriarchy in the Ancient World'. In *Myth, Religion, and Mother Right: Selected Writings of J.J. Bachofen*, translated by Ralph Manheim, 67–208. Princeton, NJ: Princeton University Press, 1992.

Bailey, Derrick S. *Sponsors at Baptism and Confirmation: An Historical Introduction to Anglican Practice*. London: SPCK, 1952.

Banner, Michael. *Christian Ethics and Contemporary Moral Problems*. Cambridge: Cambridge University Press, 1999.

Banner, Michael. *The Ethics of Everyday Life: Moral Theology, Social Anthropology, and the Imagination of the Human*. Oxford: Oxford University Press, 2014.
Barclay, John M. G. *Paul and the Gift*. Grand Rapids, MI: Eerdmans, 2015.
Barclay, John M. G. 'The Family as the Bearer of Religion in Judaism and Early Christianity'. In *Constructing Early Christian Families: Family as Social Reality and Metaphor*, edited by Halvor Moxnes, 66–80. London: Routledge, 1997.
Barth, Karl. *A Christian Directory: Or, a Sum of Practical Theology, and Cases of Conscience, Part 4. Christian Politics, (or Duties to Our Rulers and Neighbours)*. The Works of the Rev. Richard Baxter 4. London: James Duncan, 1830.
Barth, Karl. *A Holy Commonwealth*. Edited by William Lamont. Cambridge Texts in the History of Political Thought. Cambridge: Cambridge University Press, 1994.
Barth, Karl. *Church Dogmatics: The Doctrine of Creation*. Edited by G. W. Bromiley and T. F. Torrance. Translated by J. W. Edwards, O. Bussey and H. Knight. Vol. III/1. Edinburgh: T&T Clark, 1958.
Barth, Karl. *Church Dogmatics: The Doctrine of Creation*. Edited by G. W. Bromiley and T. F. Torrance. Translated by H. Knight, G. W. Bromiley, J. K. S. Reid, and R. H. Fuller. Vol. III/2. Edinburgh: T&T Clark, 1960.
Barth, Karl. *Church Dogmatics: The Doctrine of Creation*. Edited by G. W. Bromiley and T. F. Torrance. Translated by A. T. Mackay, T. H. L. Parker, H. Knight, H. A. Kennedy, and J. Marks. Vol. III/4. Edinburgh: T&T Clark, 1961.
Barth, Karl. *Church Dogmatics: The Doctrine of the Word of God*. Edited by G. W. Bromiley and T. F. Torrance. Translated by G. T. Thompson, H. Knight, H. A. Kennedy, and J. Marks. Vol. I/2. Edinburgh: T&T Clark, 1956.
Barth, Karl. *Church Dogmatics: The Doctrine of the Word of God*. Edited by G. W. Bromiley and T. F. Torrance. Translated by A. T. Mackay, T. H. L. Parker, H. Knight, H. A. Kennedy, and J. Marks. 2nd edn. Vol. I/1. Edinburgh: T&T Clark, 1975.
Barth, Karl. *Die Kirchliche Dogmatik: Die Lehre von Der Schöpfung*. 3rd edn. Vol. III/1. Zürich: Evangelischer Verlag, 1957.
Barth, Karl. *Die Kirchliche Dogmatik: Die Lehre von Der Schöpfung*. Vol. III/4. Zürich: Theologischer Verlag Zürich, 1980.
Barth, Karl. *Gildas Salvianus; The First Part: I.e. The Reformed Pastor. Shewing the Nature of the Pastoral Work; Especially in Private Instruction and Catechizing*. London, 1656.
Barton, Stephen C. *Discipleship and Family Ties in Mark and Matthew*. Society for New Testament Studies Monograph Series 80. Cambridge: Cambridge University Press, 1994.
Barton, Stephen C. 'Family'. In *The Oxford Companion to Christian Thought*, edited by Adrian Hastings, Alistair Mason, Hugh Pyper, Ingrid Lawrie and Cecily Bennett, 235–6. Oxford: Oxford University Press, 2000.
Basil of Caesarea. *Letters* in *Patrologia Graeca*, edited by J.-P. Migne, vol. 32. Paris: Imprimerie Catholique, 1857.
Basil of Caesarea. *The Rule of St. Basil in Latin and English: A Revised Critical Edition*. Translated by Anna Silvas. Collegeville, MN: Liturgical Press, 2013.
Baxter, Richard. *A Breviate of the Life of Margaret, the Daughter of Francis Charlton of Apply in Shropshire, Esq. and Wife of Richard Baxter*. London, 1681.
Baxter, Richard. *A Christian Directory: Or, a Sum of Practical Theology, and Cases of Conscience, Part 2. Christian Economics (or Family Duties)*. The Works of the Rev. Richard Baxter 4. London: James Duncan, 1830.
Beauvoir, Simone de. *The Second Sex*. Edited by H. M. Parshley. London: Penguin, 1972.

Becker, Gay. *The Elusive Embryo: How Women and Men Approach New Reproductive Technologies*. Berkeley: University of California Press, 2000.

Benedict. *The Rule of St. Benedict*. Edited by Timothy Fry. Collegeville, MN: The Liturgical Press, 1981.

Bennett, Jana Marguerite. *Singleness and the Church: A New Theology of the Single Life*. Oxford: Oxford University Press, 2017.

Bennett, Jana Marguerite. *Water Is Thicker than Blood: An Augustinian Theology of Marriage and Singleness*. Oxford: Oxford University Press, 2008.

Bestard, Joan. 'Knowing and Relating: Kinship, Assisted Reproductive Technologies and the New Genetics'. In *European Kinship in the Age of Biotechnology*, edited by Jeanette Edwards and Carles Salazar, 19–28. New York: Berghahn, 2008.

Biale, David. *Blood and Belief: The Circulation of a Symbol Between Jews and Christians*. Berkeley: University of California Press, 2007.

Bildhauer, Bettina. *Medieval Blood*. Religion and Culture in the Middle Ages. Cardiff: University of Wales Press, 2006.

Bildhauer, Bettina. 'Medieval European Conceptions of Blood: Truth and Human Integrity'. *Journal of the Royal Anthropological Institute* 19 (1 May 2013): 557–76.

Bildhauer, Bettina. 'We Have Never Been Unbloody'. *Syndicate Theology* (blog). Accessed 26 July 2019. https://syndicate.network/symposia/theology/blood/.

Billings, J. Todd. *Union with Christ: Reframing Theology and Ministry for the Church*. Grand Rapids, MI: Baker, 2011.

Bodenhorn, Barbara. '"He Used to Be My Relative": Exploring the Bases of Relatedness among Iñupiat of Northern Alaska'. In *Cultures of Relatedness: New Approaches to the Study of Kinship*, edited by Janet Carsten, 128–48. Cambridge: Cambridge University Press, 2000.

Bonhoeffer, Dietrich. *Creation and Fall: A Theological Interpretation of Genesis 1-3*. Translated by J. C. Fletcher. London: SCM, 1959.

Bonhoeffer, Dietrich. *Ethics*. Edited by C. J. Green. Translated by R. Krauss, C. C. West and D. W. Scott. Dietrich Bonhoeffer Works 6. Minneapolis, MN: Fortress Press, 2009.

Bonhoeffer, Dietrich. *Life Together and Prayerbook of the Bible*. Edited by Geffrey B. Kelly. Translated by Daniel W. Bloesch and James H. Burtness. Dietrich Bonhoeffer Works 5. Minneapolis, MN: Fortress Press, 2005.

Boswell, John. *The Kindness of Strangers: The Abandonment of Children in Western Europe from Late Antiquity to the Renaissance*. Chicago: University of Chicago Press, 1988.

Bradford, William. *Bradford's History of the Plymouth Plantation 1606-1646*. Edited by W. T. Davis. Original Narratives of Early American History. New York: Scribner, 1908.

Brighouse, Harry and Adam Swift. 'Family'. In *The International Encyclopedia of Ethics*, edited by Hugh LaFollette. Vol. 4. Oxford: Wiley-Blackwell, 2013.

Brighouse, Harry and Adam Swift. *Family Values: The Ethics of Parent-Child Relationships*. Princeton, NJ: Princeton University Press, 2014.

Brown, Peter. *The Body and Society: Men, Women, and Sexual Renunciation in Early Christianity*. Chichester, NY: Columbia University Press, 2008.

Brown, Peter. *Through the Eye of the Needle: Wealth, the Fall of Rome, and the Making of Christianity in the West, 250–550 AD*. Princeton, NJ: Princeton University Press, 2012.

Browning, Don S. 'A Natural Law Theory of Marriage'. *Zygon* 46, no. 3 (September 1, 2011): 733–60.

Burke, Trevor J. *Adopted into God's Family: Exploring a Pauline Metaphor*. New Studies in Biblical Theology. Downers Grove, IL: IVP, 2006.

Bynum, Caroline Walker. *Wonderful Blood: Theology and Practice in Late Medieval Northern Germany and Beyond*. Philadelphia: University of Pennsylvania Press, 2007.
Caesarius of Arles. *Sermons, Volume 1 (1–80)*. Translated by Mary Magdeleine Mueller. Fathers of the Church 31. Washington, DC: Catholic University of America Press, 2010.
Cahill, Lisa Sowle. 'Family'. In *Encyclopedia of Christian Theology*. Vol. 3. London: Routledge, 2005.
Cahill, Lisa Sowle. *Family: A Christian Social Perspective*. Minneapolis, MN: Fortress Press, 2000.
Cahill, Lisa Sowle. *Sex, Gender, and Christian Ethics*. Cambridge: Cambridge University Press, 1996.
Calvin, John. *Institutes of the Christian Religion*. Edited by John T. McNeill. Translated by Ford Lewis Battles. Louisville, KY: Westminster John Knox Press, 1960.
Calvin, John. *The First Epistle of Paul the Apostle to the Corinthians*. Edited by David W. Torrance and Thomas F. Torrance. Translated by John W. Fraser. Calvin's Commentaries. Grand Rapids, MI: Eerdmans, 1996.
Capp, Bernard. 'Republican Reformation: Family, Community and the State in Interregnum Middlesex, 1649–60'. In *The Family in Early Modern England*, edited by Helen Berry and Elizabeth Foyster, 40–66. Cambridge: Cambridge University Press, 2007.
Carsten, Janet. *After Kinship*. New Departures in Anthropology. Cambridge: Cambridge University Press, 2004.
Carsten, Janet. 'Substance and Relationality: Blood in Contexts'. *Annual Review of Anthropology* 40, no. 1 (September 2011): 19–35.
Carsten, Janet. 'What Kinship Does - and How'. *HAU: Journal of Ethnographic Theory* 3, no. 2 (2013): 245–51.
Cassian, John. *The Conferences*. Translated by Boniface Ramsey. Ancient Christian Writers. Mahwah, NJ: Newman Press, 1997.
Catechism of the Catholic Church. Geoffrey Chapman-Libreria Editrice Vaticana, 1994.
Cavanaugh, William T. *Being Consumed: Economics and Christian Desire*. Grand Rapids, MI: Eerdmans, 2008.
Cavanaugh, William T. *Torture and the Eucharist: Theology, Politics and the Body of Christ*. Challenges in Contemporary Theology. Oxford: Blackwell, 1998.
Chapais, Bernard. *Primeval Kinship*. Cambridge, MA: Harvard University Press, 2008.
Church of England. *Common Worship: Ordination Services*. London: Church House Publishing, 2007. https://www.churchofengland.org/prayer-and-worship/worship-texts-and-resources/common-worship/ministry/common-worship-ordination-0#mm012.
Cicero. *De Inventione*, n.d.
Cicero. *De Officiis*, n.d.
Cicero. *On Obligations*. Oxford: Oxford University Press, 2000.
Cliffe, J. T. *The Puritan Gentry: The Great Puritan Families of Early Stuart England*. London: Routledge & Kegan Paul, 1984.
Coakley, Sarah. *God, Sexuality, and the Self: An Essay 'On the Trinity'*. Cambridge: Cambridge University Press, 2013.
Coakley, Sarah. '"In Persona Christi": Who, or Where, Is Christ at the Altar?' In *A Man of Many Parts: Essays in Honor of John Westerdale Bowker on the Occasion of His Eightieth Birthday*, edited by Eugene E. Lemcio, 95–112. Eugene, OR: Wipf and Stock Publishers, 2015.

Collier, Jane Fishburne and Sylvia Junko Yanagisako. 'Toward a Unified Analysis of Gender and Kinship'. In *Gender and Kinship: Essays Toward a Unified Analysis*, edited by Jane Fishburne Collier and Sylvia Junko Yanagisako, 14–52. Stanford, CA: Stanford University Press, 1987.

Cooper, Kate. 'Approaching the Holy Household'. *Journal of Early Christian Studies* 15, no. 2 (Summer 2007): 131–42.

Cooper, Kate. 'Poverty, Obligation, and Inheritance: Roman Heiresses and the Varieties of Senatorial Christianity in Fifth-Century Rome'. In *Religion, Dynasty, and Patronage in Early Christian Rome, 300–900*, edited by Kate Cooper and Julia Hillner, 165–89. Cambridge: Cambridge University Press, 2007.

Cooper, Kate. *The Fall of the Roman Household*. Cambridge: Cambridge University Press, 2007.

Cornwall, Susannah. *Un/Familiar Theology: Reconceiving Sex, Reproduction and Generativity*. Rethinking Theologies. London: Bloomsbury, 2017.

Crawford, Patricia. *Blood, Bodies and Families in Early Modern England*. Harlow: Pearson, 2004.

De Jong, Mayke. *In Samuel's Image: Child Oblation in the Early Medieval West*. Leiden: Brill, 1996.

Delille, Gérard. 'The Shed Blood of Christ: From Blood as Metaphor to Blood as Bearer of Identity'. In *Blood and Kinship: Matter for Metaphor from Ancient Rome to the Present*, edited by Christopher H. Johnson, Bernhard Jussen, David Warren Sabean and Simon Teuscher, 125–43. New York: Berghahn Books, 2013.

Du Boulay, Juliet. *Cosmos, Life, and Liturgy in a Greek Orthodox Village*. The Romiosyni Series 18. Limni: Denise Harvey, 2009.

Dunn, Marilyn. 'Asceticism and Monasticism, II: Western'. In *Constantine to c. 600*, edited by Augustine Casiday and Frederick W. Norris, 669–90. The Cambridge History of Christianity. Vol. 2. Cambridge: Cambridge University Press, 2007.

Durston, Christopher. *The Family in the English Revolution*. Oxford: Basil Blackwell, 1989.

Edwards, Jeanette. 'Explicit Connections: Ethnographic Enquiry in North-West England'. In *Technologies of Procreation: Kinship in the Age of Assisted Conception*, edited by Jeanette Edwards, Sarah Franklin, Eric Hirsch, Frances Price and Marilyn Strathern. Manchester: Manchester University Press, 1993.

Engels, Friedrich. *The Origin of the Family, Private Property and the State*. London: Penguin, 2010.

Essner, Cornelia. 'Nazi Anti-Semitism and the Question of "Jewish Blood"'. In *Blood and Kinship: Matter for Metaphor from Ancient Rome to the Present*, edited by Christopher H. Johnson, Bernhard Jussen, David Warren Sabean and Simon Teuscher, 227–43. New York: Berghahn Books, 2013.

Faubion, James D. 'Introduction: Toward an Anthropology of the Ethics of Kinship'. In *The Ethics of Kinship: Ethnographic Inquiries*, edited by James D. Faubion, 1–29. Lanham, MD, Oxford: Rowman & Littlefield, 2001.

Fontaine, Jacques. 'Education and Learning'. In *The New Cambridge Medieval History, Vol. 1, c.500–c.700*, edited by Paul Fouracre, 735–59. Cambridge: Cambridge University Press, 2005.

Foucault, Michel. *The Use of Pleasure*. Translated by Robert Hurley. The History of Sexuality 2. London: Penguins, 1985.

Franklin, Sarah. *Embodied Progress: A Cultural Account of Assisted Conception*. London: Routledge, 1997.

Franklin, Sarah. 'From Blood to Genes? Rethinking Consanguinity in the Context of Geneticization'. In *Blood and Kinship: Matter for Metaphor from Ancient Rome to the Present*, edited by Christopher H. Johnson, Bernhard Jussen, David Warren Sabean and Simon Teuscher, 285–306. New York: Berghahn Books, 2013.

Franklin, Sarah. 'Making Miracles: Scientific Progress and the Facts of Life'. In *Reproducing Reproduction: Kinship, Power, and Technological Innovation*, edited by Sarah Franklin and Helena Ragoné, 102–17. Philadelphia: University of Pennsylvania Press, 1998.

Geertz, Clifford. 'Deep Play: Notes on the Balinese Cockfight'. In *The Interpretation of Cultures: Selected Essays*, 412–54. New York: Basic Books, 1973.

Geertz, Clifford. *The Interpretation of Cultures: Selected Essays*. New York: Basic Books, 1973.

Gregory of Nyssa. *Great Catechism*.

Gregory of Nyssa. 'The Life of Macrina'. In *Ascetical Works*, translated by Virginia Woods Callahan, 161–91. Fathers of the Church, a New Translation 58. Washington, DC: Catholic University of America Press, 1967.

Gregory of Nyssa. *To Ablabius, On Not Three Gods*.

Gregory the Great. 'Dialogue Two'. In *Dialogues*, translated by Odo Zimmerman. Fathers of the Church 39. Washington, DC: Catholic University of America Press, 1959.

Guerreau-Jalabert, Anita. 'Flesh and Blood in Medieval Language about Kinship'. In *Blood and Kinship: Matter for Metaphor from Ancient Rome to the Present*, edited by Christopher H. Johnson, Bernhard Jussen, David Warren Sabean and Simon Teuscher, 1–17. New York: Berghahn Books, 2013.

Gunton, Colin. 'Persons'. In *Dictionary of Ethics, Theology and Society*, edited by Paul Barry Clarke and Andrew Linzey. London: Routledge, 1996.

Hall, Amy Laura. *Conceiving Parenthood: American Protestantism and the Spirit of Reproduction*. Grand Rapids, MI: Eerdmans, 2007.

Harders, Ann-Cathrin. 'Agnatio, Cognatio, Consanguinitas: Kinship and Blood in Ancient Rome'. In *Blood and Kinship: Matter for Metaphor from Ancient Rome to the Present*, edited by Christopher H. Johnson, Bernhard Jussen, David Warren Sabean and Simon Teuscher, 18–39. New York: Berghahn Books, 2013.

Harrison, Carol. 'The Silent Majority: The Family in Patristic Thought'. In *The Family in Theological Perspective*, edited by Stephen C. Barton, 87–105. Edinburgh: T&T Clark, 1996.

Haslanger, Sally. *Resisting Reality: Social Construction and Social Critique*. Oxford: Oxford University Press, 2012.

Hays, Richard B. *Echoes of Scripture in the Letters of Paul*. New Haven, CT: Yale University Press, 1989.

Heine, Ronald E. 'Hippolytus, Ps-Hippolytus and the Early Canons'. In *The Cambridge History of Early Christian Literature*, edited by Frances Young, Lewis Ayres and Andrew Louth, 142–51. Cambridge: Cambridge University Press, 2004.

Heine, Ronald E. 'The Beginnings of Latin Christian Literature'. In *The Cambridge History of Early Christian Literature*, edited by Frances Young, Lewis Ayres and Andrew Louth, 131–41. Cambridge: Cambridge University Press, 2004.

Heywood, Colin. *A History of Childhood: Children and Childhood in the West from Medieval to Modern Times*. Cambridge: Polity, 2001.

Hippolytus of Rome. *Against Noetus* in *Patrologia Graeca*, edited by J.-P. Migne, vol. 10. Paris: Imprimerie Catholique, 1857.

Hodge, Caroline Johnson. *If Sons, Then Heirs: A Study of Kinship and Ethnicity in the Letters of Paul*. Oxford: Oxford University Press, 2007.

Holmes, Christopher R. J. *Ethics in the Presence of Christ*. London: T&T Clark, 2012.
Hughes, Ann. 'Puritanism and Gender'. In *The Cambridge Companion to Puritanism*, edited by John Coffey and Paul C. H. Lim, 294–308. Cambridge: Cambridge University Press, 2008.
Inwagen, Peter van. 'Free Will Remains a Mystery: The Eighth Philosophical Perspectives Lecture'. *Philosophical Perspectives* 14 (2000): 1–19.
Irvine, Richard. 'The Everyday Life of Monks: English Benedictine Identity and the Performance of Proximity'. In *Monasticism in Modern Times*, edited by Isabelle Jonveaux and Stefania Palmisano, 191–208. London: Routledge, 2016.
Isidor of Seville. *Etymologies*, 623.
Jerome. 'Against Jovinianus'. In *Jerome: Letters and Select Works*, edited by Philip Schaff and Henry Wace, translated by W. H. Fremantle. Vol. 6. Nicene and Post-Nicene Fathers: Second Series. New York: The Christian Literature Company, 1893.
John Paul II. *On the Family: Apostolic Exhortation Familiaris Consortio of His Holiness Pope John Paul II to the Episcopate to the Clergy and to the Faithful of the Whole Catholic Church Regarding the Role of the Christian Family in the Modern World*, 1981.
Johnson, Christopher H. 'Class Dimensions of Blood, Kinship, and Race in Brittany, 1780–1880'. In *Blood and Kinship: Matter for Metaphor from Ancient Rome to the Present*, edited by Christopher H. Johnson, Bernhard Jussen, David Warren Sabean and Simon Teuscher, 196–226. New York: Berghahn Books, 2013.
Johnson, James Turner. 'Marriage As Covenant in Early Protestant Thought'. In *Covenant Marriage in Comparative Perspective*, edited by John Witte Jr. and Eliza Ellison, 124–52. Grand Rapids, MI: Eerdmans, 2005.
Jussen, Bernhard. *Spiritual Kinship as Social Practice: Godparenthood and Adoption in the Early Middle Ages*. Translated by Pamela Selwyn. Newark: University of Delaware Press, 2000.
Krawiec, Rebecca. '"From the Womb of the Church": Monastic Families'. *Journal of Early Christian Studies* 11, no. 3 (Fall 2003): 283–307.
Lamont, William. 'Introduction'. In *A Holy Commonwealth*, by Richard Baxter. Cambridge Texts in the History of Political Thought. Cambridge: Cambridge University Press, 1994.
Lancy, David F. *The Anthropology of Childhood: Cherubs, Chattel, Changelings*. 2nd edn. Cambridge: Cambridge University Press, 2015.
Leach, Edmund. 'Virgin Birth: The Henry Myers Lecture 1966'. *Proceedings for the Royal Anthropological Institute of Great Britain and Ireland for 1966* (1966): 39–49.
Lee, Harper. *To Kill a Mockingbird*. London: Heinemann, 2015.
Lester, Rebecca J. *Jesus in Our Wombs: Embodying Modernity in a Mexican Convent*. Berkeley: University of California Press, 2005.
Lévi-Strauss, Claude. *The Elementary Structures of Kinship*. Edited by Rodney Needham. Translated by J. H. Bell and J. R. von Sturmer. Rev. edn. Boston, MA: Beacon, 1969.
Lévi-Strauss, Claude. *Totemism*. Harmondsworth: Penguin, 1969.
Lindemann Nelson, Hilde and James Lindemann Nelson. 'Family'. In *Encyclopedia of Bioethics*, 801–8. New York: Macmillan, 1995.
Luther, Martin. 'A Sermon on the Estate of Marriage (1519)'. In *The Christian in Society I*, edited by James Atkinson, 3–14. Luther's Works 44. Philadelphia, PA: Fortress Press, 1966.
Luther, Martin. 'Confession Concerning Christ's Supper (1528)'. In *Word and Sacrament, Volume Three*, edited by Robert H. Fisher, translated by Robert H. Fischer. Luther's Works 37. Philadelphia, PA: Fortress Press, 1961.

Luther, Martin. 'The Estate of Marriage (1522)'. In *The Christian in Society II*, edited by Walther I. Brandt, 11–50. Luther's Works 45. Philadelphia, PA: Muhlenberg Press, 1962.
Luther, Martin. 'The Persons Related by Consanguinity and Affinity Who Are Forbidden to Marry According to the Scriptures, Leviticus 18 (1522)'. In *The Christian in Society II*, edited by Walther I. Brandt, 3–10. Luther's Works 45. Philadelphia, PA: Muhlenberg Press, 1962.
Lynch, Joseph H. *Christianizing Kinship: Ritual Sponsorship in Anglo-Saxon England*. Ithaca, NY: Cornell, 1998.
Lynch, Joseph H. *Godparents and Kinship in Early Medieval Europe*. Princeton, NJ: Princeton University Press, 1986.
Maine, Henry. *Ancient Law*. London: J.M. Dent & Sons, 1917.
Malinowski, Bronisław. *The Family Among the Australian Aborigines: A Sociological Study*. Monographs on Sociology 2. London: University of London Press, 1913.
Malinowski, Bronisław. *The Sexual Life of Savages in North-Western Melanesia*. 3rd edn. Malinowski Collected Works 6. London: Routledge, 1932.
Martin, Emily. 'The Egg and the Sperm: How Science Has Constructed a Romance Based on Stereotypical Male-Female Roles'. *Signs* 16, no. 3 (1991): 485–501.
Mather, Cotton. 'Family Religion Urged'. In *Dr. Mather's Reasonable Religion*, edited by Daniel Williams, 109–34. London, 1713.
Mauss, Marcel. 'A Category of the Human Mind: The Notion of Person; the Notion of Self'. In *The Category of the Person: Anthropology, Philosophy, History*, edited by Michael Carrithers, Steven Collins and Steven Lukes, translated by W. D. Halls, 1–25. Cambridge: Cambridge University Press, 1985.
Mauss, Marcel. *The Gift: The Form and Reason for Exchange in Archaic Societies*. Translated by W. D. Halls. London: Routledge, 2002.
May, Elaine Tyler. *Barren in the Promised Land: Childless Americans and the Pursuit of Happiness*. Cambridge, MA: Harvard University Press, 1995.
McKearney, Patrick. 'Enabling Ethics: L'Arche, Learning Disability, and the Possibilities of Moral Agency'. PhD, University of Cambridge, 2016.
McKenny, Gerald. *The Analogy of Grace: Karl Barth's Moral Theology*. Oxford: Oxford University Press, 2010.
McLennan, J. F. *Primitive Marriage: An Inquiry Into the Origin of the Form of Capture in Marriage Ceremonies*. Edinburgh: A&C Black, 1865.
McPartlan, Paul. 'Person'. In *Encyclopedia of Christian Theology*, edited by Jean-Yves Lacoste. Vol. 3. London: Routledge, 2005.
Meeks, Wayne A. *The Origins of Christian Morality: The First Two Centuries*. New Haven, CT: Yale University Press, 1993.
Meilaender, Gilbert C. *Not by Nature but by Grace*. Notre Dame, IN: University of Notre Dame Press, 2016.
Modell, Judith S. *A Sealed and Secret Kinship: The Culture of Policies and Practices in American Adoption*. Public Issues in Anthropological Perspectives 3. New York: Berghahn Books, 2002.
Moreau, Philippe. 'The Bilineal Transmission of Blood in Ancient Rome'. In *Blood and Kinship: Matter for Metaphor from Ancient Rome to the Present*, edited by Christopher H. Johnson, Bernhard Jussen, David Warren Sabean and Simon Teuscher, 40–60. New York: Berghahn Books, 2013.
Morgan, Edmund S. *The Puritan Family: Religion and Domestic Relations in Seventeenth-Century New England*. Rev. edn. New York: Harper and Row, 1966.

Morgan, J. H. 'Introduction'. In *Ancient Law*, by Henry Maine, vii–xv. London: J.M. Dent & Sons, 1917.
Morgan, Lewis Henry. *Systems of Consanguinity and Affinity of the Human Family*. Smithsonian Contributions to Knowledge 218. Washington, DC: Smithsonian Institution, 1871.
Mosko, Mark. 'Partible Penitents: Dividual Personhood and Christian Practice in Melanesia and the West'. *Journal of the Royal Anthropological Institute* 16, no. 2 (1 June 2010): 215–40.
Moss, Candida R. and Joel S. Baden. *Reconceiving Infertility: Biblical Perspectives on Procreation and Childlessness*. Princeton, NJ: Princeton University Press, 2015.
Moxnes, Halvor. 'What Is a Family? Problems in Constructing Early Christian Families'. In *Constructing Early Christian Families: Family as Social Reality and Metaphor*, edited by Halvor Moxnes, 13–41. London: Routledge, 1997.
Mumford, James. *Ethics at the Beginning of Life: A Phenomenological Critique*. Oxford: Oxford University Press, 2013.
Nathan, Geoffrey. *The Family in Late Antiquity: The Rise of Christianity and the Endurance of Tradition*. London: Routledge, 2000.
Nelson, J. L. 'Monks, Secular Men and Masculinity, *c*. 900'. In *Masculinity in Medieval Europe*, edited by Dawn Hadley, 121–42. London: Routledge, 2014.
Otten, Willemien. 'Augustine on Marriage, Monasticism, and the Community of the Church'. *Theological Studies* 3, no. 59 (1998): 385–405.
Papanikolaou, Aristotle. 'Is John Zizioulas an Existentialist in Disguise? Response to Lucian Turcescu'. *Modern Theology* 20, no. 4 (October 2004): 601–7.
Philo. *Works*. Translated by F. H. Colson. Cambridge, MA: Harvard University Press, 1962.
Plato. *The Republic*. Edited by G. R. F. Ferrari. Translated by Tom Griffith. Cambridge: Cambridge University Press, 2000.
Pseudo-Dionysius. *Dionysius the Pseudo-Areopagite: The Ecclesiastical Hierarchy*, translated by Thomas L. Campbell. Lanham, MD: University Press of America, 1981.
Ragoné, Helena. 'Chasing the Blood Tie: Surrogate Mothers, Adoptive Mothers and Fathers'. *American Ethnologist* 23, no. 2 (May 1996): 352–65.
Ramsey, Paul. 'Human Sexuality in the History of Redemption'. *Journal of Religious Ethics* 16, no. 1 (Spring 1988): 56–86.
Robbins, Joel. *Becoming Sinners: Christianity and Moral Torment In a Papua New Guinea Society*. Berkeley: University of California Press, 2004.
Robbins, Joel. 'Dumont's Hierarchical Dynamism: Christianity and Individualism Revisited'. *HAU: Journal of Ethnographic Theory* 5, no. 1 (June 2015): 173–95.
Roberts, Christopher. *Creation and Covenant: The Significance of Sexual Difference in the Moral Theology of Marriage*. London: T&T Clark, 2007.
Rogers, Eugene F. 'The Genre of This Book'. *Syndicate Theology* (blog). Accessed 26 July 2019. https://syndicate.network/symposia/theology/blood/.
Roukema, Riemer. *Jesus, Gnosis and Dogma*. London: T&T Clark, 2010.
Rowe, Jonathan Y. *Michal's Moral Dilemma: A Literary, Anthropological and Ethical Interpretation*. London: T&T Clark, 2011.
Rubenson, Samuel. 'Asceticism and Monasticism, I: Eastern'. In *Constantine to c. 600*, edited by Augustine Casiday and Frederick W. Norris, 637–68. The Cambridge History of Christianity, vol. 2. Cambridge: Cambridge University Press, 2007.
Ruddick, William. 'Family'. In *Encyclopedia of Ethics*, edited by Charlotte Becker and Lawrence Becker, vol. 1. London: Routledge, 2001.

Ruddick, William. 'Family, Ethics and The'. In *Routledge Encyclopedia of Philosophy*, edited by Edward Craig. London: Routledge, 1998. https://www.rep.routledge.com/articles/thematic/family-ethics-and-the/v-1.

Ruether, Rosemary Radford. *Christianity and the Making of the Modern Family*. London: SCM, 2001.

Ruiz, Teofilo R. 'Discourses of Blood and Kinship in Late Medieval and Early Modern Castile'. In *Blood and Kinship: Matter for Metaphor from Ancient Rome to the Present*, edited by Christopher H. Johnson, Bernhard Jussen, David Warren Sabean and Simon Teuscher, 105–24. New York: Berghahn Books, 2013.

Sabean, David Warren. 'Descent and Alliance: Cultural Meanings of Blood in the Baroque'. In *Blood and Kinship: Matter for Metaphor from Ancient Rome to the Present*, edited by Christopher H. Johnson, Bernhard Jussen, David Warren Sabean and Simon Teuscher, 145–74. New York: Berghahn Books, 2013.

Sabean, David Warren and Simon Teuscher. 'Introduction'. In *Blood and Kinship: Matter for Metaphor from Ancient Rome to the Present*, edited by Christopher H. Johnson, Bernhard Jussen, David Warren Sabean and Simon Teuscher, 1–17. New York: Berghahn Books, 2013.

Sahlins, Marshall. *What Kinship Is – And Is Not*. Chicago: University of Chicago Press, 2013.

Salazar, Carles. 'Are Genes Good to Think With?' In *European Kinship in the Age of Biotechnology*, edited by Jeanette Edwards and Carles Salazar, 179–96. New York: Berghahn, 2008.

Saller, Richard P. 'Pater Familias, Mater Familias, and the Gendered Semantics of the Roman Household'. *Classical Philology* 94, no. 2 (April 1999): 182–97.

Saller, Richard P. *Patriarchy, Property and Death in the Roman Family*. Cambridge: Cambridge University Press, 1997.

Saller, Richard P. 'Roman Kinship: Structure and Sentiment'. In *The Roman Family in Italy: Status, Sentiment, Space*, edited by Beryl Rawson and Paul Weaver, 7–34. Oxford: Clarendon, 1997.

Saller, Richard P. 'Symbols of Gender and Status in the Roman Household'. In *Women and Slaves in Greco-Roman Culture: Differential Equations*, edited by Sandra R. Joshel and Sheila Murnaghan, 85–91. New York: Routledge, 2005.

Schneider, David M. *A Critique of the Study of Kinship*. Ann Arbor: University of Michigan Press, 1984.

Schneider, David M. 'Afterword'. In *Schneider on Schneider: The Conversion of the Jews and Other Anthropological Stories*, by David M. Schneider, edited by Richard Handler, 219–24. Durham, NC: Duke University Press, 1995.

Schneider, David M. *American Kinship: A Cultural Account*. 2nd edn. Chicago: University of Chicago Press, 1980.

Schneider, David M. 'Kinship, Nationality, and Religion in American Culture: Toward a Definition of Kinship'. In *Symbolic Anthropology: A Reader in the Study of Symbols and Meanings*, edited by Janet L. Dolgin, D. S. Kemnitzer, and David M. Schneider, 63–71. New York: Columbia University Press, 1977.

Shaw, Brent D. 'The Family in Late Antiquity: The Experience of Augustine'. *Past & Present*, no. 115 (May 1987): 3–51.

Silver, Lee M. 'Confused Meanings of Life, Genes and Parents'. *Studies in History and Philosophy of Science Part C: Studies in History and Philosophy of Biological and Biomedical Sciences* 32, no. 4 (December 2001): 647–61.

Slater, Miriam. *Family Life in the Seventeenth Century: The Verneys of Claydon House*. London: Routledge & Kegan Paul, 1984.

Song, Robert. *Covenant and Calling: Towards a Theology of Same-Sex Relationships*. London: SCM, 2014.
Soskice, Janet Martin. *The Kindness of God*. Oxford: Oxford University Press, 2007.
Spiro, Melford. *Kinship and Marriage in Burma. A Cultural and Psychodynamic Analysis*. Berkeley: University of California Press, 1977.
Spurr, John. 'Richard Baxter'. In *Puritans and Puritanism in Europe and America: A Comprehensive Encyclopedia*, edited by Francis J. Bremer and Tom Webster. Vol. 1. Santa Barbara, CA: ABC-CLIO, 2006.
Strathern, Marilyn. *Kinship, Law and the Unexpected: Relatives Are Always a Surprise*. Cambridge: Cambridge University Press, 2005.
Strathern, Marilyn. *Property, Substance and Effect*. London: Athlone Press, 1999.
Strathern, Marilyn. *The Gender of the Gift: Problems with Women and Problems with Society in Melanesia*. Berkeley: University of California Press, 1988.
Tanner, Kathryn. *Christ the Key*. Current Issues in Theology 7. Cambridge: Cambridge University Press, 2009.
Taylor, Jeremy. 'The Marriage Ring; or the Mysteriousness and Duties of Marriage'. In *Sermons*, edited by Charles Page Eden. The Whole Works of the Right Rev. Jeremy Taylor, D.D., vol. 4. London, 1861.
Tertullian. *Against Praxeas* in *Patrologia Latina*, edited by J.-P. Migne, vol. 2. Paris: Imprimerie Catholique, 1844.
Teuscher, Simon. 'Flesh and Blood in the Treatises on the Arbor Consanguinitas (Thirteenth to Sixteenth Centuries)'. In *Blood and Kinship: Matter for Metaphor from Ancient Rome to the Present*, edited by Christopher H. Johnson, Bernhard Jussen, David Warren Sabean and Simon Teuscher, 83–104. New York: Berghahn Books, 2013.
Thatcher, Adrian. *Theology and Families*. Oxford: Blackwell, 2007.
Theodoret of Cyrus. *Ecclesiastical History* in *Patrologia Graeca*, edited by J.-P. Migne, vol. 82. Paris: Imprimerie Catholique, 1864.
Thomas, J. M. Lloyd. *The Autobiography of Richard Baxter, Abridged by J.M. Lloyd Thomas*. Edited by N. H. Keeble. London: Dent, 1974.
Thomas, Todne, Asiya Malik, Rose Wellman (eds). *New Directions in Spiritual Kinship: Sacred Ties across the Abrahamic Religions*. New York: Palgrave Macmillan, 2017.
Todd, Margo. *Christian Humanism and the Puritan Social Order*. Cambridge: Cambridge University Press, 1987.
Tolstoy, Leo. *War and Peace*. Translated by Richard Pevear and Larissa Volokhonsky. London: Vintage, 2009.
Torrance, Alan. *Persons in Communion: Trinitarian Description and Human Participation*. Edinburgh: T&T Clark, 1996.
Treggiari, Susan. 'Marriage and Family in Roman Society'. In *Marriage and Family in the Biblical World*, edited by Ken M. Campbell, 132–82. Downers Grove, IL: InterVarsity Press, 2003.
Turcescu, Lucian. '"Person" versus "Individual," and Other Modern Misreadings of Gregory of Nyssa'. *Modern Theology* 18, no. 4 (1 October 2002): 527–39.
Turcescu, Lucian. 'Prosōpon and Hypostasis in Basil of Caesarea's "Against Eunomius" and the Epistles Author(s)'. *Vigiliae Christianae* 51, no. 4 (November 1997): 374–95.
Walker, G. S. M. 'Calvin and the Church'. In *Readings in Calvin's Theology*, edited by Donald K. McKim, 212–31. Eugene, OR: Wipf and Stock, 1998.
Walsham, Alexandra. 'Holy Families: The Spiritualization of the Early Modern Household Revisited'. In *Religion and the Household: Papers Read at the 2012 Summer Meeting*

and the 2013 Winter Meeting of the Ecclesiastical History Society, edited by John Doran, Charlotte Methuen, and Alexandra Walsham, 122–60. Suffolk: Boydell, 2014.

Walsham, Alexandra. 'The Godly and Popular Culture'. In *The Cambridge Companion to Puritanism*, edited by John Coffey and Paul C. H. Lim, 277–93. Cambridge: Cambridge University Press, 2008.

Ward, Graham. 'The Erotics of Redemption – After Karl Barth'. *Theology and Sexuality* 8 (1998): 52–72.

Waters, Brent. *The Family in Christian Social and Political Thought*. Oxford: Oxford University Press, 2007.

Weber, Max. *The Protestant Ethic and the Spirit of Capitalism*. Translated by Talcott Parsons. 2nd edn. London: George Allen and Unwin, 1978.

Webster, John. *Barth's Ethics of Reconciliation*. Cambridge: Cambridge University Press, 1995.

Welby, Justin. 'A Personal Statement from the Archbishop of Canterbury'. Accessed 14 April 2016. http://www.archbishopofcanterbury.org//articles.php/5704/a-personal-statement-from-the-archbishop-of-canterbury.

Wilhite, David E. *Tertullian the African: An Anthropological Reading of Tertullian's Context and Identities*. Berlin: Walter de Gruyter, 2007.

Wittgenstein, Ludwig. *Philosophical Investigations*. Edited by G. E. M. Anscombe and Rush Rhees. Translated by G. E. M. Anscombe. 2nd edn. Oxford: Blackwell, 1958.

Zelizer, Viviana. *Pricing the Priceless Child: The Changing Social Value of Children*. Princeton, NJ: Princeton University Press, 1985.

Zizioulas, John. *Being as Communion: Studies in Personhood and the Church*. Crestwood, NY: St. Vladimir's Seminary Press, 1997.

Zizioulas, John. *Communion and Otherness: Further Studies in Personhood and the Church*. Edited by Paul McPartlan. London: T&T Clark, 2006.

Zizioulas, John. *Lectures in Christian Dogmatics*. Edited by Douglas Knight. London: T&T Clark, 2008.

INDEX OF NAMES

Abraham   19, 69–70
Aelred of Rievaulx   126–7, 162–3
Ambrose   80
Anidjar, Gil   68 n.90
Aquinas, Thomas   63, 70
Aristotle   60, 62, 63 n.64, 92, 98–9,
   122 n.36, 143
Arius   144
Athanasius of Alexandria   136, 143–4
Atkinson, Jane   107
Aubert, Guillaume   66
Augustine of Hippo   61, 64 n.66, 70–3,
   78, 80–1, 86, 95–6, 104, 118–23,
   121–6, 148–9, 153–4, 157, 162–3
Ayres, Lewis   136

Bachofen, Johann   31–2
Bailey, Derrick   148
Banner, Michael   23, 50–1, 84, 98 n.133,
   133, 150–1
Barclay, John M. G.   12 n.20, 104 n.112,
   135–6, 164
Barth, Karl   17–22, 47, 108, 113–24, 129,
   139, 146, 153, 170–2
Barton, Stephen C.   13–15
Basil of Caesarea
   monasticism   73, 78, 80, 83–4, 86,
      96, 100
   personhood   144–5
Baxter, Richard   16–17, 26, 77–8, 86–99,
   103–4, 160–1, 163, 166
Beauvoir, Simone de   106
Becker, Gay   51
Benedict   19, 77–86, 89–90, 93–104,
   123–4, 160–1
Bennett, Jana Marguerite   22–3, 81 n.22,
   109–10, 127 n.111
Bestard, Joan   54, 153
Biale, David   71
Bildhauer, Bettina   62, 64
Billings, J. Todd   146

Bodenhorn, Barbara   151–3
Bonhoeffer, Dietrich   17–18, 163
Bossuet, Jacques-Bénigne   66
Boswell, John   85–6
Bradford, William   88 n.76
Brighouse, Harry   8–9
Brown, Peter   80–3, 109, 111
Browning, Don   13, 41–3
Burke, Trevor J.   146
Butler, Judith   123, 129–30, 162
Bynum, Caroline Walker   64–6

Caesarius of Arles   73, 149
Cahill, Lisa Sowle   10–13, 15, 36–8
Calvin, John   91–2
Capp, Bernard   88 nn.77–9
Carsten, Janet   2, 4, 45–7, 50–3, 57, 68,
   106–8, 131–3, 162
Cassian   78, 81, 84, 86, 104, 124
Cavanaugh, William   72, 56–6
Chapais, Bernard   13, 41–3
Cicero   60–61, 78, 96, 112
Cliffe, J. T.   89 n.83
Coakley, Sarah   122–4, 126, 128, 162
Collier, Jane Fishburne   116–17
Cooper, Kate   78–82
Cornwall, Susannah   74
Crawford, Patricia   89 n.80
Curzon, Lord Frederick   50–1

De Jong, Mayke   85 n.60
Delille, Gérard   65–6
Du Boulay, Juliet   83–4, 150–1, 174–5
Dunn, Marilyn   78, 80–1
Durston, Christopher   87

Edwards, Jeanette   52–3
Engels, Friedrich   98–9
Essner, Cornelia   67

Faubion, James D.   45–6

Fontaine, Jacques 82
Foucault, Michel 128–30
Franklin, Sarah 30, 52, 55–8

Geertz, Clifford 39 n.61, 40 n.65
Gregory of Nazianzus 141, 144
Gregory of Nyssa 83–4, 141–5, 146 n.75
Gregory of Tours 149
Gregory the Great 82
Guerreau-Jalabert, Anita 62–4
Gunton, Colin 136

Hall, Amy Laura 67 n.87
Harders, Ann-Cathrin 59–60
Harrison, Carol 111
Haslanger, Sally 10
Hays, Richard B. 69
Heine, Ronald E. 143 nn.56–7
Herodotus 62
Heywood, Colin 85
Hippolytus 143, 148
Hodge, Caroline Johnson 61–2, 69
Holmes Christopher R. J. 170
Hughes, Ann 92–3

Inwagen, Peter van 147 n.75
Irvine, Richard 99–102
Isidor of Seville 60

Jerome 84 n.44, 119
John Paul II 15–16
Johnson, Christopher H. 67
Johnson, James T. 91 n.102
Joseph (father of Jesus) 61
Jussen, Bernhard 149–50
Justinian 78, 149

Krawiec, Rebecca 83

Lamont, William 87
Lancy, David 89 n.81
Leach, Edmund 39–40
Lee, Harper 152
Lester, Rebecca 101
Lévi-Strauss, Claude 35, 40–2, 47
Lindemann Nelson, Hilde 9
Lindemann Nelson, James 9
Livy 60

Luther, Martin 17–18, 120–2, 145, 150 n.97, 154
Lynch, Joseph H. 148–50

McKearney, Patrick 102–4
McKenny, Gerald 19 n.57, 139
McLennan, John 30, 32
McPartlan, Paul 141–5
Maine, Henry 31–2
Malik, Asiya 48 n.90
Malinowski, Bronisław 33–6, 39–40
Martin, Emily 44
Mary (mother of Jesus) 61, 66
Mather, Cotton 97 n.127
Mauss, Marcel 134, 142, 145, 164
May, Elaine Tyler 56
Meeks, Wayne 150
Meilaender, Gilbert 155 n.121
Modell, Judith 155–6
Moreau, Philippe 59, 61
Morgan, Edmund S. 97
Morgan, Lewis Henry 30, 32–3, 35, 68 n.90, 98
Mosko, Mark 137–8, 164
Moss, Candida 125 n.101
Moxnes, Halvor 12 n.20
Mumford, James 153–5, 165

Nathan, Geoffrey 78–9
Nelson, J. L. 125–6

Otten, Willemien 81

Papanikolaou, Aristotle 147 n.75
Paul 19, 21 n.68, 61–2, 69, 71–2, 91, 93–4, 102, 109–12, 114, 117–19, 120, 122–7, 129–30, 132–7, 139, 146, 156–7, 160, 162–4, 169, 172–5
Philo 62
Plato 98–9, 143
Pseudo-Dionysius 149

Ragoné, Helena 50
Ramsey, Paul 109–11, 122
Robbins, Joel 133–8, 164
Roberts, Christopher 116
Rogers, Eugene F. 75

Rowe, Jonathan Y.   45 n.82
Rubenson   84 n.44
Ruddick, William   6–8
Ruether, Rosemary Radford   97 n.128
Ruiz, Teofilo R.   64–5

Sabean, David   58–9, 66
Sahlins, Marshall   131
Salazar, Carlos   53–4
Saller, Richard P.   79
Schneider, David
   American Kinship   25–9, 49, 57, 97, 99, 105–7, 151
   A Critique of the Study of Kinship   11–13, 25, 30, 33–9, 44–5
   defining kinship   12–13, 25–30, 35–8, 44–7, 56, 169 n.7
   theory of knowledge   54
Shaw, Brent D.   78–80, 111–12
Silver, Lee   53
Slater, Miriam   89 nn.81–2
Song, Robert   125–8
Soskice, Janet   146, 171
Spiro, Melford   35, 39–40
Spurr, John   89 n.87
Strathern, Marilyn   50, 53–6, 132–4, 153
Swift, Adam   8–9

Tanner, Kathryn   139, 146

Taylor, Jeremy   88
Tertullian   45, 143, 148
Teuscher, Simon   58–9, 63–4
Thatcher, Adrian   150
Theodoret of Cyrus   144
Thomas, Todne   48 n.90
Todd, Margo   92
Tolstoy, Leo   131
Torrance, Alan   147 n.75
Treggiari   78 n.6, 111 n.31
Turcescu, Lucian   145, 147 n.75

Ulpian   69, 71

Walker, G. S. M.   91
Walsham, Alexandra   89, 92 n.104
Ward, Graham   116–17
Waters, Brent   15 n.31
Weber, Max   96–8
Webster, John   19
Welby, Justin   138–9, 174
Wellman, Rose   48 n.90
Wilhite, David   45 n.82
Wittgenstein, Ludwig   9, 45

Yanagisako, Sylvia Junko   116–17

Zelizer, Viviana   135
Zizioulas, John   139–41, 145, 150, 164–5

INDEX OF SUBJECTS

abortion   153–4
adoption
   divine   69, 73, 95, 146–7, 172, 176
   practice of   10–11, 21, 27, 43, 56, 60, 104, 149, 153, 155–7, 160–1, 165–6, 175, 177
Ambeli   73–4, 150–1, 172, 174–5
Ancient Greece   61–2, 68–9, 111, 128, 140–3
Ancient Roman   59–61, 78–82, 92, 111–12, 142–3, 148–9
anti-Semitism   65, 67–8, 113
ARTs. *See* Assisted Reproductive Technologies
Assisted Reproductive Technologies (ARTs)   49–51, 54, 56, 73–6, 153, 160, 177. *See also* egg donation; IVF; mitochondrial donation; sperm donation
aunts   27–8

baptism   2, 50, 64, 69–70, 72–3, 76, 119 n.20, 132–3, 136, 146–51, 156, 165, 169, 172–5
biogenetic substance   8, 20, 27–9, 36, 39, 41 n.70, 42–3, 47, 49, 51–8, 68, 73–4, 163, 173–4
biological kinship   1–2, 5–14, 20–1, 27–30, 34–43, 56, 74, 138, 152, 155 n.121, 160, 177
blood
   of Jesus   50, 63–74, 85 n.123, 86, 125, 130
   kinship by   2–3, 7, 9, 16, 20, 27–8, 30, 33–4, 36–7, 45–76, 79, 83, 105, 114, 130, 132, 149–51, 159–60, 169–70, 173–4
Body of Christ. *See* Church; flesh, of Christ
breastfeeding   41, 66, 89, 108

Cappadocians   73, 78, 80, 83–4, 86, 96, 100, 141–5, 146 n.75
Caro (flesh)   62–3
Carolingians   62, 125–6
Catechism of the Catholic Church   16
celibacy   2, 43, 80, 85, 99–101, 108–12, 118–27, 129–30, 162–3, 166, 174
childlessness   21, 50, 56, 73, 133, 168
children
   bearing   40, 50–1, 56, 73, 107–12, 126–30, 153–6, 162
   and monasticism   83, 85–6
   and parents   8–9, 12–21, 30, 32, 34–8, 41–2, 47, 50–7, 60, 66, 80, 87–8, 91, 94, 98, 135, 136, 151–3, 160, 165–7
christ
   anonymous Christ   82
   as bridegroom   112, 114, 119, 153, 163
   as gift   135–6
in Christ
   identity   15, 18, 70–1, 124, 126, 138–9, 146, 164, 169–70, 173–4, 177
   kinship   62, 69–73, 95, 101, 121, 124–30, 151, 157–8, 163–6, 168–78
   personhood   132–3, 138, 145–6, 147 n.75, 164–6 (*see also* in persona Christi)
Chukchee   40–1
Church
   history of   2–3, 14, 63–7, 69–70, 73–4, 77, 92, 100, 112, 125–7, 142, 148–51, 174–5
   household as   87, 91–2
   theology of   17, 63–5, 70–6, 81, 86, 91 n.102, 93, 95, 99, 110, 114–15, 119, 121, 127, 129–30, 132–3, 136–7, 140–1, 146, 148–53, 157–8, 160, 173–4

Communion. *See* Eucharist
conception   12, 16–17, 20, 30, 32, 34–9, 55, 62, 66, 73, 127, 155, 166
contraception   110–11
Corban   175
Council, Fourth Lateran   59, 64
Council of Toledo   85
Council of Vienne   63
Council of Worms   85
cousins   28–9, 41
covenant
   God's   69, 72, 91–2, 113–17, 120–5, 129, 157, 162
   marriage   108, 113, 121–2, 127 n.112, 130, 153, 165–6, 175–6
   parental   155, 165

desire   40–1, 108, 111, 117, 122–4, 127–9
dividualism *vs.* individualism   133–8, 143, 164–5
divorce   55, 106, 118, 153, 159–60, 166
DNA. *See* biogenetic substance
Doctrine of the Genealogical Unity of Mankind   13, 29
Dominicans   65–6
Downside Abbey   99–104, 168 n.6

egg donation   51, 54, 73, 153
English Puritanism   16–17, 26, 77–8, 86–99, 103–4, 142, 160–1, 163, 166
ethnicity   27, 73
Eucharist   2, 50, 58–9, 63–76, 99–100, 104, 125, 130, 132, 160–1, 175
evolutionism   31–3, 40, 43

faith   135–8, 148, 150 n.97, 170, 176
Fall, Doctrine of   18, 86, 119, 123–4, 129, 137, 154, 176
Familiaris Consortio   15–16
family. *See* kinship
flesh
   of Christ   61–5, 70–6
   kinship by   16, 20, 61–4, 73, 83, 159
   life in the   136
   one flesh   66, 93 n.112, 115–18
fostering   27, 43, 56, 86, 104, 156–7, 160–1, 165
Franciscans   65–6

freedom   114, 139–41, 147 n.75, 164, 173
friendship   98–9, 110–11, 126–8, 150, 157, 162–3
functionalism   33–9

gender
   anthropology of   2, 8, 16, 44 n.77, 46, 48, 105–8, 123, 128–9, 161–2
   and diet   125–6
   history of   79–80, 91–4, 99 n.136, 109, 125–7
   theology of   73–4, 91–4, 99 n.136, 108–30, 161–2, 168
generation. *See* procreation
genes, genetics. *See* biogenetic substance
Gentile   69, 76, 135–6
Gestation. *See* pregnancy
gift economy   134–57
godparenthood. *See* spiritual kinship
grace   19, 91–2 n.102, 135–6, 138–9, 145
grandparents   28, 55

as Head of the Church   114, 119, 121, 123, 130
   likeness of   150, 175 (*see also* in Christ)
home. *See* house
homosexuality   116–17, 127–8
house   16, 28, 48, 59–60, 77–105, 121, 126–7, 135, 150–1, 160–1
household codes   93–4
House of Lords   50–1
human nature   16–17, 27, 31, 41–3, 53, 57, 87, 90–4, 97 n.127, 105–7, 129–32, 139, 164–8

Imago Dei   113–14, 123, 142, 162–3
Incarnation, Doctrine of   109–10, 123, 125–6, 129, 135–6, 143–6
incest   30, 41–2, 88, 105, 149–51, 157
individualism. *See* dividualism *vs.* individualism
inheritance   2, 59, 66, 79–85, 104, 126, 149–50, 156, 177
in-laws   27
In Persona Christi   63, 123
Islam   65, 73
IVF   51. *See also* Assisted Reproductive Technologies (ARTs)

Judaism   45 n.82, 65, 67–9, 71, 148 n.78

Kingdom of God   3, 25 n.1, 83, 95, 120 n.82, 130, 162, 166, 169–74, 176
King Gunthcramn   3
kinship
  Agnatic   60, 66
  australian aboriginal   34, 36, 39
  bioethics   9
  by bone   62, 115–18, 173
  cognatic   60–1, 105–6
  contemporary Euro-American   14, 28–9, 31, 35, 38–9, 43–5, 49–58, 68, 76, 132, 165
  cultural construction   6–10, 12–13
  defining the concept   1–23, 25–6, 44–8, 91, 106–8, 156–7, 159–60, 164–9, 177–8
  by effort   152, 157
  fictive   14
  folk theory   30
  french   66–7
  Iñupiaq   43, 151–3, 157
  Iroquois   32–3
  Melanesian   34, 134
  natural *vs.* classificatory   33
  philosophy   6–9
  political philosophy   17, 78, 91
  recent Christian ethics   10–15, 36–8, 41–3
  social *vs..* physical   33–4
  substance and code   27–8
  Trobriand   34–5, 39–40
  Urapmin   134
  Wana Kinship   108
  Yapese Kinship   13, 36–9 (*see also* adoption; biological kinship; blood; children; flesh; fostering; in Christ; Monasticism; spiritual kinship)

L'Arche   99, 102–4, 161, 171–3
love
  God's   18 n.46, 111, 119, 128, 130, 136, 139–41, 162
  human   11, 13, 15, 28, 76, 81 n.20, 86, 105–6, 118, 122, 127, 130, 140–1, 150, 157, 162

marriage
  anthropology of   11–17, 27–9, 32–3, 37, 40–3, 48–9, 55, 105–8, 132–3, 153
  history of   60, 66–7, 78–9, 88–94, 96, 98, 111–12, 124–7, 149–50
  theology of   80, 88–101, 105–30, 149–51, 156–8, 162–3, 165, 167, 172, 174
milk. *See* breastfeeding
mitochondrial donation   50–1, 153
monasticism
  history of   2, 14, 77–8, 81–6, 93 n.112, 124–7
  as kinship   2, 11, 15, 19, 73, 75–6, 80–6, 95, 101, 124–7, 155, 168 n.6, 171–5
  recent Mexican   101, 161 (*see also* Downside Abbey)
Monte Cassino   78, 82, 99

New England Puritanism   86–8, 96–8
nuclear family   1, 55, 166–8
nursing. *See* breastfeeding

oblation   85–6

parenthood   17–21, 55
Paterfamilias   59, 78–82, 86, 112, 135
paternity   13, 32–8, 69
personhood
  divine   132–3, 135, 139–47, 158, 164–5, 170–2
  human   2, 7, 28, 46, 48, 121, 131–58, 162–5, 168–70, 172
  Melanesian   134, 137–8, 164
  Urapmin   133–8
polygamy   88, 98
poverty   80, 82, 90, 98, 167, 177
pregnancy   20, 42–3, 54, 73–4, 76, 130, 154–5, 160, 165
procreation
  and gender   106, 109–11, 119–22, 125–30, 156, 162
  procreative ties   2, 7–8, 11–20, 22–49, 60–1, 66–8, 74–6, 94–5, 110, 130, 154–6, 165

race   65–8, 73–4, 110, 113, 173

relatedness. *See* kinship
reproductive ties. *See* procreation

Sanguis 59–66
Sardica, Synod of 144
seed, seedbed 12, 38, 69, 96, 112
sexuality 11–13, 32, 34–6, 38–40, 81–2, 88, 110–11, 116–17, 120, 122, 125–30, 162–3, 166
shared substance 2, 20–1, 27–9, 36, 46, 49–58, 68, 75–6, 117, 152, 159–60, 163, 173
slavery 78–9, 81–2, 88, 93 n.112, 98, 173
sperm donation 153

spiritual kinship 2–34, 48 n.90, 56, 64, 73–6, 119 n.20, 133, 145–51, 165
sponsorship. *See* godparenthood
step-family 27, 55, 159–60
sterilisation 67–8
structuralism 39–44
surrogacy 50, 153, 155

Trinity, Doctrine of 135, 140, 143–7, 164

uncles 27–8, 79

vocation 120–2, 126, 129–30

INDEX OF BIBLE REFERENCES

Genesis
1–2   116–17
1–3   46
1.25   113
1.27-8   110, 120
2   118
2.18-25   114, 118
2.24   117, 119
9.4-6   63
12.1   19
17.8   157 n.127
17.9   69

Exodus
20.12   18
Leviticus
17.11   63
17.14   63
26.12   157 n.127

Deuteronomy
5.16   18
7.6   92

Proverbs   21

Song of Songs   116–17, 163

Isaiah
63.15   21 n.68

Jeremiah
30.22   157 n.127

Ezekiel
16.49   90
36.28   157 n.127

Matthew
3.17   146
5.28   153

12.46-50   94, 174
16.17   139
19   120 n.82
19.4-6   118 n.71, 153
19.8-9   153
22.30   109 n.20
23.9   21 n.68, 146, 157, 167
25.1-13   134, 137–8
25.31-46   72
25.36   82 n.32

Mark
3.33   78
7   175
12.25   119

Luke
2.41-51   19
9.23   160
9.61-2   83
10.16   95
11.27-8   21
14.26   94
20.35-6   110, 125
22.20   69

John
1.18   141
3.5-7   149
6.56   71

Acts
2.43-7   81
15.10   172

Romans
1.3   61
1.26-7   117, 120
8.9-10   139
8.15-16   146
8.29   146

11   69
12.2   160
12.5   136

1 Corinthians
1.9   146
6.16   118 n.71
7   110–12, 119, 122, 127, 162
7.32-4   124
10.16-17   72
11   127
11.3-6   114, 123
11.27-9   71–2
12.12   136

2 Corinthians
6.16   157 n.127
12.10   102

Galatians
2.19-20   122, 136, 146
3.17   157 n.128
3.29   69
4.6-7   146, 173

Ephesians
3.15   21 n.68
4.22-4   139
5.21   130
5.25   130
5.28-33   118 n.71

5.29-30   137
5.29–6.9   93, 114, 123, 127
6.1   19

Philippians
2   93 n.112

Colossians
3.20   19

1 Thessalonians
5.20-2   174

1 Timothy
5.8   175
6.1-2   94
6.6   172

Titus
2.1-10   94

Hebrews
1.3   143
12.2   170

1 John
4.16   141

Revelation
21.3   157 n.127

www.ingramcontent.com/pod-product-compliance
Lightning Source LLC
Chambersburg PA
CBHW061829300426
44115CB00013B/2299